JEWISH IDEALS

AND OTHER ESSAYS

JEWISH IDEALS

AND OTHER ESSAYS

BY

JOSEPH JACOBS

Essay Index Reprint Series

BOOKS FOR LIBRARIES PRESS
FREEPORT, NEW YORK

First Published 1896
Reprinted 1972

Library of Congress Cataloging in Publication Data

Jacobs, Joseph, 1854-1916.
  Jewish ideals.

  (Essay index reprint series)
  Reprint of the 1896 ed.
  CONTENTS: Jewish ideals.--The God of Israel: ì
history.--Mordecai: a protest against the critics.
[etc.]
  1. Jews--History--Addresses, essays, lectures.
2. Hagin family. I. Title.
DS102.5.J2 1972   296   72-311
ISBN 0-8369-2795-8

PRINTED IN THE UNITED STATES OF AMERICA
BY
NEW WORLD BOOK MANUFACTURING CO., INC.
HALLANDALE, FLORIDA 33009

To Lady Magnus

DEAR LADY MAGNUS,

You were pleased to be pleased with some of these Essays when they first appeared. Indeed, it was to the earliest of them, my defence of " Daniel Deronda," that I owed my first acquaintance with you. They may, therefore, be fitly connected with your name now that they come together between the same boards. They may serve as a memorial of a friendship which has been tried and tested throughout the years during which they have been written.

On Jewish matters I think it may be said of us, as of other friends, that we agree in everything except in opinion. Of all that I have written—and I am beginning, I fear, to be a rather voluminous writer—my Jewish studies have been those that have engaged my deepest thought and my sincerest feeling. You, too,—for we are fellow-authors,— have put most of your large heart into what you have written on Jewish affairs. These Essays, then, are offered you as from friend to friend, as from one Jewish author to another; I would they were more worthy of your acceptance.

I remain, dear LADY MAGNUS,

Yours very sincerely,

JOSEPH JACOBS.

b

PREFACE

THE following Essays have appeared in various perio-
dicals during the past eighteen years. They range over
nearly all the problems which the peculiar position of
Modern Judaism has brought into prominence. The
spiritual walls of the English Ghetto have only fallen
during the present generation. I may lay claim, I
think, to have been almost the first who stepped outside them, and regarded the position of Judaism from
the standpoint of Modern Thought. Others have
followed, and there is every sign of a rise of a New
Judaism which attempts to combine fidelity to Jewish
history with the requirements of Modern Thought
and Culture. I am hoping that these Essays in their
collected form will contribute something towards the
new movement.

INTRODUCTION

ONE collects a series of essays like these, spreading over such a long series of years, with mingled feelings of wonder and dismay. One wonders, "Was it indeed I who wrote these things? How much I knew in those days!" One is dismayed to find how inadequately one managed to put one's deepest thoughts. Self-praise and self-blame may be summed up in the single exclamation, "How young I was then!"

It is a mistake, I consider, to attempt to rewrite the essays written in youth. One is so different from one's former self in such a case, that it seems like rewriting another man's work. I have avoided this mistake in the present instance. I thought it would be more interesting, both to myself and to others, if I were to summarise here the points on which my views have changed, or which I would nowadays put otherwise, with regard to the topics discussed in some of the following papers.

The essay which I should probably find most difficulty in rewriting nowadays is that entitled "The God of Israel." This was no less than an attempt to write the history of European thought from a Jewish standpoint. It is only when one is young that one dares to tackle so large a theme. Yet boldness has its reward as well as its dangers. I know more about the subject now, yet I doubt if I should be able to present as clear a view of the interlaced action and reaction of the Aryan and the Semitic elements in European culture. Coming fresh to the subject, I could see more clearly those broad aspects of it which lie on the surface. "It is only the superficial," it has been well said, "who do not judge by what lies on the surface." There are three stages in any investigation into a complicated subject. When we first review the field we arrive at provisional and general results, which, as often as not, give the outline of the truth so far as it will ever show itself to us. When we come to closer quarters, and plunge into details, it is impossible to rise out of them to any general conception of the subject at all. We only arrive at this again when we have worked our way through, and got out on the other side, as it were. I have never since succeeded in getting outside the subject of Jewish metaphysics; I doubt if I ever shall. The "God of Israel" must, therefore, remain for a long time to come all that I can profitably say about the development of the Jewish conceptions of the Deity. I can only wish that I had said it in a less priggish and technical form.

The essay was written and published before the star of Wellhausen had arisen and caused all the other planets of Old Testament criticism to pale beside it. But after all, brilliant as has been the light Wellhausen has thrown on the subject, he only concentrated rays which had been coming for many years from the Leyden school. I have, therefore, very little to retract or modify in the first part of my essay. I am glad also to find that I there adumbrated, and to some extent applied, the methods of institutional archæology to Old Testament problems, of which I have given more detailed examples in my "Studies in Biblical Archæology." I fancy, too, that later research has justified my protest against the "meteorological" explanation of mythology in the note on page 29, though I should be no longer prepared to claim historic reality for the Patriarchs.

Somewhat more has been done to advance our knowledge on the various Jewish philosophers of whom I have spoken in the second part of my essay. But in the main, my summary outline of the chief moments in the development of Jewish mediæval thought remains accurate and adequate enough for the special purpose I had in view, that of leading up to its culmination in Spinoza. The summary I give on pp. 53, 54, as to the Jewish elements of his thought, requires now to be supplemented by an allusion to the influence of Gersonides on Spinoza's views on intellectual immortality, to which Sir Frederic Pollock has drawn attention in his monograph, p. 291.

The whole essay is a pæan in honour of Spinoza, and represents in my own intellectual development the profound influence that thinker had upon me while I was in my metaphysical stage. In later life it is somewhat difficult to understand the passionate eagerness with which a young man attacks the metaphysical problems. That burning desire to get at the root of things, to clutch at reality amid the flux of phenomena, has its pathetic as well as its amusing side. For us in later years the curtain of life is the picture. Its phenomena are the only true reality for us. But there was a time when one dared to hope to raise the veil of Isis and pierce to the truth of things *sub specie æternitatis.* Of all the prophets that have claimed to raise that veil, Spinoza speaks to the neophyte in most authoritative accents. Yet when we peer into his Holy of Holies we shrink back, awed by the vacant gloom.

As the "God of Israel" was written under the influence of Spinoza, so the essay on "Daniel Deronda," which follows it here, but was the first thing I ever wrote, points to the other great influence on my early intellectual life. It is difficult for those who have not lived through it to understand the influence that George Eliot had upon those of us who came to our intellectual majority in the "seventies." Darwinism was in the air, and promised, in the suave accents of Professor Huxley and in the more strident voice of Professor Clifford, to solve all the problems of humanity. George Eliot's novels were regarded by us not so much as novels, but rather as applications of Darwinism to life and art. They were to us *Tendenz-Romane*, and we studied them as much for the *Tendenz* as for the *Roman*. Nowadays, when their *Tendenz* is discredited, their artistic qualities have been depreciated far below their just value. But of this I have spoken elsewhere.[1] In the "seventies," however, she spoke to us with the combined authority of the artist and the thinker. She was, in Mr. Myers' memorable phrase, our "Sybil in the gloom."

I had come under her influence before the appearance of "Daniel Deronda." When it appeared, I was just at that stage which comes in the intellectual development of every Jew, I suppose, when he emerges from the Ghetto, both social and intellectual, in which he was brought up. He finds the world outside pursuing a course quite oblivious of the claims of his race and his

---

[1] "Literary Studies," second edition, in the Introduction.

religion. This oblivion is in itself a tacit condemnation of the claims which justified his former isolation.
He is forced to reconsider them, and the result is,
either that he re-enters the Ghetto never to emerge,
or comes outside never to re-enter. Just as I was at
these cross-paths "Daniel Deronda" appeared, and I
found the thinker for whom I had the greatest reverence justifying from the standpoint of the most
advanced thought the historic claims of the position
of Judaism. I cannot trust myself to say with what
eagerness I read the successive monthly instalments of
"Daniel Deronda" as it appeared during 1876. The
enthusiasm it aroused in me is sufficiently indicated by
the somewhat gushing tone of the review of the book
given in the following pages. On the whole, I am
gratified to find that my enthusiasm did not outstrip the
bounds of reason. Except a single sentence on page 71,
of which I seemed to recognise the boldness even at the
time, there is scarcely a passage to which I would not still
adhere after the lapse of twenty years. It is not every
one who can say that about the first thing he wrote.

George Eliot's influence on me counterbalanced that
of Spinoza, by directing my attention, henceforth, to
the historic development of Judaism. Spinoza envis-
aged for me the Jewish ideals in their static form,
George Eliot transferred my attention to them in their
dynamic development. Henceforth I turned to Jewish
history as the key to the Jewish problem, and most of
the remaining essays in this volume deal with various
aspects of that history; while I have, in two separate
works,[1] added a considerable mass of material to our

---

[1] "Jews of Angevin England;" "Inquiry into the sources of the History
of the Jews in Spain."

knowledge of the Jewish past in England and in Spain.

These historical essays are, in the main, archæological. I have ventured to bring them up to date in point of facts, so that there is no need for me to dilate upon them here. They deal chiefly with special points of interest or difficulty in the early history of the Jews in this country, and were the direct outcome of the interest aroused in me on that subject by the Anglo-Jewish Historical Exhibition, initiated by my friend Mr. Isidore Spielman, and held in the Royal Albert Hall in 1887. Somewhat to my surprise I found, on looking into the matter, that vast unused materials existed for the early history of the Jews in this country, which have hitherto been passed over both by Jewish and English historians. I have since done something to utilise these materials. The three essays here—on the "London Jewry," "Hugh of Lincoln," and "Aaron Son of the Devil"—may serve as examples of the new light that can be obtained from this source.

In the paper on the "London Jewry" I would also call attention to the method there employed, I believe for the first time, of ascertaining the boundaries of town holdings by the parish boundaries, which seem to have run along the back fences. In the essay on "St. Hugh of Lincoln" I have endeavoured to ascertain, as impartially as I could, what amount of complicity can fairly be attributed to the Jews of Lincoln in the disappearance of little Hugh. As a folklorist, I am convinced that at the back of every such tradition there must be at least some foundation of fact. In the case of little St. Hugh, I find it in the injudicious conduct of the Jews in not handing over the body of the lad when they first discovered it. In some of the reviews of the paper where it first appeared, I observed a tendency to consider the charge against the Jews as merely an anti-Semitic concoction. But I regard this as unscientific; that hypothesis will not explain all the facts of the case. The short paper on "Aaron Son of the Devil" is chiefly of interest as containing the earliest dated portrait of the mediæval Jew. Since I first drew detailed attention to the subject, the portrait has been used in the illustrated edition of Green's "Short History," p. 393, and I have to thank Messrs. Macmillan for lending me their block, which was more accurate than my rough tracing.

In the "Hugh of Lincoln" study I have endeavoured to utilise the folklore records contained in the ballads dealing with the subject, and have shown how tradition often fills up gaps left in the historical and antiquarian records. In another of the papers I have dealt with Jewish contributions to mediæval folklore, especially to that part of the subject to which I have especially directed my attention. I have been unable to find any traces of the influence of Jews in the spread of folktales from Europe by means of oral tradition. It has been mainly by their activity as translators and literary transmitters that they have exercised any influence in this direction. Since I wrote, Dr. Steinschneider of Berlin has produced his monumental work on "Jewish Translators in the Middle Ages," in which this position is fully confirmed.

The paper on "Jehuda Halévi" deals with the most fascinating figure in mediæval Jewry. He sums up almost all the qualities that make for romance in the history of Israel in Europe. Even the scoffer Heine felt his attraction, and it elicited from him one of the finest efforts of his muse, which Matthew Arnold recognised as such in his essay on the poet. I have heard it stated that Matthew Arnold at one time contemplated translating a selection of Jehuda Halévi's poems. I do not know why the idea was not carried out, but the loss was a great one for English literature, and still more for English Judaism. Since his death, Mrs. Lucas has given some specimens of the poems in her charming little volume, "Songs of Zion." Perhaps the absence of an adequate edition of the poet's works may partly explain the abandonment of Matthew Arnold's intention. It is satisfactory to know that this reproach to Jewish scholarship and Jewish patriotism is about to be removed by an edition of the complete poetical works of Jehuda Halévi, about to be issued by a Jewish learned society in Berlin.

If these essays had appeared anywhere on the Continent, there can be little doubt that many of them would have dealt with the so-called Jewish Question. Here in England we are almost absolutely free from any taint of anti-Semitism. Yet it is impossible for any Jew who thinks on the condition of his race in these days to avoid asking himself why it is that the Jewish character, with its many fine qualities, fails to attract. The absence of charm is as distinct a characteristic of Jews as the presence of capacity. In a semi-humorous letter to the *Jewish Chronicle* some twelve years ago, I endeavoured to diagnose the former characteristic. I have thought it worth while to reprint the letter here, as, though ironic in form, it contains my sincere conviction that much of the ill-will against Jews is due to the over-intellectuality of their educational and social training. To this should have been added their neglect of their own ideals, and the consequent absence of high sentiment and noble motive in their corporate and social activity. It would seem, indeed, as if the age of Jewish chivalry was no more.

It is for this reason that I have given the first and eponymous position in this volume to the paper in which I have attempted, so far as I know for the first time, to extract and expound the fundamental ideals underlying the Jewish life, and to justify them from the standpoint of modern thought. Judaism requires some such justification if it is to continue its existence as a separate activity amid the world's spiritual forces. The mere appeal to the Bible and its promises has lost its force when addressed to modern thought. Jewish separatism must be put on a rational basis if it is to continue. The monotheistic ideal has been in substance accepted by the civilised world, Christian and Moslem. It remains to be seen if the other Jewish ideals are also acceptable. But to ascertain this they must become clearly conscious to Jews themselves, and expounded and promulgated by them. On the other hand, if these be accepted, there need be no defence of the separatism of Jews due to their small numbers. From this we are saved by the comfortable doctrine of the "Remnant," first preached by the Greater Prophets, and endorsed by that latter-day prophet, Matthew Arnold. The Book of Numbers is not the only gospel, whatever modern democracy may say. To use its own language, "The future always lies with minorities." It remains to be seen whether the "Remnant" of Israel has still that future before it which its prophets and sages have claimed for it at the cost of tears and blood.

If Israel have no future, man's past has no clue. Alone among the nations the Jews have preserved their existence as a separate spiritual entity throughout historic time. The Catholic Church alone, the spiritual daughter of Israel, can claim anything like the same authority of tradition. But the Catholic ideals have proved themselves incapable of withstanding the onslaughts of modern reason. Will it be the same with the Jewish ideals when they are given a full opportunity of appealing to modern men? That is for Jews to say, for Jews to try and avoid. If they fail, the long travail of Israel through the ages has been for naught, and man must look back upon his past, and forward to his future, without seeing the visible presence of God.

CONTENTS

JEWISH IDEALS [1]

(" *Jewish Quarterly Review*," *October* 1890)

WE are all of us artists in life, and very poor daubs most of us make of it. If we were to examine into the causes of this failure, which by universal consent is more general nowadays than ever before in the world's history, we should find it, I fancy, in the multiplicity of ideals which are being held up before us as exemplars. The truth is, we are carrying the principle of being all things to all men a little too far. We desire to be ascetic with the Buddhists, and natural with the Greeks, law-abiding as the Romans, and free as the French, socialistic like the early Christians, and individualistic as the modern Briton. Doubtless, in the millennium, all these diverse ideals will be reconciled and fused into one perfect ideal of society ; but, alas ! the millennium is not yet. Meanwhile the presentation of all these ideals in their most attractive colours only produces the effect of making them all seem equally true and equally false, or, at least, one-sided.

I may seem to be only helping to make confusion still more confounded by proposing this evening to bring before your notice another set of ideals for your sympathetic admiration. But I hope to show that this is not the case. For among the principles of ethical

[1] A Lecture delivered before the Ethical Society, Sunday, May 12, 1889.

action which seem to me to underlie the Jewish conception of life, that of rigid fidelity to the system of
ideals into which you are born is, perhaps, the most
conspicuous. I say "seem to me," for you must not
take anything I am about to say as authoritative statement of Jewish views of life. I doubt, indeed, whether
there exists any authority competent to speak in the
name of all Jews on the *rational* basis of Jewish
ideals. For speaking on such a subject before this
Society, I am debarred from all reference to the theological basis on which Jews found their claim to
live the Jewish life. I believe that life is, to quote
your charter of incorporation, " capable of rational
justification," which is tacitly taken to mean : apart
from theological suppositions. The justification I
shall offer shall not transgress that proviso, but it
thereby becomes only a personal one, and is only
founded on many years of reflection and observation
of the facts of Jewish life, literature, and history. I
suppose I share, with most members of this Society,
that curious nineteenth-century attitude towards our
ancestral creed, in which we stand, as it were, outside
ourselves, and attempt to look at our ideals and aspirations with the eyes of others. But yet we remain ourselves, and true to ourselves, during the process. And
if we observe any flaws in our ideals, it is as if
we were scanning critically a dear mother, wife, or
daughter. We may recognise in her some lapse or
deviation from our ideal of perfect beauty, but yet we
love her—but yet we love her.

After these preliminaries, let us to our theme. I
have spoken above of a "system of ideals," and I wish
first to develop that conception as a key to what I
am to say further. When we examine any specific
system of ethics—say the Buddhist or the Homeric—

we are struck by the fact that in broad detail it almost exactly resembles our own. It was no discovery of the ancient Hebrews that man must not slay his fellow-man, or forswear his faith, or steal what is not his own. No civil society could exist in which those principles were not recognised as binding. And what applies to the broader principles, applies in a large measure to the minor moralities. The content of the ethical code is everywhere among nations who can claim to be civilised practically the same. This is true of Judaism, even in its mediæval phases, when the terrible persecutions which Jews underwent might almost have justified anti-social interpolations. Jewish apologists have culled from Jewish writings of all time ethical maxims of the highest moral import, which vie in loftiness of spirit with those of the most favoured nations or creeds. A useful collection of these utterances has recently been compiled by a Jewish minister, the Rev. Morris Joseph, to whose *brochure*, "Jewish Ethics,"[1] I may refer those who doubt their existence, or who are otherwise interested in Jewish gnomic wisdom. For myself, I will venture to assume the practical identity of the contents of Jewish ethics with those of all the great religions, and am prepared in turn to grant the same to them.

I am more concerned to claim for Jews that they have been the first to grant this identity of the ethical principles adopted by humanity. I can illustrate this by a quotation from one of the few works written by Jews during the early middle ages in England, before they were expelled. Most of you will have read Browning's powerful poem, "Rabbi Ben Ezra." Mr.

---

[1] Published at the office of the *Jewish Chronicle*. It is also included in the volume on "Religions of the World," published by Messrs. Sonnenschein & Co.

Browning was probably unaware that the hero of his poem, Abraham ibn Ezra, a Spanish Jew of great attainments, an astronomer, grammarian, Biblical critic, mathematician, and traveller, visited England in 1158, and while here wrote a book on the Foundations of Religion (*Yesod More*), in which occurs the following passage on the Laws of Moses :—

"There is a fundamental law which commands us to observe all the Divine enactments, positive and negative. This precept, 'Ye shall serve the Lord your God' (Ex. xxiii. 25), includes all the laws to be kept by heart, word, or deed, whether primary laws or those serving to record them in memory. . . . Many commands have lost their force, as that of hyssop (Ex. xii. 22), of the manna (ibid. xix. 11). . . . Some commands are imposed on the whole people, as burnt offering, shew-bread, libations ; others belong to certain distinct families, as the duties of a prince, of a high priest, and the rest of the priests and Levites, the number of whose duties is very great. Several precepts are given to male and female indiscriminately ; some to men alone, as the redemption of the first-born ; others to women alone, as concerning vows. . . . There are many laws relating to a certain time . . . but many laws depend neither on time nor anything else, and these are imposed on all, male and female, king, priests, rich and poor, Israelites and proselytes, whole and sick. There is one law for all, and such precepts are primary. These primary laws are ingrained in the mind . . . and were known by the power of the mind before the law was declared by means of Moses; and there are many of this kind as, *e.g.*, those of the Decalogue except the Sabbath : these were only repeated by Moses. . . . There are also commanded certain pious works by which we are reminded of the primary precepts, as the observance of the Sabbath in memory of the creation of the world, Passover, unleavened bread, tabernacles, inscriptions on our doors, phylacteries of hand and head, fringes of garments. . . .

"All the precepts are to be referred to three things : (1) to piety of the heart, (2) to words, (3) to deeds. And as unity is contained in every number, so the beginning of every pious act by deed or word is internal piety, without which all worship is false and of none avail."

There are two points to which I wish to draw your attention in this passage. The first is, the remarkable statement—remarkable, that is, for a mediæval writer —that the primary laws of morality are ingrained in the human heart, and are not due to revelation, so that all human beings are cognisant of them, and they are binding on all. This is put more clearly, perhaps, by Ibn Ezra than any other mediæval Jewish thinker; but it underlies all Jewish thought and practice. Combined with the principle that salvation rests on works, it leads at once, and logically, to the dictum, "The pious of all nations have a part in the world to come"—a sentence which comes upon most people as a surprise, as emanating from a creed which is supposed to be so exclusive and narrow. It likewise accounts for the absence of all proselytising zeal, which is characteristic of Judaism, and comes equally as a surprise to most persons. The second point I will here only advert to, and that is the full recognition of the necessary inwardness of morality. That I will refer to later on ; but at present I wish to emphasise the Jewish recognition of the substantial identity of the ethical code of all nations. But while we allow that the raw materials of ethics are the same in all the great creeds or ethical systems, we are far from asserting that the way in which these materials are built up into the Jewish and into other systems of ethics is by any means identical. In the house of ethics there are many mansions : the bricks may be the same in each, but the order of architecture varies vastly. To any system of ethics we may address numbers of questions which can receive divers answers. To which of the virtues does it give most prominence ? What motives does it hold out for the performance of duty ? How does it propose to inculcate morality on its adherents ? And, lastly, what general principles does it posit by which it welds all the elements of morality into one system of ethics ? It is these general principles that I propose to deal with to-night, under the name of "Jewish Ideals," for want of a better.

The first and most striking of these—the one that occurs doubtless to most of you as the characteristic side of Jewish ethics, as you know it in the Old Testament and in the contests of the New—is the conception of *Morality as Law.* This involves the idea that the details of morality can be expressed verbally, and codified somewhat in the form of a legal code, and can be taught as such. The moral life in Jewish conception consists in conformity to such a law: sin consists in transgression of any of its enactments. Now, this is at first sight incongruous with much that you have been accustomed to hear in this Society. Whenever I have had the pleasure of listening to any of your lecturers, whatever the theme has been, the central conception has always been to put forth the ideal of Morality as Freedom. "The Good consists in the Good Will, and the Good Will is the Free Will;" that is the kind of -formula with which you are here familiar. Or to put it in another way, it is the intention that makes the morality of the act, not the conformity with any moral law imposed from without. True, to that we are all agreed. You will remember that Abraham ibn Ezra, in the passage quoted above, was as emphatic on this point as the most advanced Kantian can be. But the further question arises : How are you going to create good intentions in the human subject? Jewish ethics replies, by inculcating the practice of good actions in conformity with the moral law.

Here we come upon one of those differences of stress which constitute the divergences of various moral systems. Jewish ethics and Christian ethics agree in saying that good acts are desirable, and that good intentions are praiseworthy. But each lays stress on a different member of the pair. Jewish ethics says: Do good acts, and you will feel good; Christian ethics says: Feel good, and you will do good. The contrast is as old as the breach between the two Churches: you are familiar with it as the contrast between the Letter and the Spirit, a way of putting the distinction which scarcely does justice to the Jewish attitude, as is but natural in polemical pamphlets. I do not feel called upon to decide between the two contrasting principles of moral training. In putting before you the Jewish view, I do not defend, I expound. But I would point out that the matter in dispute is a question of pædagogics: in inculcating morality we are *ex hypothesi* dealing with the young, and I fail to see how else we are to proceed with them than by training them to acts. Freedom if you like for adults, but moral law for the growing spirit. And the freedom that is ultimately to be obtained by this means is not absence of all control, but willing obedience to a law self-imposed—*Frei und eins mit dem Gesetz,* as Berthold Auerbach put it. And in developing this relation between Morality as Freedom and Morality as Law, I fancy I but interpret that saying of the man who first brought out the contrast: "I come not to annul the Law, but to fulfil it." Another great Jew, Spinoza, also founds his conception of man's freedom on the notion of law. So far as I understand the fourth and fifth books of his "Ethics," perhaps the most difficult of all philosophical reading, he bases Freedom on Law, and does not oppose it to Law. Just at present one of the great wants of the age is the recognition of this conception of Morality as Law. A friend of mine even goes so far as to urge that a distinct Moral Code should be

drafted for instruction to children. Without entering
into the question how far this is practicable, I would
point out that the idea is eminently a Jewish one.
I would also point out that a large part of morality
is already codified as Law, and there is a distinct
tendency to increase this amount. A few years ago
it was a moral act to inform purchasers that certain
articles were made in Germany; nowadays it is
legally obligatory. I do not mean to infer that all
moral acts should become Acts of Parliament: they
would cease to be moral acts, pure and simple, then.
The truly moral act is that which is not punished by
the law if left undone, and is thus performed for its
own sake; and of this character are the enactments
of the so-called Jewish Law, which has no sanction
but the approval of conscience. There was a kind of
customary morality in England under the old *régime*
which partook of the same character, though it was
not formally codified. This has almost entirely disappeared, and there is nothing taking its place. Now
customary and conventional morality may not be the
highest type of morals, but it is surely better than
nothing at all; and that is practically what the urban
lower classes are coming to, who attend no Church,
and have no recognised authority in any moral problem. The Talmud, with all its casuistic minutiæ,
would be better than that state of things.

I have here incidentally touched upon the main charge
that is brought against the idea of Morality as Law.
There is in it a tendency to degrade moral acts into
mere mechanical custom, as when prayer, the free intercourse between man and his Maker, may degenerate
into a meaningless gabble, or a custom like that of not
eating pork may be raised to the same level as the
moral principle of not telling lies. I will grant at

once that there is this danger attaching to the Jewish conception of morality. But we have to reflect that the majority of men are creatures of habit, and only susceptible for the most part of a morality of conventions. Judaism accepts this fact, and legislates for' this class without at the same time preventing the rarer spirits from rising, as occasion serves, into the higher region of Morality as Freedom. Christianity battles strenuously against this tendency to convention, which it calls the World, and enlists on its side the more enthusiastic spirits who form the noble army of its martyrs and saints. But it is only enabled to do this by crippling the free exercise of men's speculative powers, whereas Judaism leaves these almost entirely unfettered, and by the very exercise of legal controversy in moral matters tends to lay an almost exaggerated stress on intellect and its function in life. Each system, it will be seen, has its own disadvantages : Christianity fetters the intellect, and fails to train the masses morally; Judaism tends to confuse morality, law, and custom. The morality of the Jew may become merely conventional; the morality of the Christian may only result in gush.

Before I pass on, I would disabuse your minds of at least one misconception which clings about the Jewish idea of Morality as Law ; and that is to regard the Law under the aspect of a burdensome yoke. As a matter of fact, this is for the most part utterly erroneous, and is indeed incongruous with the other charge brought against Jewish morality of being conventional or customary. The Jewish child grows accustomed to the yoke, and so it ceases to be burdensome to the Jewish man. And in so far as the Law does demand some sacrifice from Jewish children, it performs a distinctly moral function as a training in self-restraint. At almost

every moment of its life the Jewish child is taught to
consider life a discipline, in which it has to learn to
give up some of its selfish inclinations for the sake of
a principle. The conception of the Jewish Law as a
yoke is thus a distinctly moral principle.

Meanwhile, we may now direct a somewhat closer
scrutiny at the Law with which morality is identified
in Jewish conceptions. For practical purposes, it was
sufficiently characterised and analysed in the extract
from Abraham ibn Ezra, which has hitherto formed
our text. The Law consists of (1) the primary laws of
morality, (2) customs associated with certain seasons,
and (3) customs commemorative of certain events.
Now we have already seen that it is a characteristic
of the Jewish system of ethics to raise these customs
to the same level as the primary laws of morals. The
grounds adduced for this by Jewish authorities are
theological, and with these we are not at liberty to deal.
But apart from theology, a fair case may be made out
for the worship of

"Old Use and Custom, sisters grey,"

as Lord Tennyson calls them in a passage that points
to a defence of Custom as a foster-sister of Morality.
The utility of custom in the moral life, it seems to me,
is to create a fund of tender emotion which will be at
the service of the moralities. The abuse of custom, as
we all know, is its tendency to harden into superstition.
The dislocation of custom among the English peasantry
illustrates both. They are less superstitious, but less
considerate for others than they were in older days.
Jewish customs also illustrate both; but I desire to
regard them as illustrating the second great Jewish
ethical principle, which differentiates it from others,
and that is what I should term the *Holiness of Home.*

By Holiness, I mean something specific and intimately connected with those customs of which we have just been speaking. I mean the association of certain times and seasons in the Jewish home with certain ceremonial customs regarded as sacred. These ceremonies become "object lessons" in religion and in morality. They are interesting historically in many ways, to two of which I wish to call your attention. A wicked wit has called Judaism a "religion of survivals;" and the epigram is the more biting since it contains the proverbial half-truth, though not in this instance 'the better half of truth. The dietary laws have been plausibly explained as a survival of totemism; the rite of Abraham is still practised by a majority of the non-civilised races; the objection to intermarriage is known elsewhere as the rule of endogamy, and much of Jewish fidelity to faith and kindred bears a suspicious resemblance to ancestor-worship. The probabilities are that in their origin these were all savage, or, as we used to term them, idolatrous customs, and it was the policy of the Mosaic legislators to raise these to a higher power, to use a mathematical expression, by connecting them, as they are now connected, with a purer faith. Just at present, however, I wish to point out that in the Judaic conception of the Holiness of the Home, there has been raised to a higher power the most moral and most touching side of the ancient religions. When we think of the noble and dignified type of character produced in the Greek and Roman world, we may be sure that there was something more in their religion than mere external pageantry and impure idolatry. And that purer side of their religion was represented by the worship of the Penates, or ancestral gods, of which we know but little in detail, but which clearly dominated the whole home-life of the ancients, and, as has been shown by

M. Fustel de Coulanges, was made the basis of their
social organisation.   Not a meal, not a family meeting
occurred which was not ushered in by a solemn libation
to the spirits of the ancestors, who were conceived to be
present and sanctified the whole of the home.   Judaism
preserves this noble trait of the ancient world, with the
difference of regarding the spirit that is present and is
invoked as the spirit of all flesh, the Divine Majesty
of the Universe.   It is impossible to describe to those
who have not experienced it, the feeling of holy joy
which is diffused throughout the humblest Hebrew
home by the solemn repetition of acts which in themselves may be regarded as mere customs, without vital
connection with the souls of men.   In speaking thus,
I am not thinking of the so-called upper classes of Jews,
who aim at an electro-plate imitation of the manners of
their neighbours, and think it " cultured " to drop these
customs.   I refer more particularly to the home-life of
the ordinary Jewish artisan, even of the poor Polish
Jews, who have in other respects been degraded by
ages of persecution, but in this particular possess a
dignity in their homes which is not shared by those of
their neighbours which are quite free from " survivals,"
even of decency.

This aspect of Jewish morality is perhaps more
familiar to you than any other, because it is that in
which English life has been most deeply affected by
Hebraic conceptions, as represented by the Bible.   And
the particular institution in which it is embodied most
characteristically, both for Jews and Christians, is that
of the Sabbath.   I do not know how it has come about
—or rather, I do know, but cannot linger to discuss—
that a " Judaic Sabbath " means a day of austere gloom.
As a matter of fact, it is the one bright spot in the
Jewish life.   Heine, to the last a Hebrew of the

Hebrews in his severer moods, has written a beautiful
poem about the Princess Sabbath, in which Israel has
been condemned by a wicked fairy to wander about
during the week as a hound, but on Sabbath is transformed once more into human shape, and resumes his
natural dignity. All is joy and good-humour in the
Jewish home on the Friday night, when Sabbath
" comes in." I would attribute a good deal of the
difference between the Jewish and the Christian
Sabbath to the seemingly mechanical difference, that
the one begins and ends at an hour when its advent
or exit can be solemnised by ceremonial, whereas the
other comes and goes, if I may use the phrase, " as
a thief in the night." Curiously enough, the other
work, written by the Rabbi Ibn Ezra while in England,
was an elaborate defence of the Eastern method of
beginning the day with the eve. It is indeed to the
Sabbath primarily, and the other home ceremonials
which embody the Hebraic conception of the Holiness
of the Home, that we can trace the remarkable per-
sistence of the Jewish race through the ages. This
is generally spoken of as due to their fidelity to their
faith, and so on ; but we have to seek for the social
institutions in which that faith was embodied before
we can adequately understand the attraction it had
for its adherence. Life itself seemed to the Jew little
worth having without the Holiness of Home, to which
he had been accustomed from his early days, and which
kept its attraction even for the arch-scoffer Heine.

We may now pass to a third leading principle that
dominates Jewish ethics, which we may call its Messianic tone, due to the idea of the *Mission of Israel*.
In speaking of the hallowing of custom, which forms
so large a part of the Jewish discipline, I should have
said that it not only strengthens family love, the nurse

of all the moralities, but it forms a bond of common custom between family and family, and between Jews of one country and those of another. But a bond for what? it may be asked. Is Judaism a mere trades union designed to promote the benefit of its members against the competition of others who are not "on the statement," as the trade phrase runs? It would seem as if the anti-Semites thought so; and so far as their criticisms touch Jews who have lost the Messianic hope, their view might seem to be justified. But these are just the Jews who are not under the influence of the bond of custom, which they have mostly thrown off. The mass of Jews are still influenced by the Messianic hopes, and keep up their separateness from others, and their bonds with one another under the influence of the conviction that there is a Divine mission for Israel to play in the world's history. The conviction is somewhat vague and indefinite; some look forward to a personal Messiah and a political future, others anticipate a Messianic age and a spread of Hebraic conceptions and Jewish ideals. But a hope need not be the less vivid because it cannot be expressed in a formula, or rather, I would say, the more clear and definite you make it, the nearer it is to its last hour. Judaism is here at one with the last and greatest of the philosophers, Hegel, in regarding "abstraction" as the least vital form of thinking and of aspiration. The moment you can reduce your ideal to a formula, you may prepare for its funeral, or you may as well nail it at once to your barn-door as a scarecrow; it has no more vitality left in it, no further potentialities of development. To come back from this abstract way of looking at the matter—the very thing against which I am inveighing—I would remark that a hope that is vague is one that cannot be disappointed, and can therefore live on through all vicissitudes of fortune, as the Messianic hope has done in Israel.

I feel a difficulty of speaking of this Jewish ideal under the limits I have imposed upon myself of speaking without reference to any theological conceptions. But I would remark that there is no reason why a similar conception could not be adopted by all nations. What, indeed, is involved in the conception of a nationality, but the profound conviction of its members that they have developed a special type of character which peculiarly fits them for some special function in the development of humanity ? Would that England were more conscious of some Divine mission to perform in the world's history! Once it was Protestantism that gave enthusiasm to the majority of Englishmen, the eradication of slavery has still some of the vitality of an ideal, and even the latter-day apology for a mission, " Peace on earth and Free Trade among men," can still rouse Englishmen's energies on behalf of an ideal. Even if the mission turn out to be an illusion, I say it is better for men to have an illusory ideal than none at all. Puritanism braced up Englishmen's souls, though its ideals have crumbled away under the assaults of modern thought and sentiment. Acute observers are of opinion that the only hope of raising France from the Slough of Despond is in keeping alive the seemingly futile hope of the *Révanche*. And reverting to Israel, one feels that the only thing that idealises the too often prosaic figure of the modern Jew is the halo of the Divine promises to which he still clings, and so justifies his separateness from the rest of mankind. Consider what dignity is given to the function of maternity when every Jewish mother may feel the hope that from her may issue one who will restore moral peace to mankind.

Underlying the whole conception, or presenting another aspect of it, is the fourth Jewish ideal of the *Hallowing of History*. Here again I am hampered by my own bonds, and am prevented from describing this in the shortest way as the recognition of God in History. But looking at the matter merely on psychological grounds, this conception is the recognition of the fact that man is made man by history. It is history that, as represented by its medium language, differentiates man from the brute. It is history that causes the men of the historic nations to be more civilised than the savage. The Jew recognises practically, if not consciously, that he is made what he is by the history of his fathers, and feels he is losing his better self so far as he loses his hold of his past history; for he regards himself as having gone through the vicissitudes of his fathers. Many of the customary ceremonials which make up the holiness of the Jewish home are purely history raised into religion. One of them, the Passover, has passed over into Christianity as its most sacred function, still retaining survivals of its historic origin and connections; the wine and wafer of the Mass (or Communion) representing the wine and unleavened bread still tasted by Jews at the inaugural banquet of the Passover Service. At one part of the ceremonial, which is mainly made up of the story of the Exodus, it is remarked: "Every Jew should regard himself as if he had personally come out of Egypt." That spirit dominates the whole of Jewish life and ceremonial.

Here, again, I see no reason why the Judaic conception of history should not be adopted and adapted by all nations that have a history. The idea of giving history a continued life in ceremonial has altogether died out among modern nations, and especially among

Englishmen, where its only survival is "Guy Fawkes' Day." A distinct loss of national dignity results from this, and we may notice that the virtue of patriotism no longer holds the place it once did in the hierarchy of English virtues. Some years ago the question was raised, "Can Jews be patriots?" implying, Could Jews feel themselves at once Jews and Englishmen? The answer is, that the very reason that makes an English Jew conscious of his Judaism makes him equally conscious that he is an Englishman. For certain sides of his character and ideals he feels his indebtedness to his Jewish parentage and breeding; other sides, his freedom as a citizen, his language, and the intellectual acquirements that go with it, he feels he owes to his position as an English citizen.

Before leaving this side of the subject, I would remark on certain corollaries on the Messianic Ideal and the Hallowing of History that have a characteristic bearing on Jewish ethics. These have a distinctly moralising effect by making the ideal of each individual 'something other than himself—in the first place his co-religionists, and in the final issue humanity. The unit is the family, which is a permanence; hence the pertinacity and patience with which Jews have borne the tribulations of ages, buoyed up by the Messianic hopes. "If not in my time, at least in that of my children," thinks many a Jewish parent. This idea has results not so desirable from an economic point of view in the early marriages of Jews and their all too numerous results. It concentrates, too, attention on this world as the true field of the Divine drama. Jews escape by this means "other-worldliness," it is true; but I doubt whether that is so much inferior to "this-worldliness" to which Jews are thereby restricted. There

B

is finally involved an optimistic conception of the world which is in reality involved in every Theistic conception. That can be no good God who has made, or who rules, a world radically evil. But here, again, I am trenching on the province of the theologian.

I have now called your attention to the four chief principles on which Judaism deals with the material of ethics, and works them up into a specific Jewish ethics—the ideas of Morality as Law, the Holiness of Home, the Mission of Israel, and the Hallowing of History. If there were time, I might show how these are interconnected together into an organic system, and may be ultimately resolved into the first and last—Morality as Law and the Hallowing of History. But I prefer to look at the subject from another point of view, and exhibit the organic character of Jewish ethics as shown in its subjective aspects. "We live by admiration," says Wordsworth; and by the imitation that expresses our admiration, we may add. By holding up certain ideals before men's eyes you create certain types of character which differ morally, not by any difference in the contents of the moral code, but by emphasis on different parts in it, and by special selection of the various virtues by which morality can be realised. Such a type of character is an organic one; you cannot lop off one ideal and suppose the rest of the character to remain the same. You cannot change the relative importance of the characteristic virtues without modifying the whole system; you cannot get the heart to perform the functions of the brain. Now each nation and each religion tends to develop its special type; there is a distinct English character, and even an ideal of a specific Christian character, and so there is a special

Jewish type of character. I suppose if we were to hit upon the pet virtue of an Englishman, it would be justice; and, similarly, the most prominent characteristic at which the Jewish character seems to aim is fidelity to race and religion. In other words, the Jew stands up for differentiation in character. It is not his ideal that all men should be alike in character just at present, and in the practical expression of that aim he lives and dies.

This is the much abused separateness of the Israelite which brings down upon him the ill-will of nearly the whole world. Strangely enough the opposition comes most strongly from those new-fledged patriots of Germany and Austria, who insist most strenuously on the need of living up to a specific German or Austrian ideal of character. Or rather not strangely, for it is a necessary element of a specific national character that it feels opposition to any rival ideal. The interesting point to observe is, that what these gentlemen object to in the Jewish character is not its too great narrowness, but its cosmopolitanism. Indeed, it is generally characteristic of Jews to confound their accusers in this way. While Christians have preached humility and forgiveness of enemies for centuries, Jews have been content to practice those virtues, the former rather laxly, perhaps, but the latter in all its fulness. And so while the Austrian is preaching the necessity of all men becoming brothers ("German cousins" they really mean), the Austrian Jews have no more than taken him at his word, in feeling an interest in the rest of the world, even though it be but a portion of that remainder.

At the beginning of this lecture I promised you a "rational justification" for the Jewish ideals which I was about to present to you, and you may think

I shall be hard put to it to find a justification from a universalist standpoint for this one of Jewish separateness. Not at all. That remaining apart of Jews, while still joining in all the world's work that is unsectarian and beneficial, is fully justified by the great danger that begins to loom before us as never before in the world's history. I refer to a process which is best exemplified in the Chinese Empire, and which I would therefore call *Chinesism*. This is the tendency among huge masses of people to crush individuality, and reduce all its members to one dead level of mediocrity. The ideals of such a mass are formed, its type of character fixed, and for it there rests no more hope of progress, either in elevation of ideal or ennobling of character. Its individual members may live happy lives, but from that mass the world has nothing to hope for in moral teaching. Something of this kind is beginning to be noticed in the United States of America. In Europe, too, there are signs of the creation of a European type, to which we shall all conform. One of the outward signs of this, which all artists lament, is the spread of the chimney-pot hat and black cloth coat throughout Europe, and even in joyous Japan, displacing the picturesque and characteristic national dresses. In one hundred years things will be worse; there will then remain only five or six types of human character out of which the final human character can develop. The nationalist movements of this century have been unconscious protests against this tendency of things. Now, the evil of this is that whenever a distinct ideal or specific type of character is crushed out, the resultant human type that seems so rapidly approaching will be so much the less rich and varied. This, then, is why the Jews, ay, or the Irish, or the Japanese, should be allowed, and encouraged, to preserve any characteristic they have which differentiates them from the great masses of humanity whose characters are becoming ossified. Suppose for a moment that the whole 100,000 Jews of Great Britain were made, to-morrow, completely indistinguishable from the rest of Englishmen, what advantage would accrue to humanity from the transformation? Is it not possible that the English character might have thereby lost the chance of being enriched at a favourable moment by one or other of the specific Jewish ideals that I have put before you?

Of course there are disadvantages connected with the present state of things—disadvantages, mark you, which fall upon Jews for the most part, and not on the peoples among whom they dwell. One of these disadvantages I consider a serious one, though it seems at first sight somewhat ludicrous. I refer to the vanity which is almost necessarily involved in keeping alive the feeling of special mission. I fear, however, that it is necessary in the present state of human nature. If you are to believe in your ideals and in your ideal character, you must believe in yourself, and have the courage of your self-opinion. I have myself blown a somewhat loud fantasia on the Hebraic horn, with variations of my own. Not that I could not have introduced a few discordant notes. There are lapses in every ideal, or we should have reached the end of our tether in idealisation. The cumbrousness of the Jewish code, the obsolete character of some of its customs, the theoretical injustice done to women, and other points, might be adduced. But, with your permission, I prefer putting these, if I have an opportunity, before my own community. To you it would do no good to rehearse them. I have preferred putting before you those points of Jewish ethics which, in my opinion, it would be well if they could be adopted into other national systems.

"If, then, you believe so strongly in your ideals, why do you not strive to spread them among the nations?" is the final retort you will have for me. To that the reply is, that character ideals and types can only be spread by living up to them, and thus prompting to admiration and imitation by others. Of course, if Judaism and the Jewish ideals were mere matters of faith, one could spread them by preaching. Truths or untruths of the intellect can be spread abroad by preachments, but not ideals of character. If now and again a Jewish thinker were to give to an Ethical Society a rose-coloured picture of the Jewish ideals, I doubt if the characters of the members, already formed as they are, would be much modified, unless possibly in their home life they aimed at adapting the Jewish ideals for the benefit of those coming after. Character cannot be passed from person to person in neat little parcels wrapped up in brown paper. It is only by working out your own character to the highest pitch of which it is capable that you can influence the characters of others, especially of the young. Jewish practice in this regard has the countenance of two great German thinkers. Kant, who lived the most non-human life of any mortal that ever breathed, and by his very detachment from life was enabled to see most clearly and profoundly into it, declared that you can directly aid a man's happiness, but he must work out his perfection for himself. So, too, Goethe, who lived perhaps one of the most human and natural lives ever passed by men, gives the same moral in the mystical final scene of his "Faust." The soul of Faust is handed over to the care of the spirit of Margaret, who earnestly asks how she is to conduct him to the highest peaks. " Go up higher ; he will follow thee," is the response—simple words, but there is the whole philosophy of human fellowship in them.

No ; I see nothing for it but that each should live up to the highest that he himself can grasp, trusting that in the final issue the supreme highest will prevail, and hoping that his ideal will at least form a part of the final aim of humanity. Ideals have their life and development, and, as with all life, development depends on conflict, which subjectively means renunciation. We should not be disheartened while the conflict goes on, since the longer it lasts the higher the final stage of development. Meanwhile, in the strife of creeds and ideals, all we can ask for, and give, is a fair field and no favour. Let each man bear himself as bravely as he may, and let the battle-cry be, as of old, " God for us all ! "

THE GOD OF ISRAEL: A HISTORY

(" *Nineteenth Century,*" *September* 1879)

HISTORICAL science is laying its hand on the ark of the Lord. Undeterred by the fate of the men of Beth-shemesh (1 Sam. vi. 19), the men of Leyden [1] have looked into the Bible with reverential, yet critical, eyes to discover the historical nature of the God of Israel.[2] Abating not a jot of the reverence of their gaze, we may yet venture to disagree with the critical method that has directed their vision. They have opposed the supernaturalists and the doctrine of verbal inspiration, but, as almost always happens in the history of thought, they have retained the psychological method of their opponents. The older science of mind regarded man as separated from his fellows, and as being much the same at all stages of the world's history. Super-naturalism, accepting this view, drew a hedge round the children of Israel, and regarded the Deity as inspiring certain isolated individuals with a conception of His nature which remained the same throughout sacred history. The Leyden naturalistic school with-

[1] Professor Kuenen's *Religion of Israel* and *Prophets and Prophecy in Israel* have been translated into English, as well as Knappert's *Religion of Israel*, a useful summary of Kuenen's results. It is to be regretted that Kuenen's *Historisch-kritisch Onderzoek*, the critical foundation of his views, and Professor Tiele's important *Vergelijkende Geschiedenis van de Egyptische en Mesopotamische Godsdiensten* (Amsterdam, 1872), still remain buried in so tribal a tongue as the Dutch.

[2] This phrase has been employed throughout as a convenient abbreviation of the unwieldy expression "the views about the Highest Being held by the children of Israel."

draws the hedge, but still regards the inspired ones as isolated, and chiefly differs from its opponents in restricting the period of inspiration to the times of the prophets. Both schools think of history as a collection of disconnected pools, instead of regarding it as a stream of living waters.

Meanwhile in Germany, the home of history, Professors Steinthal and Lazarus have laid the foundations of the science of National Psychology (*Völkerpsychologie*) as the basis of historical investigation. The Psychology of Nations has to investigate the traits which, in addition to his common humanity, make a man a Greek, a Jew, an Englishman, or a German, and in doing this it has arrived at the scientific treatment of the national spirit (*Volksgeist*) existing in all the members of a nation, and having its life in the national history. From this point of view—and it is the fundamental conception of all German historiography—we should have to treat gifted individuals as merely the voice of the national spirit, and not as an isolated phenomena. Again, in making the nation and not the individual our starting-point we introduce the idea of continuity into history, and with it the conception of development and growth of the national spirit. We have accordingly to trace in the earlier stages of a nation's life the germs of later developments of the national genius. In retaining the individualistic view of mind and thus neglecting the influence of the social medium, in overlooking the fact of growth and thus making no distinction between seed and fruit, the Leyden critics have left out of account the determining factors of the problem.

In the following pages an attempt is made to treat the development of the religious conceptions of the children of Israel from the new standpoint of historic method reached by Professors Steinthal and Lazarus. Hitherto they had not applied their principles to any particular history, and it is, no doubt, owing to this that they have overlooked a most important influence at work, which will here be termed the *cross-fertilisation* [1] *of national ideas.* Given, with the Berlin professors, that each nation has its peculiar mental traits, the problem remains to be determined how far these are influenced by communication with the thought of other nations. In giving due prominence to this phenomenon we have been led to trace the development to a latter stage of the national life of the Jews than is usually attempted. Indeed, it was in tracing the antecedents of Spinozism in Judaism that this influence was seen to have been at work all down the line. There has thus been obtained a continuous development of the religious ideas of the Jews from the Jehovah [2] of Abraham to the *Substantia* of Spinoza, each stage of change being due to some cross-fertilisation by the thought of another nation, the influence of Greece being specially prominent. Nor, on the other hand, has the influence of Israel on the world's thought been unworthy of notice. Christianity is but the most striking example. This cross-fertilising influence of Israel has accordingly been touched upon as forming episodes in the history of the God of Israel.

---

[1] This metaphor is here introduced as being more definite and suggestive than the vague term "influence." By the biological analogy suggested there is implied (1) that the ideas cross-fertilised belong to nearly allied species of *Volksgeist* (the ideas of a Hottentot and of a Hindoo cannot cross-fertilise) ; (2) that the resultant idea is more fitted to survive in the struggle for spiritual existence.

[2] The writer of Ex. vi. 3, who evidently considers that there had been such a development between the patriarchal age and the times of Moses, gives "El Shaddai" as the name of the earlier conception, and Semitic comparative philology seems to confirm his view. "Jehovah" is here used to indicate the specific Hebraic element.

That history divides itself into two periods which are of nearly equal length, but which differ greatly in familiarity to the ordinary reader. The first, which may be roughly termed the Biblical period, reaching down to the foundation of Christianity, comprises that part of the world's spiritual history with which Englishmen are, or used to be, most familiar. All that was here necessary was to give a rapid summary of the chief spiritual movements in Israel, attempting, more consistently than hitherto has been done, to give the logical connection of each stage. More importance is to be attached to the method employed than the results obtained. The Leyden school, it is here contended, has not given due attention to the need of tracing in earlier stages the beginnings of later movements.

The second period of the national history of the Jews, from the second century A.D. to the present time, is practically unknown to the English reader, and has only lately received adequate attention in Germany. And notwithstanding the mass of monographs on separate Jewish thinkers and systems, no complete history of Jewish thought in its logical development exists as yet in any language. This is mainly due to an erroneous conception of the position of Spinoza in the history of philosophy. Till very recent years Spinozism has been regarded as merely a more consistent Cartesianism, the outward similarity of method obscuring the essential difference of spirit in the two systems. With regard to Spinoza's relation to Judaism, the excommunication of the *Beth-Din* (ecclesiastical tribunal) of Amsterdam, a purely defensive act, was held to have settled the question of his connection with Jewish speculation by a decided negative. But Dr. M. Joel's researches have conclusively shown that

the philosopher-martyr took his problem from Jewish
predecessors, and was mainly indebted to Descartes—
a heavy debt—for the method which he applied to its
solution. And we maintain that the recognition of
Spinoza as the goal of the long line of Jewish thought
gives its history a unity which has been universally
overlooked. In a first attempt like the present, and
with the limited space at disposal, no more could be
done than roughly to map out the ground for future
investigation. This is especially the case with the
latter part of the post-Biblical period, where individual
philosophers come into the foreground, and it becomes
difficult to see strictly national movements. The
national organism, as it were, had in them differentiated a brain, an organ of self-consciousness; and, on
our historic method, the successive philosophers must
be treated as stages of the Jewish mind in its progress
towards Spinozism. We have, so to speak, to trace
the course of an intellectual tunnel through the
Middle Ages which only comes to the light of day
with Spinoza.

With these necessary words as to plan and method
we may now proceed to our inquiry, viz., the history of
the *views of the children of Israel* about the Deity—in
short, the history of the God of Israel.

I

At the outset of the inquiry — *i.e.*, the Biblical
period—we are met by a number of preconceptions,
theological and anti-theological, which render the
adoption of a scientific attitude extremely difficult.
Let it be enough if we say here that, in assuming the
Bible to be the work of man, we hold that the assump-

tion tends rather to dignify man than to degrade the Bible. But once having assumed the Bible to be a human production, there follow several prosaic yet important corollaries, such as that it was composed, written down, copied, and finally edited. Further, as the use of writing cannot be regarded as an early mode of transmission of thought, that portion of the Bible which relates to the earlier fortunes of the Hebrews must have been handed down by tradition for many centuries, subject to the imaginative colouring of the narrators for that long period. Assuming the mytho-pœic[1] tendency of the transmitters, the "personal equation" of the composers, and finally the antagon-istic attitude of the editors towards stages of thought which the nation had outgrown, we must recognise that the source of history has become very impure, and requires a strong solution of psychological criticism to precipitate the impurities and render the troubled waters clear. We have consequently to guard against a fourth source of error—historically, perhaps, the most important—the inadequate nature of the psychological apparatus which earlier investigators applied to the problem.

The *origines* of Hebraism treated with these pre-cautions can scarcely be settled with even tolerable certainty, as is proved by the widely divergent recon-

---

[1] Bernstein and Goldziher would have it that all the earlier history, reaching down almost to the time of David, is purely mythical. This is, however, going too far; however much myths may gather round the stories of national heroes (we have their "survival" in modern scandal), the heroes have existed, and have done heroic deeds. The personification of the sun and moon, of the dawn and eve, which the followers of Max Müller would posit in place of actual personalities, appear to the present writer a most instructive warning against dealing with words instead of things. Abraham and Isaac, Jacob and Joseph, may not have done all the Bible tells of, but they are certainly not different aspects of the sun-god or varying forms of the dark and dewy eve.

structions of the Biblical narrative put forward of late
years. Nor can we place much reliance on the new
science of Comparative Religion. Here, too, national
psychology has to moderate the too sanguine expecta-
tions of the Semitic specialists by calling attention to
a radical defect in their method. Granting that all the
Semitic tribes have a number of generic similarities of
character, we must not overlook the co-ordinate fact
that each has its specific differences. And it is extremely probable that the diversities from the Semitic
type form the most important characteristic of so
unique a nation as the Hebrews. The late Salomon
Munk defended with great force the position that the
Hebrews alone of all the Semites rose to monotheism ;
and Renan's brilliant and specious contention for a
Semitic monotheistic instinct is now ruled out of court
by all scholars. We are not enlightened as to the
development of religion among the Hebrews by
guesses as to the gods of Phœnicia, or by ingenious
conjectures as to the pre-Islamite development of the
Arabian conceptions of religion. The comparative
method will find its proper application in the problems
of cross-fertilisation which occur in the history of the
Hebrews, in the determination of the influence of
Egypt, Canaan, Phœnicia, Babylon, and Persia on the
religion of Israel. For the actual development of the
specifically Hebraic conceptions our only source, unsatisfactory as it may be in some respects, is the
Hebrew Bible itself.

Having thus cleared the way, however roughly,
through the mass of obstructions of method which
form the real obstacles to Biblical research, let us
attempt to sketch in very bold outline the development
of the Hebraic conception of the Deity during the
Biblical period. Broadly speaking, that development

consists in the continual universalising of the national
God Jehovah.[1] And we must add that the characteristic
of the Hebraic conception, as distinguished from that
of the other Semitic tribes, was the lofty ethical character ascribed to Him. Or rather, we may say that
the views about conduct which the old Hebrews held
in connection with their religious conceptions have
become the moral or ideal views of conduct for the
civilised world. What were once Hebraic opinions on
social conduct, are now the moral instincts of civilised
humanity. The "strictness of conscience" was once
the "spontaneity of [the Hebrew] consciousness," to
apply Mr. Matthew Arnold's attempted distinction between Hebraism and Hellenism in the fourth chapter
of his "Culture and Anarchy." The glory of the
Hebrews is not that they never had a "tribal" God,
but that they held practical opinions in connection
with religion which have become the ideal of civilised
morality. It was in consequence of this, as we shall
see, that they alone rose from the "tribal" conception
of a divine protector of the children of Israel to that of
the one Divine Father of all (Mal. ii. 10). The stages
of development are not clear, but the following may be
put forward as probable.

The HEBREWS were originally a nomad tribe, perhaps in the beginning resident in Mesopotamia, if we
may trust the national tradition of the origin of Abraham in Ur of the Chaldees. As far as we can gather
from later accounts, Jehovah was but a family god,
though even then a just and righteous one (*cf.* the

---

[1] I use the more familiar form in preference to the possibly more correct Jhwh, Jahveh, or Yahweh, on the same principle which makes us still
speak of Homer and Horace instead of Homeros and Horatius. At the
same time, it expresses dissent from the current hypothesis, first started
by Astruc (1753), of an Elohistic and Jahvistic redaction of the Bible,
which has not yet been established by any complete induction.

legend of Sodom and Gomorra). From their primeval home, whether Mesopotamia (Tiele) or North Arabia (Schrader), they wandered west till they found suitable pasturage in Lower Egypt. Here they came in contact with the higher civilisation of an agricultural state of society. The effects of this cross-fertilisation is one of the first problems of the comparative method. Here we can only refer to the conjectured relation between the *Nuk-pu-nuk* of Egyptian hierology and the "I am that I am" of the Hebrew legislator (*cf*. Ex. vi. 3). After a stay of uncertain duration, their prosperity brought upon them the tyranny of the Egyptian king (Ramses the Second), and in the reign of his successor they resumed their nomad life, accompanied, it would seem, by a number of Egyptians. This deliverance from the "house of bondage" made a profound impression on the national mind, and rendered their attachment to the "tribal" God deep and abiding. But the more important point to notice is the ethical character of their conception of God. The Ten Words are unique in history as a covenant of a nation with its God to bind itself to righteousness. The importance attached to the moral law, to social conduct, as distinguished from penal legislation and political life, is a distinguishing mark of the Hebrews, which they have carried with them throughout their history. And if we are to retain our scientific attitude, we must recognise at least the germ of this in the very beginnings of the national life. Thus the science of history seems to confirm the national tradition that Jehovah had been made known to Israel before the residence in Egypt. And in the moral attributes of the "tribal" Jehovah are the elements which ultimately lead to the conception of the God of all. A just God cannot be conceived as partial to one body of men, unless they have deserved it by some service which must be to the rest of mankind. In the conception of a just "tribal" Jehovah we have the germs of the later conceptions of the God of all and of Israel as the Messiah of the nations. The supernaturalists who assert that the Hebrews had as universal a God as the greater prophets thereby prove themselves the worshippers of a tribal deity, while the Leyden critics who deny the existence of a universalistic element in the Hebraic conception of the "tribal" Jehovah must trace its source from another nation, or relegate its explanation to the mystics.

The next stage of the national history is the conquest of the tribes of Canaan and the formation of the ISRAELITE nation out of the nomad tribe of Hebrews. The latter result was finally consummated under David, who commenced to centralise at Jerusalem. Throughout this period we have a struggle between the religion of Canaan and of the Hebrews, and we have here another instance of cross-fertilisation. Like all other conquering nations, from the days of Veii to those of Alsace-Lorraine, the Hebrews could only consolidate their conquest by permitting the conquered to amalgamate with them. Along with this political there went a religious amalgamation. The lower orders of the Hebrews joined with the Canaanite *peregrini* (to borrow a term of Roman law [1]) in the worship of the gods of the country, Baal, Asteroth, &c., who appear, from recent researches, to have had their original home in Assyria. And even the highest classes were influenced by the Canaanitish theory of things, as is natural when a less civilised nomad tribe conquers a more highly cultured agricultural nation.

---

[1] To the unprejudiced observer, one of the most light-giving books on the Old Testament which have appeared in late years is Sir H. S. Maine's "Ancient Law."

There seems reason to believe that the Hebrews bor-
rowed their cosmogony from the Canaanites (if it was
not brought later from Assyria) and connected with
it the institution of the Sabbath. But even more
important was the necessary change in their views of
Jehovah : He had to be put in connection with the
"other gods." This relation was naturally one of
superiority as the God of a conquering tribe. And
this superiority was strengthened by the centralisation
carried on by David and his successor, till among the
higher minds the view gained currency that the "other
gods" were as nothing compared with the almighty
Jehovah. With the disruption of the kingdom under
the tyranny of Solomon's son, the centrifugal forces
became very strong, and local divine government
ensued in the worship of Baal, Moloch, and the other
foreign gods. But at this critical moment the national
spirit of the Israelites expressed itself in a series of
men whose thoughts and words have moulded the
religious belief of the civilised world for upwards of
1500 years. The prophets strove valiantly to uphold
the honour of Jehovah among the people, laying stress
on the ethical elements implicit in the earlier conception in contrast to the cruel and bloodthirsty gods
of Phœnicia and Canaan. In politics they held fast
to the principle, unique among all political principles,
that the greatness of a nation depended on its righteousness, and endeavoured to oppose seeking for aid
in the struggle between North and South Judæa from
Assyria or Egypt. They were unsuccessful, and both
kingdoms were subdued, and a large body of the
Israelites carried over to Babylon. They were unsuccessful as politicians, but they had succeeded in a
spiritual sense. They had purified the national conception of their God from the ignoble elements which

form so large a part of the views of their Semitic
kinsmen about their deities. But here again it must
be insisted that these nobler elements had been implicit in the earlier Hebraic conception. For man at
least there is no creation *ex nihilo*, and the prophets
could only have given back to the Israelites as rain
what they had received from their nation as vapour,
to use Mr. Gladstone's fine metaphor. We contend
against Kuenen and Tiele that the note of righteousness must have been a mark of the Hebraic God from
the very beginning.

The stay in Babylon was productive of changes in the
national mind of world-historic importance. During
this period the chief traits of the character of the
JEWS were permanently formed—their intense historic
consciousness of the national past and passionate regard for the national future, their cosmopolitan
tendencies, their strict theocratic legislation, their
plasticity of intellect, and rigidity of social observance.
All these traits are represented in the redaction of
the Biblical canon which took place on their return.
The Bible, which thus represents the Judaic or mature
phase of the national mind, has ever remained the
centre of the national literature. The literary activity
of the Jews for the next thousand years after the final
settlement of the canon is entirely a development of
the Bible in paraphrase (Targum), codification of the
law (Halacha), or expansion of legend (Hagada,
Midrash). The national character became fixed, and
in its maturity commenced to cross-fertilise the growth
of the world's thought at various intervals. They
were prepared for this by the assimilation of new
elements. In Babylon they had come in contact with
the noblest Aryan religion—Erânian Mazdeism—and
their conception of the Divine nature was heightened

and broadened by the cross-fertilisation. Jehovah
was conceived as the Universal Father, inexpressible
by material images, unapproachable by material sacrifices. The tribalism of the earlier conception was
raised to the lofty view that Israel is only His chosen
people in order that through them the nations should
be blessed. The Jews had returned from the captivity
chastened by adversity, and with the national ideal of
spreading among the nations the prophetic conception
of ethical monotheism. The influence of Mazdeism
is shown in the second Isaiah and possibly in the
Book of Job, where the existence of evil is the first
puzzle disintegrating the older conception of the God
of Righteousness. It indicates the first beginnings of
subjectivity among the Hebrews, the rise of the distinction between the individual and the nation, and
with it the striving after personal immortality. This
remained a mere germ for future fertilisation. The
Jews in their sacred books do not show any signs of
having been influenced by fears or hopes of a future
state in their views of morality; they show no signs
of a clutching "otherworldliness" in their views of
conduct. In adversity each member of a nation loses
his individuality, his subjectivity—his ideal is the
public good; and this objectivity was fostered among
the Jews by their conception of the Deity as the just
Jehovah into whose hands each felt he could entrust
his fate.

At the same time that Israel was being tried by
adversity, Greece was in the first flush of victory over
the common enemy. But the national prosperity of
the Greeks was not without its evil results. There
arose the feeling of a life away from the social life
which we have called above subjectivity, and which
is expressed in history by the rise of the Sophists.

Throughout the ethical thought of Greece, remarks Mr. Sidgwick, egoism was an implicit assumption. While Israel was commencing its long career as the People of Sorrows, the Greeks in their glory were developing traits which led to the "hungry Greekling" of Juvenal's pages. Yet we may trace the spiritual history of the civilised world in the action and counter-action of the national spirits which were maturing and becoming fixed in Hellas and Judæa in the fifth century before the present era. The remainder of these remarks will be devoted to the chief stages in the history of the interlaced development of Hebraism and Hellenism.

With the conquests of Alexander and the spread of Hellenism among the barbarians, we have the first contact of the two influences. The results on the Jewish mind are to some extent preserved for us in the Septuagint version. The Greek had risen to the idea of an intellectual monotheism, a cosmic conception of a highest principle without emotional or historic elements. We accordingly find the intensely personal view of God in many cases toned down in the Greek version, and the general spirit of the version is naturalistic. Later on, the individualism of Hellenistic culture vitalised the corresponding germ which had been transplanted from Persian soil, and brought the question of personal immortality into the foreground, giving rise to disintegration of the national life into sects. The Sadducees, the conservative priestly party, held to the older view or instinct of non-belief; as far as we can gather from the Talmud, they rather denied the relevancy of the question in the spiritual life than dogmatically denied the possibility of the fact. The Pharisees, or liberals, the party of progress, were not opposed to assimilation of foreign modes of thought,

and believed in immortality as essential to individualism.
With this rise of freethought there naturally arose a
tendency to mysticism, attempting to solve intellectual problems by emotional conceptions. The sect of
Essenes in Judæa, and the mystic union of Moses and
Plato in the pages of the Alexandrian Philo, are two
instances of this tendency among the many which
might be given. Mysticism, psychologically considered,
may be regarded as the incomplete fusion of new
thought and of emotion or compressed ancestral thought.
It consequently very frequently contains the germs of
new developments, which are to be resultants of new
and old spiritual influences. It is a problem of extreme
complexity, but of extraordinary interest, to trace in the
mysticism of the Apocrypha and Midrash the beginnings of Christianity.

Meanwhile Greece was being moved to higher things
in her fall by a touch of Semitic fervour if not of
Hebraic faith. The new tone of Greek ethical thought
displayed in the rise of Stoicism must have been due,
according to our national psychological standpoint, to
some cross-fertilisation by the ideas of a different race.
And Sir Alexander Grant [1] has shown that all the eminent Stoics were of Semitic origin. The similarity which
has struck most observers between Stoicism and Christianity receives it explanation from our present standpoint when we remember that both were cross-fertilisa-
tions of Hellenism by Semitism. The difference, too,
may be due to the fact that in one case the less intense
Semites were the missionaries while Christianity was
propagated by the fiery zeal of the Jews. The spread
of Stoicism among the Romans cannot but have had
some influence in preparing the way for Christianity.

In approaching the subject of Christianity, we must

[1] Aristotle's *Ethics* (3rd edit.), i. p. 307.

distinguish between two problems. The *rise* of Christianity among the Jews, it cannot be too often repeated, will only receive its explanation when the mental and moral atmosphere of the time is made known to us as crystallised in the pages of the Talmud. The question of the originality of Jesus is merely one example of the general question of the relation of the individual and his nation. But more important than any question of origin is that of the *spread* of Christianity among persons of different race and different views of the world. This is the most important problem of cross-fertilisation in the history of the world's thought. The Judaic Deity had to be Indo-Germanised or Hellenised before He could become the God of Aryan worship. This transformation, the outcome of the Pharisaic movement, was the great work of Saul of Tarsus and of the Alexandrian-pseudo-John. To become fruitful among another nation than that of its origin, an idea must conform to the laws of assimilation of the new nation's mind. Thus in Christianity, the just and righteous God becomes the God of love; instead of objective Hebrews, His worshippers are subjective Hellenists. He appeals to each man separately instead of to a nation collectively. The egoism of the Hellene was elevated (for it was elevation) into the "other-worldliness" of the Christian. Each man became separate from the world, and antagonistic to society. So far from being universal, Christianity has its logical outcome in the "twa or aiblins three elec'" of the Scotch blacksmith. The universal, integrating element was given by the Church, the spiritual successor of the Roman Empire. To use logical terminology, the "God of All" of the Hebrew took the All collectively; Hellenistic Christianity made the All distributive. At the same time the moral or practical view of the Semite

gave way to the metaphysical or speculative view of
the Aryan. Men are made holy by faith, not practice.
The personality of the Deity is analysed and subtilised
into a Trinity. From our present standpoint this
receives illustration from the analogous Aryan Triune
Deity of post-Buddhistic Brahmanism. That racial
influences were at work is confirmed by the later rejection of Aryan Christology by Semitic Islam.

II

But we must now return to the history of the Divine
idea among the Jews during the post-Biblical period.
Their dispersion after the last heroic stand at Bethar
brought them into contact with the world's thought at
every point. Greece, Rome, Egypt, Persia, Assyria, all
meet in the pages of the Talmud, which faithfully
represents the incomplete assimilation of multifarious
views of the world. It is useless to attempt to give
any systematic account of Jewish belief from the Talmud : there is no such system. We can only recognise
in it germs of later development. In the struggle
between the Pharisees and the Sadducees, the former,
the progressive and assimilative party, gained the
victory, though not without being influenced by the
conservatism of the Sadducees. And the Talmud is
the production of the Pharisees, and represents their
cosmopolitan tendencies. In particular, we recognise
the influence of Greek rationalism, Persian dualism,
and by their side the mystic tendency which came
later to a head in the Cabbala. The Talmud is a law
book, and is a pre-eminent example of the practical
social tendency of the Hebraic genius. Thought is
free when it does not come into conflict with social

observance. The crystallising touch which was to precipitate NEO-JUDAISM from the confused syncretism
of the Talmud was to come from the Arabs, Semitic
kinsmen.

We need not here retell the story of the adoption of
Hebraism by Mahomet, told so well as it has been by
Geiger, Dozy, and Deutsch. We are here rather concerned with the reaction of Islam upon Judaism. The
milder rule of the Moslem gave the Jew a needed
pause in the struggle for existence, and the similarity
of the Semitic genius in both prevented the perceptible
tendency to narrowness, and brought the Jewish mind
again into free contact with the world's thought. To
the Semite, wisdom is the jewel of life: witness the
excellent Talmudic system of education—witness, too,
the Semitic ideal of kingship, the wise Solomon, the
wise Haroun-al-Raschid. The first aim of the Caliphs,
after the victory of Islam was assured, was to resus-
citate Greek science and philosophy. Translators were
employed to bring forth from their Syriac tombs Aristotle
and Galen. And the Jews at once took part in this
Semitic Renaissance (the counterpart of the later new
birth of the Aryan mind, when the latter was stirred
anew by contact with the great spiritual heritage of
its ancestors). And as the first contact with Hellenism showed its influence in the differentiation of the
national life into the sects of Pharisees and Sadducees,
so this second contact with Semitised Hellenism gave
rise to new sects. The beginnings of *Karaism* are
involved in much obscurity, but it may be generally
described as a revolt against authority—Jewish Protestantism—a struggle against the fetters which the
Talmudic doctors were placing round Jewish reason.
And the revolt was successful : though Karaism itself
dwindled away into a still narrower traditionalism, it

forced its opponents, the Rabbinites, to adapt tradition
to the reason of the time, and, in so doing, brought.
about a radical change in the Judaic views of the
Deity. The history of that change must now be
roughly traced.

As the pre-Christian era was characterised by a
continual universalising of the Divine idea, so the
post-Islamite development consisted in a still further
extension of universalism in the depersonalising of the
Divine conception. This was caused by the influence
of the Arabic Aristotle, and the consequent rise of the
inevitable struggle between a philosophical or intellectual and a religious or emotional view of the universe.
Such a struggle is really a conflict between old and
new thought, though the older conceptions have
become embedded in the national mind as feelings.
That process which goes on in the mind of the thinker
till he gets to apply his ideas instinctively, and they
become feelings rather than propositions to him, takes
place also in the history of a nation's mental development. Thus feeling is, as it were, condensed ancestral
thought, and thought is the personal element by which
we increase or alter the wisdom of the ages organically
registered as feeling in our frames—*i.e.*, we feel as our
ancestors thought, and think as our descendants will
feel. And from the standpoint of national psychology,
thought is the blank form of feeling without historic
content. Specifically national emotions cannot accordingly cross-fertilise. But abstract thought being
divested of the historic element is international, and,
therefore, the chief agent in cross-fertilisation. New
thought in a nation, as distinguished from the natural
growth of the specifically national conceptions, may
come from new experience, or by contact with the
experience of other nations. Now, the Jewish mind

is peculiarly open to this latter influence. Experience
has shown that a man may be an exemplary father of
a family and a respectable member of society while
believing in the eternity of the πρώτη ὕλη. And the
practical tendency of the Jewish genius led them to
accept this teaching of experience. How far they were
aided in this toleration by the absence of an established
Church in Judaism is an interesting problem which
we cannot here discuss. At any rate, this assimilative
characteristic of Judaism causes the history of Jewish
philosophy [1] to be one of the most instructive examples
of the cross-fertilisation of national ideas, leading
finally to an organic union of Hellenism and Hebraism
in Spinoza. At first we get a merely mechanical ad-
mixture. The two theories of the world lie alongside
each other without commingling. The God of intellect
is conceived in Hellenic forms of thought; the moment
we turn to practice, the Jewish doctors (of law as well
as of divinity) treat of the God of emotion under the
older conceptions. While feeling to the Greek was
intensely personal, egoistic, his intellect viewed the
universe quite impersonally. To the Hebrew the
universe was charged with personal conceptions—
not thought of except in relation to an *ab extra*
Creator—while his practical views were altruistic, non-
subjective. There was thus in the objective practical
feeling of the Jew a basis for an impersonal view of
the Deity. Yet this view took centuries to become
a really vital principle in Hebrew thought, owing
probably to the unconscious reaction of Christian and
Moslem thought and the intense veneration for the
Bible. But it gained a nominal victory almost from
the very first. The first stage of Jewish, as of Moslem,

[1] I hope one of these days to sketch the *Outlines of the History of Jewish
Philosophy down to Spinoza*, as a study in national psychology.

thought is an attempt to determine the Divine attributes,[1] to bring the Hebraic Deity under Hellenic
forms of thought—in effect to depersonalise the conception. Along with the question of the Divine attributes, forming indeed the crucial problem between
Hellenism and Hebraism, there was connected the
question of a creation *ex nihilo*. The relation of
Jehovah to the material universe had been conceived
as exactly similar to that of man and the work of
his hands. God was outside the world, and could
interfere at any moment with its working to produce
miracles. Opposed to this, the Jewish Aristotelians
found their master teaching the eternity of matter, and
with it a conception of the Deity as continuously exer-
cising His influence on the material universe in giving
it form. The difference between the two views is of
vital importance : the first chapter of Genesis strikes
the keynote of Hebraism, especially of its Christian
form, where the relation of the individual and his
Maker is more direct, more charged with subjective
craving for Divine favour than in Judaism, where the
Divine preference is desired more for the race than
the individual. The creation *ex nihilo* dogma becomes
more and more prominent, and comes into the foreground of Jewish speculation in the second post-
Maimonidean stage. Throughout the later stage,
mysticism attempts to assimilate the new conceptions
in emotional forms. Finally, in Spinoza the Hellenic
conceptions are at last thoroughly assimilated as feelings rather than abstract truths, and Hellenic thought

[1] See Professor Kaufmann's *Geschichte der Attributenlehre in der jüdischen
Religionsphilosophie des Mittelalters von Saadja bis Maimûni* (Gotha, F. A.
Perthes, 1877), rather the annals than the history of Jewish thought
during that period, but presenting a rich mass of materials nowhere else
accessible.

becomes Hebraic feeling. It might be of interest to treat of the development more in detail. All that can be here attempted is roughly to characterise the Hellenic factor in the thought of each prominent philosopher: our exposition must, therefore, be taken as one-sided, though that side was the fruitful one containing the germs of future development of the world's thought. The Rabbis themselves would probably have been aghast at the logical results of their views, and there were not wanting signs of an uneasy instinct of their tendency.

(1) During the first period (933–1204) we should have to take into account the influence of the parallel line of Arabic philosophy, more especially of the eclectic cyclopædia of the Græco-Arabic thought by the Brothers of Purity. All the works of the Jewish philosophers of this period were written in Arabic, and imbued with the philosophic phraseology of the Arabs, itself entirely derived from the Greek. But the line of thought taken was somewhat different, owing chiefly to two causes: the influence of the Bible, and the greater toleration of free thought. In Islam there was from the first a continual battle between theology and philosophy, in which theology finally conquered under the philosophic theologian Al-Ghazzâli. Still at first the distinction between Jewish and Moslem thought was slight. The most trustworthy exposition of the *Kalâm*, or first philosophic movement among the Arabs, is to be found in a treatise by a Karaite Jew, Josef el Basr.[1] His treatise, *Al Muḥtawi*, or the Book of Roots, commences the documentary history of Jewish philosophy

---

[1] See Dr. P. F. Frankl, *Ein mütazilitischer Kalâm als Beitrag zur Geschichte der Muslimischen Religionsphilosophie* (Wien, Karl Gerold's Sohn, 1872 : reprinted from the *Sitzungsberichte* of the Royal Vienna Academy of Science).

by discussing the specifically Hebraic conceptions of
the Deity. His unity and justice, creation *ex nihilo*,
and the connected dogma of free will, are proved by
ingenious applications of Greek logic to cosmology.
Opposed to him on the question of the authority of
tradition, but at one with him in results if not in
method, is his Rabbinite contemporary Saadja, the
Gaon or chief of the Theological College at Bagdad
which carried on the tradition of the Talmudic doctors
of the law. He sums up and defends the traditional
beliefs in his book on "Dogmas and Opinions" (*Emu-
nuth Wedeoth*), discussing them with all available
appliances of Greek philosophy. He sees the connection of the incorporeal attributes of the Deity with
the dogma of creation, and accordingly brings all his
logic to bear on the proof of a creation. The next
link in the chain is formed by Bachja ibn Pakuda,[1]
who proves most elaborately the unity of the Godhead
to be a real substantial unity unlike that of man. Yet
after he has passed through the "Gate of Unity" (the
Hebrew title of book i.) and proceeds to treat of the
subject of his treatise, the "Duties of the Heart"
(*Choboth Halebaboth*), he returns to the ordinary anthropomorphic modes of expression. He, like the two
preceding, is uncompromising in his adherence to the
dogma of creation *ex nihilo*. The difficulties of the
latter conception were more clearly perceived by
Salomon ibn Gebirol, one of the greatest poets of the
Synagogue, whom Munk has shown to be the same
as Avicebron, the author of the *Fons Vitæ*, the most
original philosophic production written in Arabic. He
attempted to evade in mysticism the dogma of creation, which his profound metaphysical genius felt was

---

[1] A full account of his views has been given by Professor Kaufmann in
the *Sitzungsberichte* of the Royal Vienna Academy of Science, 1874.

uncongenial with the new thought. In the midst of Aristotelian diversities of matter and form he places a mystic Neoplatonic Will as an attribute of the Deity, which is to explain, or to evade explaining, the creation. He had not much influence on Jewish thought, but is quoted with great respect by Albertus Magnus and Thomas Aquinas, and later on his views were adopted by Giordano Bruno. He is interesting here as the first who attempted to assimilate the new thought into a consistent system, whereas previous thinkers had merely used Greek philosophy as a clothing for their Hebraic faith. He attempted, at least, to make it the flesh.

Jehuda Halevi, the sweetest singer of the New Exile, marks a turning-point in Jewish thought. He first attempted to check the influence of Greek thought and its threatened overthrow of the dogma of creation which he felt to be essential to the old faith. His poet-soul gave utterance to prophetic warnings with a meaning something like this :—

> Go not near the Grecian wisdom ; [1]
> It has not fruit, but only blossoms.
> For its fruit is that the heavens
> And the earth can have no Maker,
> The creation no Creator,
> And the moon no end to changing.
> Follow that delusive doctrine,
> Whose foundation is unfounded,
> Then your heart is void and bitter,
> And your mouth is full of phrases.

He consequently attempted to rival the feat of Al-Ghazzâli, who, within the pale of Islam, had so suc-

---

[1] Kaufmann, p. 129; Munk, *Mélanges*, 484, n. ; Geiger, *Divan*, 86. The Talmud (Sot. 49 b ; Menach. 64 b) had already said, "Cursed is the man who allows his son to learn the Grecian wisdom," but Jehuda Halevi sees the specially dangerous doctrine of the Greeks.

cessfully philosophised against philosophy. To support
the probability of a creation, he laid great stress on the
omnipotence of God as the most important attribute.
Yet he owns that the argument against creation is
as weighty as that for (*Cusari*, i. 67), and resorts to
Revelation for a solution which reason cannot offer.
He is even still more interesting as a representative of
Jewish national feeling ; he it was who said : " Israel
is among the nations as the heart among the limbs."
His intense patriotism has made him a popular philosopher among the Jews, and his chivalrous love for
Jerusalem has inspired Heine's noblest poem. His
fiery zeal for Jews and Judaism led him to base their
claims on a philosophy of history which would be
ludicrous but for its poetic fervour.

But his efforts to repress speculation were unsuccessful, and the question of the Divine Attributes
continued to be discussed by the Neoplatonic Joseph
ibn Zaddik, and the Peripatetic Abraham ibn Daud.
The former denied that we could have any real knowledge of God, and rejected all attribution. He thus
prepared the way for Moses Maimonides, who marks a
halt in the march of thought, and sums up the speculation of the first period. In the sphere of practical
philosophy he performed the part of a Jewish Bentham,
codifying the " halachic " or legal portions of the Talmud in the fourteen books of his " Strong Hand " (*Yad
Hachazaka*). And in speculative philosophy he brought
about a morganatic union between Græco-Arabic philosophy and Judaic religion. He laid down the principles
of the resultant Neo-Judaism in his " Guide of the
Perplexed" (*Moreh Nebuchim*), perhaps the most remarkable metaphysical *tour de force* in the history
of human thought. He attempted to compromise all
the questions at issue between the thought of Greece

and the feeling of Judæa. Thus, with regard to the question of the Divine attributes, he grants that all attribution is anthropomorphic, and therefore degrading to God's dignity; yet he denies that we can give *negative* attributes to the Deity, and thus brings in the positive ones by a side wind. The question of creation he declared to be antinomical : the balance of evidence is equal. His views on all the great theological questions have a rationalistic tendency, as may be seen in the restatement of them contained in Spinoza's *Tractatus Theologico-Politicus*. He commences his treatise by going through all the anthropomorphic epithets applied to God in the Bible, explaining them away in every case. Indeed, the characteristic thing about the whole of the first movement, from Saadja to Maimonides, is the increasing theoretic aversion to anthropomorphism, which we can trace back through Targum and Talmud to the LXX. Yet the Bible had too strong a hold on the religious life to allow this tendency to have practical effect except in controversy with Christians, where it gave great advantages.

(2) Maimonides had a great influence on scholasticism. Albertus Magnus and Thomas Aquinas own their indebtedness to him, and it would almost seem that the Church had added the Doctor Perplexorum to the Doctor Universalis and Doctor Angelicus as one of her authorities. By his own co-religionists his views did not meet with such universal acceptance. Immediately after his death (1204) a fierce struggle took place as to his orthodoxy, and in the heat of controversy his works were publicly burned. But the anti-Maimonites ultimately gave way, and Maimonides has, since the beginning of the fourteenth century, been the rallying post of Jewish orthodoxy. Yet the rationalistic elements in his thought were not allowed

D

to slumber. Levi ben Gerson (Gersonides), in the
next century after Maimonides' death, showed so much
boldness in his "Wars of the Lord" (*Milchamoth
Adonai*), that his opponents called his book the "Wars
against the Lord." In particular he accepted the
eternity of matter, which answered in those days to
the acceptance of the theory of evolution in these.
Gersonides had no inconsiderable fame as an astronomer; Kepler writes to Johannes Remus for the fifth
or astronomical book of the *Milchamoth Adonai*, and
we may not unreasonably connect his rejection of the
creation *ex nihilo* with his training in astronomy.
Cross-fertilisation is as marked a phenomenon in the
history of sciences as in the history of nations, and
theology and cosmology have many points of contact.
It is not without reason that the creative fiat of the
first chapter of Genesis is connected with the old
Assyrian cosmology and its "revolving dish-cover"
theory of the heavens. Astronomy was in the age of
Gersonides gradually emerging from its mythologic
stage of astrology, and accustoming men's minds to a
more impersonal view of the universe and a more ex-
tended view of the cosmos. This would naturally lead
to a rejection of the creation *ex nihilo* hypothesis, and
with its rejection a modification of the conception of
God's relation to the universe. The idea of an *ab
extra* Deity interfering arbitrarily with the material
universe gave way to the conception of God as continuously manifesting Himself in the natural order.
The impersonal view of the Deity, which was the outcome of the discussion of His attributes during the
first period, must naturally have prepared the way for
the change. Psychologically, it was a change in men's
imaginative view of the world; the function of the
imagination in religion being to bridge over the gap

between the God of nature and the God of conscience, the Ruler of the " starry heavens above" and of "the moral law within." Hence the importance, theologically considered, of the Copernician theory, with its reversal of the anthropocentric view of the universe. It is not difficult to see in Gersonides' rejection of creation *ex nihilo* the first step towards the Spinozistic attribution of extension to the Deity. We meet, too, in the ἦθος of Gersonides that scientific mode of thought which is so marked a characteristic of Spinoza, and which Sir F. Pollock can only trace to the influence of Descartes (*Mind*, No. x.).[1]

But, as in the first period by Jehuda Halevi, another attempt was made to stem the progress of Hellenism in Jewish philosophy by Don Chisdai Creskas, in his "Light of the Lord" (*Or Adonai*). He made it his task to oppose the views of "the Greek [Aristotle] who in these our days darkens the eyes of Israel," in reality the Aristotelism of Gersonides. And he attempts to fight philosophy with its own weapons; he accepts, *e.g.*, determinism in a most rigid manner. But the authority of the Maimonidean Aristotle was too firmly established for Creskas to overcome, and his principal influence was to lessen the number of fundamental principles of Judaism, which Maimonides had reduced to thirteen. In a work on the " Principles " (*Ikkarim*), by Creskas' disciple Albo, they are reduced to three.

During this second period (1204-1677) we have a parallel movement to the rationalising tendencies of the followers and opponents of Maimonides—the mysticism of the Cabbala, which is often regarded as the specifically Jewish philosophy. So far from this being the

---

[1] Spinoza quoted Gersonides in one of the marginal notes to his *Tractatus*. Of him treat Joel in his *Beiträge zur Greschichte der Philosophie*, and J. Weil, *Philosophie Religieuse de Lévi-ben-Gerson* (Paris, Ladrange, 1868).

case, it may rather be regarded as heretical, and certainly as unorthodox. Its history is obscured by a mass of .pseudepigraphic writings (one, *e.g.*, attributed to Adam), but, thanks to Jellinek's researches,[1] the origin of the specifically Cabbalistic mysticism has been discovered in the twelfth century, though mystical elements may be traced in Jehuda Halevi, Ibn Gebirol, in the Talmud, Philo, and perhaps in the vision of Ezechiel. It has an interest as representing a side of the Jewish mind—the mysticism which seems common to all Orientals. It presents an interesting example of a curious psychological trait in the mystical mind—the attraction of mathematical symbols, seen in Pythagoras, Plato, Swedenborg, and cropping up in rank luxuriance in De Morgan's "Budget of Paradoxes." Like all mysticism, it is a premature attempt to register rational thought as feeling by clothing the new abstractions with the old emotions. The Cabbala thus attempts to treat the question of creation, and there seems every reason to believe that Spinoza was influenced by it in his conception of the relation of God to the universe, the so-called pantheistic element in his thought. Emanation led to immanence. The Cabbala had very great influence on Christendom in the Renaissance period, when men's hearts were craving some more substantial nutriment than the dry bones of scholasticism.[2] When, indeed, we reckon the influence on

---

[1] A useful summary of the principal doctrines of the Cabbala has been published by Dr. Ginsburg, *The Kabbalah*, Longmans, 1865.

[2] A. Stöckl in his voluminous *Geschichte der Philosophie des Mittelalters* (1862–65) gives the following analysis of the Cabbalistic influence in his third vol. (*Periode der Bekämpfung der Scholastik*), vii., Die cabbalistische Theosophie, pp. 394–608, §§ 87–129 :—(1) Die pythagoräisch-cabbalistische Theosophie : (a) *Johannes Reuchlin*, (b) *Heinrich Cornelius Agrippa*, (c) *Francesco Zorzi*. (2) Die c. T. in Verbindung mit der Naturphilosophie und Arzneikunde : (a) *Theophrastus Paracelsus*, (b) *Hieronymus Cardanus*, (c) *Johann-Baptist von Helmont*, (d) *Robert Fludd*. (3) Die c. T. in dogma-

scholasticism of Avicebron, Maimonides, and the Jewish translators of Græco-Arabic philosophy, and the cross-fertilisation of Renaissance mysticism by the Cabbala, we cannot but regret that historians of mediæval thought have enclosed their exposition of Jewish philosophy in a sort of *ghetto*. The development of the spirit in Christianity and Judaism went through the same phases during the period 1000–1500 A.D. Both in church and synagogue an attempt had been made to clothe Hebraic faith in the abstract forms of Græco-Arabic logic, and in both the harsh result drove men to mysticism in an attempt to bring home the new thought to men's hearts. And this mysticism grew mainly on the soil of Judaism, which gave the Cabbala to both Jew and Christian. Out of these discordant elements came the mixed rationalism and mysticism of Spinoza's *Ethica*, which thus sums up the whole movement of European thought during the Middle Ages. The influences that had been at work both in Christendom and Jewry came to a head in Baruch Spinoza, who thus forms a landmark in the history of the world's thought.

In him we find the flower and fruit of the cross-fertilisation of Hebraism and Hellenism which we have been tracing in its principal exponents. When we combine the deanthropomorphised Deity of Maimonides with the eternity of matter of Gersonides, the determinism of Creskas, and the immanence of Divinity

tischer Form mit altgnostisch-manichäischer Färbung : MARTIN LUTHER (4) Philosophische Versuche unter der Herrschaft der lutherischen Dogmatik : (a) *Philip Melanchthon*, (b) *Nicholaus Tamillus*. (5) Die c. T. Mystik unter dem Einfluss der lutherischen Dogmatik : (a) *Valentin Weigel*, (b) *Jacob Böhme*. To these names we may add those of Raymond Lully, Pico della Mirandula, Henry More, and the Cambridge Platonists generally : traces of Cabbala are even to be found in Dante. For the general influence of the Jews on the Renaissance, see, Steinschneider's *Letteratura Italiana dei Giudei*, and L. Geiger's notes to his edition of J. Burckhardt's *Cultur der Renaissance*.

in all things taught by the Cabbala, and cast them
into the mould of Cartesian method, we have the
materials for the so-called Pantheism of Spinoza.[1]
But it is to be observed that these positions are held
by him as implicit assumptions (I would call them
feelings) rather than as definite propositions; they
have been completely assimilated into his mental
system. He does not disprove creation *ex nihilo;* he
speaks of extension as an attribute of the Deity; he
does not discuss the personality of the Godhead;
he speaks of God as *Substantia.* We consequently
find in him a thorough application of the new thought
to ethics. In all previous Jewish thinkers the practical
and speculative spheres had been completely separate;
Aristotle ruled the one, the Bible the other. But in
Spinoza we have an attempt to apply the same objectivity to conduct as to metaphysics. And it is
here that the Hebraism of his nature displayed itself;
he combined the Hebraic objectivity of practice with
the Hellenic objectivity of thought. We find no trace
of ascetic "otherworldliness" in him, no craving for
special grace, except in so far as he had deserved it
from the God of justice. In his *Ethica* we find
remarkable coincidences with Stoicism,[2] and it is not

---

[1] Spinoza's indebtedness to his Jewish predecessors has been put beyond
all doubt by Dr. M. Joel's monographs on post-Maimunite Jewish philosophy, now bound together as his *Beiträge zur Geschichte der Philosophie*
(Breslau, 1876). A somewhat disconnected summary of his results is
given by Sir F. Pollock in *Mind*, No. x.

[2] The following passage from the *Thoughts of Marcus Aurelius* (iv. 23,
Long) gives perhaps the best example of the characteristic tone of both
Stoicism and Spinozism :—"Everything harmonises with me, which is
harmonious to thee, O Universe. Nothing for me is too early or too late
which is in due time for thee. Everything is fruit to me which thy
seasons bring ; O Nature, from thee are all things, in thee are all things,
to thee all things return." This is the very voice of the "intellectualis
amor Dei." *Cf.* Professor Clifford's "Cosmic Emotion," *Nineteenth
Century*, October 1877.

undeserving of remark that both systems are results
of cross-fertilisation of Semitism and Hellenism.   Nor
can the modern world offer any more striking example
of the Stoic ideal than that afforded by the blameless
life of Baruch Spinoza.

The characteristic of his religious emotion (and in
no man was the Divine Spirit so dominant) is happily
hit off in his own phrase, " intellectualis amor Dei."
The Hellenic intellectual conceptions had become
emotions to him; he feels that "cosmic emotion"
which the late Professor Clifford has described.   Yet
he is free from the unphilosophic agnosticism of Mr.
Herbert Spencer; his twenty-ninth letter is the best
answer to the latter's doctrine of the unknowable.
We may fairly call his views Cosmic Theism—Hellenic
philosophy filtered through Hebraic faith.   Hence his
appeal to all the great thinkers of modern times, and
especially the Spinoza-cultus of the present century;
he is the summation of Hebraism and Hellenism, the
two great factors of civilised life.   And the fact that
Hellenism has in him the victory caused the appeal to
the Aryan mind to be more urgent.   As Spencer has
been called "the poet's poet," so we may term Spinoza
"the philosopher's philosopher." [1]

With him ends the history of Jewish philosophy;
later movements in Judaism were directed towards the
attainment of social status, and, when that had been
attained, to raise again the historic consciousness,
both the reflex results of that large sweep of European thought which we may roughly term Democracy.
With him, too, culminates the long series of changes

---

[1] "But what especially riveted me to him," says Goethe, who represents
Spinozism in literature, "was the boundless disinterestedness which shone
forth in every sentence," *i.e.*, what we have above termed his objectivity
both in thought (Hellenic) and practice (Hebraic).

in the God of Israel. From a family deity it had been raised into the Divine Father of All, the Creator of the universe, and under this form had cross-fertilised Græco-Roman culture as Christianity. But "the whirligig of Time brings in his revenges;" Israel came in contact with Greek philosophy, and was in its turn cross-fertilised by Hellenism. Jehovah was gradually depersonalised, and the world was rendered independent of Him, till, under the influence of mysticism, He becomes an immanent principle of the universe, as the *Substantia* of Spinoza. From an *ab extra* Deity, the God of Israel had been changed by cross-fertilisation into a continuous energetic Principle.

If we turn our eyes away from the past and gaze upon the spiritual conflict of the present, may we not say that the struggle between religion and science is really a conflict between the Christian and Spinozistic developments of the God of Israel?[1] Among the Jews the development of thought had been comparatively free; it was far otherwise in Christendom. The creeds of the Church have crystallised the conception of God as the *ab extra* Deity of 1500 years ago, and all the progress of the world's thought has been made in opposition to the Church, which has always had an instinct that its theology was bound up with the older cosmology. Hence its opposition to Copernicus, Galileo, and science generally. The period from the rise of Christianity to the Renaissance was a pause in the development of the West Aryan mind. It was filled up by an attempt to assimilate

---

[1] On the relation of Spinozism to current scientific speculation, *cf.* Sir F. Pollock's masterly essay on "The Scientific aspect of Spinoza's Philosophy," *Fortnightly Review*, May 1873, the most important contribution on Spinozism that has been made in England.

Hebraic notions of righteousness, which could only be engrafted by an appeal to Aryan egoism in the hedonistic conceptions of a future state. The *Divina Commedia* has been rightly considered the embodiment of the mediæval mind, and we can see why the so-called ancients are really nearer in spirit to the post-Renaissance thought than the non-Aryan development of the Middle Ages. The specific Aryan development passes from 300 B.C. to 1500 A.D. With the Renaissance the souls of kinsmen of olden time came and released the Aryan mind from the Hebraic armour, which had become too narrow for it. Yet it must not be forgotten that the panoply had helped the human race mightily in its war against evil, and must ever remain as a relic of heroic battles of the spirit. That generations of men have held the Bible sacred must always keep it sacred for us. And indeed it is doubtful whether the Aryan mind has completely assimilated Hebraic righteousness. Only when it has the instinct to do right as right, apart from rewards and punishments (this is the true Hebraic objectivity), will the work of the Bible be done. Even then the Bible may be as important in the education of the individual as it has been in the education of the race.

Meanwhile some in these days have thoroughly assimilated Hebraism, and are ready for new developments of the Aryan (Hellenic) part of their nature. Their position as individuals answers to the mediæval stage of the Jews as a race. And it is natural that they should approach the position of the Hellenic Hebraism of Spinoza. Thus we have to-day two conflicting views of the world, each the outcome of the Judaic spirit.[1] Thomas à Kempis and Johann Wolf-

[1] In theology we have the opposing conceptions of an *ab extra* Deity and of a continuous energetic Principle. In cosmology the world is conceived

gang Goethe are typical examples of the opposing *Weltanschauungen*, the old and new faiths. No one who has watched the spirit of the time can doubt which of the two ideals is the goal towards which the mind of man is marching. Cosmic Theism (Spinozism with an addition to be presently mentioned) is destined to be the religion of the future.

It is natural to discuss the relation of Judaism to the two faiths which have sprung from its bosom. It has always rejected Christianity, which is utterly alien to the Jewish *Volksgeist*, but it could clearly, without loss of historic dignity, advance to the new faith. Whether it will take the latter course remains to be seen; it rejected Spinoza, and with him the history of Jewish thought, *quâ* Jewish, ceases. The nation turned to the task of gaining a position among the nations, and withdrew from abstract speculation. But there was another reason which explains the rejection and neglect of Spinoza by Judaism, and which points to the main defect in Spinozism. *Spinoza was no true Jew;* he had not that historic sense of communion with his people's past which has been the bond that has kept Judaism alive through the ages. Judaism is not alone a religion, but a philosophy of history. And herein we see the main defect of Spinozism, due to Spinoza's individualistic psychology: we should see God, not alone in Nature, but also in History. The Comtist enthusiasm for humanity has its value in the recognition of this truth. And there

on the one side as out of relation to God and man, and on the other as one in substance with mankind. In anthropology we have opposed a statical individualistic conception of man's nature with judgment of history from a hedonistic standpoint (Optimism or Pessimism) and a dynamic social conception with a progressive view of history. In ethics the opposition lies between an egoistic method which seeks for a solution of the hedonistic calculus in future rewards and punishments, and a perfectionist ideal of self-culture.

are not wanting signs that the main striving of the mind of the age is towards the foundation of a philosophy of history. And when the history of the Jews has been told as it should be, it will then be seen that they above all others have earned the title of the chosen people of God. The great question for contemporary Judaism is whether it will continue God's work or cease to be. "Prophecy is of all errors the most gratuitous," we are told, but I can see no meaning in history if the richest product of humanity, which has shared in all the progressive movements in the history of man, shall not have within it germs of mighty thoughts and deeds.

NOTE.—A table is here appended summing up the results indicated. The prehistoric and contemporary stages have been added for the sake of completeness. Reflected arrows indicate national movements which had effect on the later history of Judaism. Dates are put rather later than the appearance of movements in individuals. The numbers refer to the following remarks :—

1. This stage is unique, those who returned from the captivity being of one mind, and thus there is no spiritual division of the nation.

2. The influence of Stoicism must be reckoned, though not strictly Jewish.

3. The metaphysical nature of the Christian Deity is here omitted as an Aryan trait.

4. The Cabbalists apply to the impersonal conception the emotions previously felt towards the personal God of tradition, while the rationalists remove the emotional element from the latter, and attempt to intellectualise the conception in terms applicable to the impersonal God of reason. This is here represented by the crossed lines.

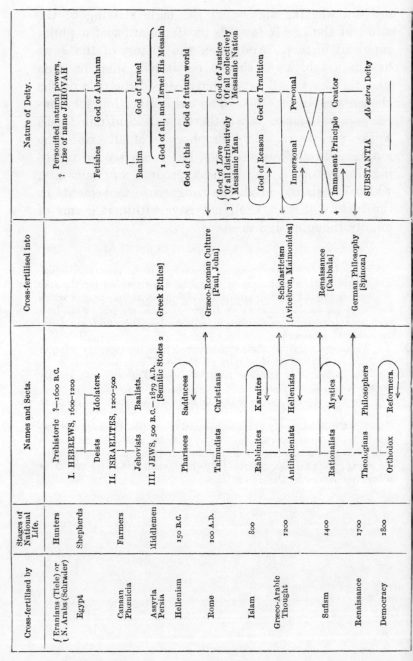

MORDECAI

A PROTEST AGAINST THE CRITICS

("*Macmillan's Magazine*," June 1877)

"*Sephardo, the Jew.*   Wise books,
         For half the truths they hold are honoured tombs."
                                                            —*Spanish Gipsy*, p. 205.

THE critics have had their say: the recording angels of literature, more sorrowful than angry, have written down "Daniel Deronda" a failure.   And there seems to be at least this much of truth in their judgment, that one of the parts of which the book is composed has failed to interest or even to reach its audience.   For the least observant reader must have noticed that "Daniel Deronda" is made up of two almost unconnected parts, either of which can be read without the other.   Every "book" after the first is divided into two parts, whose only claim to be included under the same covers is the common action or inaction of the eponymous hero.   One set of characters and interests centres round the fate and fortunes of Gwendolen Harleth, and of this part of the book we can surely say that it has excited as much interest and bitten as deeply into men's minds as any of the author's previous studies of female character.   Indeed, we would submit that George Eliot's last portrait of female egoism is in many ways her best; her hand has become more tender, and, because more tender, more true than when she drew such narrow types as Hetty Sorrel and Rosamond Vincy, so unnaturally consistent in their

selfishness. The story of Gwendolen Harleth's purification from egoism is, then, one might say, even a
greater success than the former pictures of girlish
struggles, and displays the author's distinguishing excellences in undiminished brilliancy. But there is
another part of the book with which the English-speak-
ing public and its literary "tasters" have failed to sympathise, and which they have mostly been tempted to
omit on reperusal. The tragedy of Mordecai Cohen's
missionary labours, on which the author has spent
immense labour of invention and research, must
be pronounced to have completely failed in reaching
and exciting the interest and sympathy of the ordinary
reader. Mr. Bagehot has told us that the greatest pain
man can feel is the pain of a new idea, and the readers of
"Daniel Deronda" have refused painfully to assimilate
the new idea of the Mordecai part of the book. This
idea we take to be that Judaism stands on the same
level as Christianity, perhaps even on a higher level, in
point of rationality and capacity to satisfy the wants of
the religious consciousness, "the hitherto neglected
reality," to use the author's own words (ii. 292), "that
Judaism is something still throbbing in human lives,
still making for them the only conceivable vesture of the
world." The difficulty of accepting this new idea comes
out most prominently in the jar most readers must have
felt in the omission of any explanation of the easy
transition of Deronda from the Christianity in which he
was bred to the Judaism into which he had been born.

The present notice proposes to discuss the failure of
this unsuccessful part, from the standpoint of one for
whom this initial difficulty does not exist, and who has
from his childhood seen the world habited in those
Hebrew Old Clothes of which Mr. Carlyle and others
have spoken so slightingly. And the first thing that it

is natural for a Jew to say about "Daniel Deronda" is some expression of gratitude for the wonderful completeness and accuracy with which George Eliot has portrayed the Jewish nature. Hitherto the Jew in English fiction has fared unhappily, being always represented as a monstrosity, most frequently on the side of malevolence and greed, as in Marlowe's Barabas and Dickens's Fagin, or sometimes, as in Dickens's Riah, still more exasperatingly on the side of impossible benevolence. What we want is truth, not exaggeration, and truth George Eliot has given us with the large justice of the great artist. The gallery of Jewish portraits contained in "Daniel Deronda" gives in a marvellously full and accurate way all the many sides of our complex national character. The artistic element, with the proper omission of painting and sculpture, in which Jews, though eminent, have not been pre-eminent, is well represented by Klesmer, Mirah, and the Alcharisi. Ezra Cohen is a type of the commonplace Jew, the familiar figure of prosperous mercantile dealing, the best-known trait of Jews to Englishmen; while little Jacob exhibits in a very humorous form the well-known precocity of Jewish children. The affectionate relations of Ezra Cohen and his mother, and the tender respect of Mordecai and Mirah for the memory of theirs, point to the exceptional influence of the Mother and the Home in the inner life of Jews. Then in Kalonymos, whom we feel tempted to call the Wandering Jew, we get the nomadic spirit which has worked in Israel from times long previous to the Dispersion, while all must join in the scorn the author evidently feels for Pash, the Jew who is no Jew. Yet he is the representative of what might be called the Heine side of Jewry—the wit and cynicism that reached their greatest intensity in the poet of Young

Germany. The more temperate Gideon represents, it
is to be feared, a large proportion of English Jews, one
not ashamed of his race, yet not proud of it, and willing to see the racial and religious distinctions we have
fought for so valiantly die out and perish utterly among
men. Perhaps the most successful of the minor portraits is that of the black sheep Lapidoth, the Jew with
no redeeming love for family, race, or country to preserve him from that sordid egoism—the new name for
wickedness—into which he has sunk. His utter uncon-
sciousness of good and evil is powerfully depicted in
the masterly analysis of his state of mind before pur-
loining Deronda's ring. To some extent the weird
figure of the Alcharisi serves as a sort of companion-
picture of female renunciation of racial claims, but
the struggle between her rebellious will and what old-
fashioned folk call the Will of God (Professor Clifford
would perhaps name it the Tribal Will) raises her to
a tragic height which makes Deronda's mother perhaps
the most imposing figure in the book. Deronda himself, by the circumstance of his education, is prevented
from typifying any of the social distinctions of a Jew,
yet it is not unlikely that his gravity of manner and
many-sided sympathy were meant by the author to be
taken as hereditary traits.

These, with Ram the bookseller, the English Jew of
the pre-emancipation era, and some minor characters,
give to the reader a most complete picture of Jews and
Jewesses in their habits as they live, of Jews and Jewesses as members of a peculiar people in relation to the
Gentile world. To point the moral of human falli-
bility, besides some minor slips in ceremonial details,
on which it were ungrateful to dwell,[1] we cannot but

---

[1] *E.g.*, Taliths or fringed mantles are not worn on Friday nights (ii. 292–
300); the Kaddish, or prayer in honour of the dead, is only said for eleven

think (a critic is nothing if not critical) that the author has failed to give in Mirah an adequate type of Jewish girlhood. Mirah is undoubtedly tame; and tameness, for those who know them, is the last infirmity of Jewish girls. Still, even here the sad experience of Mirah's youth may be held to have somewhat palliated any want of brightness, and the extra vivacity of Mrs. Cohen junior perhaps supplies the deficiency.

So much for the outer life of Judaism. The English reader will find here no idea so startlingly novel as to raise opposition to its admission, or to disturb his complacent feeling of superiority over Jews in all but a certain practical sagacity (he calls it sharpness or cunning), which must be postulated to explain the "differentia of success" characterising the Jewish species of commercial dealings. One new fact he may indeed profitably learn : from the large group of Jewish characters in "Daniel Deronda" he may perhaps gather that there are Jews and Jews, that they are not all Lapidoths, nor even all Ezra Cohens, as he has been accustomed to think.

But the new idea of which we have spoken is embodied in the person of Mordecai Cohen, the Jew *par excellence* of the book, the embodiment of the inner life of Judaism. The very fact of this recognition of an inner life, not to speak of the grand personality in which she has typified it, entitles George Eliot to the heart-deep gratitude of all Jews; the more so inasmuch as she has hazarded and, at least temporarily, lost success for her most elaborated production by endeavouring to battle with the commonplace and

months, not eleven years (iv. 92), and then only by a son. Mirah seems to be under the same delusion (ii. 306). Before breaking the bread (ii. 356), Cohen should have "made Kiddush," *i.e.*, pronounced a blessing over some sacramental wine. It is doubtful whether Cohen would have paid money and written a pawn-ticket on Sabbath eve, but this may be intentional.

E

conventional ideas about Judaism. The present article aims at striking another blow to convince the English world of the existence in the present day, and for all past time, of a spiritual life in Judaism. And we can conceive of no better point of defence for the position than the historic probability of the character of Mordecai, which critics have found so mystic, vague, and impossible.

For those who know anything of the great leaders of spiritual Judaism will recognise in Mordecai all the traits that have characterised them. Saul of Tarsus, Ibn Gebirol (Avicebron), Jehuda Halevi, Ibn Ezra, Maimonides, Abrabanel, Spinoza, Mendelssohn (not to mention other still more unfamiliar names) were all men like Mordecai—rich in inward wealth, yet content to earn a scanty livelihood by some handicraft; ardently spiritual, yet keenly alive to the claims of home affection; widely erudite, yet profoundly acquainted with human nature; mystics, yet with much method in their mysticism. The author seems even to have a bolder application of the historic continuity of the Hebraic spirit in view: she evidently wishes Mordecai to be regarded as a "survival" of the prophetic spirit, a kind of Isaiah Redivivus. Hence a somewhat unreal effect is produced by his use of a diction similar to what might be expected from a "Greater Prophet" stepping out of the pages of the Authorised Version. Still, it is to be remembered that we almost always see Mordecai in states of intense excitement, when his thought would naturally clothe itself in the forms in which all his literary efforts had been written. He speaks in a sufficiently prosaic and unbiblical style when the subject is prosaic, as to Daniel Deronda at their first meeting (ii. 336): "What are you disposed to give for it?" "I believe Mr. Ram will be satisfied with half-a-crown, sir," remarks suf-

ficiently on the level of nineteenth-century conversation
to give Mordecai some community with ordinary folk.

There is yet another quality which Mordecai shares
with the sages and prophets of the past: he is a lay-
man. The natural thing for a writer describing "a
spiritual destiny embraced eagerly in youth," a representative of the religious life of a nation, would be to
describe some young priest ardently striving for the
spiritual enlightenment of his flock, some Mr. Tryan,
some Savonarola; and it would have been right for all
other religions. But in Judaism the inner development of the Spirit has been carried on almost entirely
by laymen: the Jewish Summa Theologiæ, "The Guide
to the Perplexed" (*Morê Nebouchim*) of Maimonides,
was written by a physician. We shall be using more
familiar illustrations when we remind the reader that
Moses and, above all, the prophets were men from
the lay community, not members of an organised
priesthood. This may account for that spirit of Compromise (writers of the New English call it "adaptation
to environment"), which is as marked a characteristic
of the religious history of Jews as of the political
history of Englishmen. Other religions have had
churches, bureaucracies; Judaism has had a synagogue,
a representative assembly.

Mordecai shares yet another gift of his predecessors:
he is a poet. The fragment in chapter xxxviii. commencing—

> "Away from me the garment of forgetfulness,
>   Withering the heart,"

might well be a translation from a Piut of Ibn Gebirol
or a Selicha of Jehuda Halevi, and makes him a fit
dramatis persona of that "national tragedy lasting 1500
years, in which the actors have been also the heroes
and the poets."

We do not speak without knowledge of the history
of Jews, post-biblical as well as biblical, when we say
that Mordecai Cohen is a lineal successor of those
great leaders of spiritual Judaism who have fought in
the van in that moral warfare which Judaism has
waged and won against the whole world; a fitting
companion of that valiant band which has guarded
through the ages the ark of the Lord intrusted to
Israel's keeping 4000 years ago; a noble representative of that spirit of resistance that has repulsed the
most powerful disintegrating forces ever brought against
a nation or a creed. A "nation of shopkeepers" has
produced a Milton, a Shelley, a Newman; a "nation
of pawnbrokers," if you will, has given birth to a
Jehuda Halevi, a Spinoza, a Mordecai.

To believers in the principle of Heredity this would
be enough to give to Mordecai that possibility which
is sufficient for artistic existence. English critics, however, seem not to believe in hereditary influences: they
have unanimously pronounced him an impossibility.
They require, it would appear, some more tangible
proof of the existence among modern Jews of a character like Mordecai's than the *à priori* probability
afforded by the consideration of the historic continuity
of national character. Even this want could be sup-
plied. The present writer was fortunate enough to
discover [1] traces of a Jew who, allowing for the idealisation which is the privilege of the artist, might well
stand for the prototype of Mordecai. In the *Fortnightly Review* for April 1, 1866, Mr. George Henry
Lewes prefaces an article on Spinoza with an account
of a philosophers' club where he first made acquaintance with the doctrines of the Hebrew thinker, and

---

[1] The discovery was communicated to the *Academy* of July 29, 1876, by
my friend Mr. McAlister, to whom I had shown it.

which resembles in every particular the club at the
" Hand and Banner" in the sixth book of " Daniel
Deronda." The locality, Red Lion Square, near Holborn, is the same; the free and easy method of discussion is the same; the vocations of the frequenters
are the same—a freethinking second-hand bookseller
(Miller), a journeyman watchmaker (Pash), a bootmaker
(Croop), one who " penned a stanza when he should
engross" (Lilly), and so on. But above all, the leading spirit of Mr. Lewes' club was a German Jew
named Cohn or Kohn, whom he describes in words
which might be applied almost without alteration to
Mordecai. Mr. Lewes says of Cohn :

"We all admired him as a man of astonishing
subtlety and logical force, no less than of sweet
personal worth. He remains in my memory as a
type of philosophic dignity. A calm, meditative, amiable man, by trade a journeyman watchmaker, very
poor, with weak eyes and chest, grave and gentle in
demeanour; incorruptible even by the seductions of
vanity; I habitually think of him in connection with
Spinoza almost as much on account of his personal
worth as because to him I owe my first acquaintance
with the Hebrew thinker. My admiration of him was
of that enthusiastic temper which in youth we feel for
our intellectual leaders. I loved his weak eyes and
low voice; I venerated his intellect. He was the
only man I did not contradict in the impatience of
argument. An immense pity and a fervid indignation
filled me as I came away from his attics in one of the
Holborn courts, where I had seen him in the pinching
poverty of his home, with his German wife and two
little black-eyed children; indignantly I railed against
society which could allow so great an intellect to with-
draw itself from nobler work and waste the precious

hours in mending watches. But he was wise in his
resignation, thought I in my young indignation. Life
was hard to him, as to all of us; but he was content
to earn a miserable pittance by handicraft, and kept
his soul serene. I learnt to understand him better
when I learnt the story of Spinoza's life.

"Cohn, as may be supposed, early established his
supremacy in our club. A magisterial intellect always
makes itself felt. Even those who differed from him
most widely paid voluntary homage to his power."

Aut Mordecai aut diabolus. Just as Walter Scott
merely idealised Rebecca Gratz, the beloved of Wash-
ington Irving, into his Rebecca of York, so George
Eliot, by the force of her genius, has transformed
Kohn into a prophet of the New Exile. Even the
omission of the wife and two children (in whose
stead we get Mrs. Cohen junior, with Jacob and
Adelaide Rebecca) only serves to heighten the isolation which makes the pathos of Mordecai's lot.

But surely the critics had no occasion to doubt the
possibility of a Jew like Mordecai at a time when we
are still mourning the loss of one who laid down his life
for the regeneration of our views of Israel's past, as
Mordecai sacrificed his for the elevation of our hopes of
Israel's future. "I have certain words in my possession," wrote Emanuel Deutsch,[1] "which have been
given me that they might be said to others, few or
many. . . . I know also that I shall not find peace
or rest until I have said my whole say. And yet I
cannot do it. And I yearn for things which I see,
and which might have been mine, and would have
been blessing and sunshine and the cooling dew to
the small germs within me—and yet! and yet!—"

Would that Mr. Deutsch had lived to convince the

[1] "The Literary Remains of the late Emanuel Deutsch" (Murray, 1874), p. xii.

world in his own burning words that Mordecai is no inert scarecrow of abstractions, but a warm living reality!

We have laid so much stress upon the artistic truth of Mordecai's character because, if this be granted, it is inexplicable that the central incident of the Jewish part of "Daniel Deronda," the meeting on the bridge between him and Deronda, should have failed to strike readers as perhaps the most remarkable incident in English fiction. If Mordecai has artistic reality, we contend that the meeting on the bridge in chapter xl. reaches a tragic intensity which almost transcends the power of the novel, and would perhaps require the manifold emotive inlets of the Wagnerian drama to do it justice—eye, ear, brain, and heart should all be responsive. We boldly deny greater tragic intensity to any incident in Shakespeare. Nor are there wanting signs that the author herself, no contemptible critic of her own productions, sets an equal value on the incident. In the motto prefixed to chapter xxxviii., describing Mordecai's yearnings, she tells us in Brownesque English—

"There be who hold that the deeper tragedy were a Prometheus bound, not *after*, but *before*, he had well got the celestial fire into the νάρθηξ, whereby it might be conveyed to mortals. Thrust by the Kratos and Bia of instituted methods into a solitude of despised ideas, fastened in throbbing helplessness by the fatal pressure of poverty and disease—a solitude where many pass by, but none regard."

In other words, George Eliot considers the circumstances of Mordecai's fate to surpass in tragic pathos the most colossal monument of Greek dramatic art. Notice, too, the care with which she leads up to the incident. In chapter xxxvii. we have Deronda coming to the Meyricks at Chelsea to announce to Mirah the forthcoming visit of Klesmer, and the chapter finishes as he is leaving Chelsea. The next chapter (xxxviii.) is filled with a description of Mordecai's yearning for a spiritual successor, and give us *en passant* a fine picture of the scene of the meeting (iii. 137). We get here, in short, all we need to understand and sympathise with the final episode of the "book;" but lest we should come upon the fulfilment of the prophecy with too vivid a memory of the author's sublimation of the idea of prophecy, we have interposed, like a comic scene in an Elizabethan tragedy, the magnificent account of Klesmer's visit to the Meyricks in chap. xxxix., which clearly occurred *after* the events described in chapter xl., which takes up the stream of narrative from chapter xxxvii.

It seems to us clear that all this seemingly inartistic transposition of events is intended to make the incident of chapter xl. stand out more sharply into relief. We have the miracle explained away, it is true — the modern analytic spirit requires it—but the author wishes us to forget the explanation, or at least to relegate the intellectual element of chapter xxxviii. to the unconscious background, where it may be ready to assist, though not present to obstruct, emotion. All this care appears to show the importance attached by the author to the last chapter of Book v.

And in itself, apart from what the author may think of it, what a soul-moving incident is there contained! A representative of an ancient world-important people, whose royalty of wrongs makes the aristocracies of Europe appear petty, finds himself clutched by the gripping hands of want and death before he can move the world to that vision of the Phœnix-rise of Israel which the prophetic instincts of his race have brought up clear before him. Careless of his own comfort, careless of coming death, he desires only to live anew — as the quasi-Positivist doctrine of the Cabbala bids him live—in "minds made nobler by his presence." His prophetic vision pictures to him the very lineaments of his spiritual *alter ego*, whom he pathetically thinks of as differing from himself in all externals, and, as death draws nigh, the very scene of their meeting. And in this nineteenth century, in prosaic London, this inward vision of the poor consumptive Jew is fulfilled to the letter.

Would it be too bold a suggestion if we suspected the author of having typified in the meeting of Deronda and Mordecai that

"One far-off divine event
To which the whole creation moves,"

the meeting of Israel and its Redeemer? In personal characteristics, in majestic gravity (we cannot imagine Deronda laughing), in width of sympathy and depth of tenderness, even in outward appearance, Daniel resembles the great Galilean Pharisee[1] whom all Christendom has accepted as in very truth the Messiah that will restore Judæa to the Holy People. To say the least, the author suggests the audacity in her comparison of the two to the figures of Jesus and the Pharisee in Titian's "Tribute Money."

We do not remember a single criticism[2] which has referred to this magnificent scene, where, to our mind, George Eliot's power of representing soul speaking to soul has reached its greatest height. We do not

---

[1] A friend informs me that Pharisee is derived from פרש, to extend (the law), not from פרש, to separate and define it.

[2] Professor Dowden's article in the *Contemporary Review* for Feb. 1877, which appeared after the above was written, forms an exception with respect to this as to all the other deficiencies of the critics against which we here protest.

remember a single critic who seemed to think that
Mordecai's fate was in any way more pitiful than that
of any other consumptive workman with mystic and
impossible ideas. What reasons can be given for
this defect of sympathy? In addition to the before-
mentioned assumption that Mordecai does not possess
artistic reality, there has been the emotional obstruction to sympathy with a Jew, and the intellectual
element of want of knowledge about modern Judaism.
If Mordecai had been an English workman laying down
his life for the foundation of some English International with Deronda for its " Messiah Lassalle," he
would have received more attention from the critics.
But a Jew with views involving issues changing the
future history of Humanity — "impossible, vague,
mystic." Let us not be misunderstood : the past
generation of Englishmen has been so generous to
Jews, that we should be ungrateful if we accused
cultured Englishmen of the present day of being
consciously repelled by the idea of a poor Jew being
worthy of admiration. But fifteen centuries of hatred
are not to be wiped out by any legislative enactment.
No one can say that the fact of a man's being a Jew
makes no more difference in other men's minds than
if he were (say) a Wesleyan. There yet remains a
deep unconscious undercurrent of prejudice against
the Jew which conscientious Englishmen have often
to fight against as part of that lower nature, a survival of the less perfect development of our ancestors,
which impedes the Ascent of Man.

Along with this unconscious Judæophobia there
has gone the intellectual element of a tacit assumption
that modern Judaism is a lifeless code of ritual instead
of a living body of religious truth. Of course the
pathos and tragedy of Mordecai's fate depend in large

measure on the value of the ideas for which he laid
down his life. If he were a crazy believer that the
English nation is descended from the lost Ten Tribes,
his fate would only deserve a smile of contemptuous
pity. Hence the artistic necessity of the philosophic
discussion in chapter xlii., where his ideas are explained and defended. Here again we have to complain of the want of sympathy shown by the critics,
but perhaps still more of their want of knowledge.
Our author devotes the forty-first chapter to a piece
of special pleading (really addressed to the reader,
though supposed to be a philosophic musing of
Deronda's), the outcome of which is that if we
want to tell whether an enthusiast is justified in
his faith, our only test is knowledge of the subject-
matter. And the moral naturally is: study the history
of the Jews. Hegel says somewhere—"The heritage
a great man leaves the world is to force it to explain
him," and we may say the same of a great work of
art. But the critics of "Daniel Deronda" have refused
to pay the heavy probate duty of wading through the
ten volumes or so of Grätz's "Geschichte der Juden" to
see whether Mordecai's ideas have anything in them
or no: the easier plan was to denounce them as
"vague and mystical." If it be contended that the
subject is too unfamiliar for ordinary readers, and
therefore unsuited for a novel, we may answer that
similar reasoning would exalt an Offenbach over a
Beethoven. George Eliot has endeavoured to raise
the novel to heights where it may treat of subjects
hitherto reserved for the Drama or the Epic; but
instead of encouragement from English critics, she
meets with their neglect.

Apart, however, from the intrinsic value of Mordecai's ideas, the discussion would deserve our admiration

as a literary *tour de force*. It was the high praise of the Greek philosopher that if the gods spoke Greek they would talk as Plato wrote : may we not say that if Isaiah had spoken English he would have prophesied as George Eliot makes Mordecai speak ? We trace in this the influence which the Authorised Version—with all its inaccuracies, the most living reproduction of the Hebrew Scriptures—has had on our principal writers, notably in the case of so un-biblical a writer as Mr. Swinburne.

And what of the ideas which Mordecai clothes with words as of one whose lips have been touched with coals of burning fire ? What vagueness or mystery is there in the grand and simple lines of Jewish policy laid down by Mordecai ? Two ideas dominate Mordecai's arguments throughout the discussion. The resumption of the soil of Palestine by the Jews, which has often been proposed by Gentile writers as a solution of the much-vexed Eastern Question, and, as a conse-quence, the third and final promulgation of the Jewish religion to the world, are sufficiently definite ideas, however large and grand they may be. Even if one disagree with Mordecai's views, one may at any rate pay him the respect due to an energetic leader of opposition, and recognise in him the leader of those who refuse to believe that Israel's part in history is played out, and that her future policy should be to amalgamate with the nations as soon as possible, letting her glorious past sink into an antiquarian study, instead of living as a perennial spring of political action. Mordecai is not of those who hold that the millennium will come when men shall have arrived at that nicely balanced mediocrity, that the " pale abstract " man shall know his brother from other cosmopolitan beings only by some official badge necessary for distinction. He rather holds that in the world-organism of the nations each nationality will have its special function, Israel, as the Jewish poet-philosopher said, being the nations' heart.[1] The now-prevailing doctrine of Heredity, and the political enthusiasm for Panslavism, Panteutonism, Pan-what-notism, will have nought to urge against these Pan-judaic views. And to our minds Mordecai's is the profounder philosophy of history when he further thinks that the great quarry of religious truth, whence two world-religions have been hewn and shaped, but only into torsos, has yet wherewithal to completely fashion the religion of the future. The one theologic dogma of Judaism, the unity of the Godhead (involving, as Mordecai remarks, the unity of mankind), can meet with no harsh reception from the philosophies of the day, imbued as they all are with the monism of the "God-intoxicated Jew." The rationalism of Spinoza's *Tractatus Theologico-Politicus*, which has undermined mediæval Christianity, now tottering from the attack, merely represents the outcome of a long line of Jewish thought on prophecy, miracles, and the like, and is, in large measure, derived from our summa theologiæ, the *Morê Nebouchîm* of Maimonides. Again, reverence for law, as marked a trait of the Jewish spirit as of Roman pride (the Talmud is but a *Corpus Juris*), is another characteristic which Judaism shares with the *Zukunfts-religion*. The divorce between man and the world, which is the disintegrating factor in Christianity, nowhere finds a place in Judaism. Further, the teleologic tendency of the evolution doctrine must find a reason for the miraculous tenacity

[1] Cusari, ii. 36. Mordecai attributes the saying to Jehuda Halevi; Sephardo in the "Spanish Gypsy," p. 210, to the "Book of Light," the Cabbalistic book Sohar. It occurs in both. *Vide* Cassel's note *in loco*.

with which Judaism has clung to life.   If, as biologists
tell us, life consists in the adaptation of internal forces
to the relations of the environment, Judaism, of all
religions, has most truly lived, and George Eliot has
with due knowledge connected the utterances of
Mordecai on Judaism with the problem of the hour,
"What is progress?"   In this connection it were
interesting to contrast the history of the two religions
of civilisation in the ages previous to the Reformation.
While Father after Father was crystallising the freethought of Jesus into stony dogma; while Doctor after
Doctor was riveting still closer the fetters of reason ;
Rabbi after Rabbi was adapting tradition to the reason
of the time, each, when his task was done, dying with
the *shemah*[1] on his lips.   Our author has put into the
mouth of a Jew one of her noblest passages, describing
this progress in Judaism.   Sephardo, in the "Spanish
Gipsy" (p. 215), speaks thus of the principles of order
and progress in the Jewish religion—

> "I abide
> By that wise spirit of listening reverence
> Which marks the boldest doctors of our race.
> For truth to us is like a living child,
> Born of two parents : if the parents part
> And will divide the child, how shall it live ?
> Or I will rather say : Two angels guide
> The paths of man, both aged and yet young,
> As angels are, ripening through endless years.
> On one he leans : some call her Memory,
> Some Tradition ; and her voice is sweet
> With deep mysterious accords : the other,
> Floating above, holds down a lamp which streams
> A light divine and searching on the earth,
> Compelling eyes and footsteps : Memory yields,
> Yet clings with loving check, and shines anew,
> Reflecting all the rays of that bright lamp

---

[1] The assertion of the Divine Unity (*Deut.* vi. 4).

Our angel Reason holds. We had not walked,
But for Tradition : we walk evermore,
To higher paths by brightening Reason's lamp."

The pages of that history of rationalism that shall treat
of the progress of Jewish theosophy, culminating in
the epoch-making thought of Spinoza, will fully bear
out the historic truth of the above description. And
surely that represents the spirit with which we may
expect the religion of the future to be informed.

But the new birth of Judaism and its revelation to
the world are, in Mordecai's opinion, indissolubly connected with the new birth of the Jewish race as a
nation. "The effect of our separateness," he says,
"will not be completed and have its highest transformation unless our race takes on again the character of
a nationality." And here, again, history confirms his
views. For the life of Judaism has been connected
with the history of Jews in a way such as has been the
fate of no other religion. The very name of the religion
displays this intimate connection ; of all religions,
Judaism alone has been named after the race of its believers. And it is to this that we may perhaps attribute
the peculiar interest that George Eliot has felt for Jews,
which we can trace at least as far back as 1864, when
the first draft of the " Spanish Gipsy " was written. The
two chief interests of the translator of Strauss and
friend of Mr. Herbert Spencer have been the religious
consciousness, which she was the first to use for the
artistic purposes of the novel, and the influence of
hereditary forces, which she first raised into an ethical
creed. And Jews are interesting in both connections,
exhibiting in the greatest known degree what is to her
the highest virtue—fidelity to claims of race. At the
same time, this relation of believers and creed has been
the source of much misconception. No distinction is

made in the popular mind between the theologic and
ethical doctrines of Judaism and the national customs
of Jews. It is true that in the biblical times and afterwards the social and religious sanctions were not
differentiated, but their *raison d'être* nowadays, apart
from the sanitary sanction of many of the customs, is
merely the same as that which preserves many family
customs among the aristocracies of Europe. It is our
national boast to have been the first to proclaim the
true God, and the "Swiss Guards of Deism," as Heine
wittily calls us, have clothed themselves with such
customs as with a uniform. These rites and ceremonies
are not essential to the Judaism we have the mission to
preach to the world : for Jews are a missionary, though
not a proselytising people ; however our voices may
have hitherto been stifled, we have lived our mission
if we have not been permitted to preach it. Those who
become Jews in religion need not adopt the Mosaic
rites, unless they wish to be naturalised as Jews in race.
Still the religious trust that has kept the national life
throbbing through the centuries has been the conviction that the Messiah who shall spread Judaism to the
four corners of the world will be a Jew by race as well
as in creed.   And Mordecai's views of the resumption
of the soil of the Holy Land by the holy people are the
only logical position of a Jew who desires that the long
travail of the ages shall not end in the total disappearance of the race. For from the times of the Judges
periods of prosperity, such as the one upon which the
present generation has entered, have been the most
perilous for our national life : it is the struggle for
national existence that has resulted, we are vain enough
to think, in the survival of the fittest missionaries of the
true religion. The Sages say, "Israel is like the olive,
the more it is pressed, the more copious the oil ; " and

it is to be feared that the removal of the pressure will result in the cessation of the noble deeds that are typified by the oil. Unless some such project as Mordecai has in view be carried out in the next three generations, it is much to be feared that both the national life of Jews and the religious life of Judaism will perish utterly from the face of the earth. "A consummation devoutly to be wished," the scoffers may say; but not, surely, those in whose veins runs the blood of Israelites, and who have the proud heritage of God's truth to hand down to their children.

Enough has perhaps been said to show that Mordecai's views about the future of Judaism and of Jews have all history and much reason on their side, and display those powers of intellectual intuition of the future which the psychological system of Maimonides assigns to the Prophet. And we have perhaps contributed somewhat to an explanation of Deronda's acceptance of his spiritual inheritance. Like Mordecai, Deronda protests against the "blasphemy of the time," that men should stand by as spectators of life instead of living. But before he meets with Mordecai, what noble work in life has this young and cultured Englishman with his thousands a year? This age of unfaith gives no outlet for his deep, spiritual yearnings, nor for those of thousands like him. The old beliefs are gone; the world is godless, and Deronda cannot, for all the critics have said, offer to Gwendolen Grandcourt any consolation in the higher order of things instead of the vague platitudes which alone remain to be offered. Yet there comes to this young ardent soul an angel of the Lord (albeit in the shape of a poor Jew watchmender) with a burning message, giving a mission in life as grand as the most far-reaching ideal he could have formed. Is it strange that his thirsty soul should

F

have swallowed up the soul of Mordecai, in the Cabbalistic way which the latter often refers to? Is it strange that Deronda should not have refused the heritage of his race when offered by the hands of Mirah's brother? But is it not strange that the literary leaders of England should have failed to see aught but unsatisfactory vagueness in all the parts of "Daniel Deronda" which treat of the relations of the hero with Mordecai Cohen? Is it possible that they have failed to see the grandeur and beauty of these incidents because of the lack of that force of imagination necessary to pierce to the pathos of a contemporary tragedy, however powerful their capacity might be to see the romance of a Rebecca of York, or the pathos of a Baruch Spinoza?

One possible source of misconception for English readers may be mentioned. Since the time of Moses Mendelssohn the home of spiritual Judaism has been in Germany, and George Eliot, whose pages are informed with the writings of German Jews like Zunz, Geiger, and Grätz, has, with true historic insight, attributed Mordecai's spiritual birth to the teachings of his German uncle. English Judaism is without signs of life: the only working of the spirit, the abortive reform agitation, was due to a similar movement in Germany. And English Jews have themselves much to blame for the neglect that English criticism has shown for Mordecai.

What we have attempted to show has been that the adverse criticism on the Mordecai part of "Daniel Deronda" has been due to lack of sympathy and want of knowledge on the part of the critics, and hence its failure is not (if we must use the word) objective. If a young lady refuses to see any pathos in Othello's fate because she dislikes dark complexions, we blame the young lady, not Shakespeare; and if the critics have refused to see the pathos of Mordecai's fate because he is a Jew of the present day, so much the worse for the critics.

We have not attempted to criticise "Daniel Deronda" as a whole. Whether it errs in the juxtapositions of two parts appealing to such widely diverse interests, or in the position of the hero—which seems to partake of that unstable equilibrium which the proverb assigns to him that sitteth on two stools—or in the frequent introduction of psychology couched in Spencerian phraseology, we have not cared to inquire. We have only spoken because we have some of the knowledge and all of the sympathy which alone, we contend, are needed to make the Mordecai part of "Daniel Deronda" as great a success as all must acknowledge to have attended the part relating to Gwendolen Harleth. If this be so, the lovers of English literature will have the gratification of knowing that the hand of one of our greatest artists has not lost its cunning in these last days. Indeed, if a higher subject argued higher faculties, the successful treatment of a great world-problem would seem to be an advance on her previous studies of village life.

One word more of explanation. I have spoken throughout the above remarks in the plural, as feeling that most of what I have said would be shared by all Jews who have the knowledge and sympathy which enable them to recognise in Mordecai Cohen not only the finest representative of their religion and race in all literature, but also the most impressive personality in English fiction.

BROWNING'S THEOLOGY

(*From " The Jewish Quarterly Review," April* 1890)

THERE is at the first blush a superficial resemblance between a poet and a theologian. Both the one and the other give formal expression in accurate phraseology to some of our profoundest feelings. The poet, as well as the theologian, expresses explicitly what we feel most deeply. The theologian, equally with the poet, deals with the ideals of life, and especially the architectonic ideals that organise life and make it, or should make it, one vast grand poem. A little more harping on the same string, and especially a little more mixture of metaphors, and it would not be difficult to make out a good case for calling poet, priest, and theologian, poet writ large.

But when we come to the mode in which the poet and the theologian respectively give expression to the ideal elements within us, all these resemblances vanish at once. Think for a moment what is implied in the formal expression which a poet and a theologian respectively would give of the yearning after immortality. While the artist in words and moods would endeavour so to express the yearning as to invoke in his reader the same feeling that moves him with all its *nuances* of hope and doubt, rapture and shrinking, the theologian will be thinking under what section of what chapter of his Treatise on Eschatology the subject will most logically be introduced. For the theologian

as such appeals, or at least ought to appeal, solely to
the reason, whereas the poet has the whole diapason
of human nature to work upon.

I seem to have cut away the ground beneath my
own feet, if the thing be possible and the metaphor
allowable, in thus distinguishing so sharply the respective functions of poet and theologian. If they be so
distinct, how treat of Browning's theology, on which
I am to speak a few words from the Jewish point of
view? But Browning, in this as in so many things,
struck out a new line for himself. Regardless of the
canon that a poet cannot be a theologian, he wrote
theological poems, in which the reasoning is at least
as close and certainly as difficult to follow as that of
many professed theologians. It is true they are mostly
in dramatic form; instead of discussing anthropomorphism or fetishism, he gave us "Caliban on Setebos;" instead of answering Strauss directly, he wrote "Christmas
Eve" and "Easter Day;" instead of writing an essay on
miracles, he pictures for us Karshish's reflections on
the case of Lazarus. It is not, however, so difficult as
one might think to penetrate beneath the mask of the
dramatis personæ and gain access to the thoughts of
Robert Browning himself on the higher problems and
obscurest difficulties of life. It is these that constitute
him a theologian in the strict sense of the word, and
should enable us to place the poet in one or other of
the categories into which the theologians of the day
may be divided.

In one case, indeed, Browning drops the mask of
impersonation altogether, and speaks out on a theological subject of great importance. Stirred to the
inmost depths by the sudden death of a friend, he
discusses at some length in *La Saisiaz* the question
of the immortality of the soul. Interesting as his

treatment is, it scarcely comes within the scope of these remarks to consider it. For the dogma of immortality is one of natural religion, one common to all the creeds (except perhaps Buddhism). It is not more Jewish than Christian, Moslem than Greek ; and in seeking to define Robert Browning's relation to Judaism, we must deal with the dogmas more distinctive of the creeds, and consider his attitude towards them, and its relation to that of other religious thinkers of his time.

His opinions show him to have been a member of the Broad Church School, as represented by Dean Stanley and the men of "Essays and Reviews." A certain amount of sympathy is shown with what used to be known as German neologism, which in "Christmas Eve" is regarded as being even one of the ways of knowing Christ. But at the same time, the inadequateness of the rationalistic attitude towards the Divinity of Christ is also insisted upon, and the assumption is left that this, with all its consequences—the Incarnation and the Atonement—must be accepted by faith, if not to be definitely established by reason. Throughout this poem the figure of Christ appears in such a form as would be impossible without a thorough faith in His Divinity. It must, therefore, be owned that so far as the evidence of his works goes, the jubilation of the orthodox Christian over the faith of Browning is to a certain extent justified, and there is little or no reason to suppose, as some Jewish students of the poet have thought, that his creed was a pure monotheism, with a rejection of the Incarnation. Browning's theology was distinctively Christian, and in no way can be said to approximate to Judaism on the chief point that separates the two religions.

At the same time, outside "Christmas Eve" very little

stress is laid on influence of the Mediator in the spiritual life, the practical side by which the Divinity of Christ is made operative in the Christian life. But herein Browning is only at one with the rest of the Broad Church, who tend to attenuate the function of mediation till Christ becomes little more than the spiritual brother in God, and Christ-worship becomes practically impossible. Another tendency which he likewise shares with the school of thought with which I am identifying him, is the practical disappearance of the third person of the Trinity from his theology. Except in such vague form as "God's Spirit" or the "Spirit of Love," there is scarcely any reference to the Holy Spirit in his writings.

Speaking generally then, Browning's theology is that of the Broad Church with all its catholicity, but also with all its vagueness, and its want of touch with the practical religious life. So far as Browning's thought on religious matter seems Jewish, it is because of its Broad Church tone. In a fuller treatment of the subject it would be necessary, as it would be interesting, to discuss from a Jewish point of view the whole Broad Church movement before determining how far Browning approximates to the Jewish position. In many Jewish circles it was thought, and is still thought, that the Broad Church was a tendency in Christianity towards Judaism. This is, however, erroneous : it is a tendency towards Unitarianism, not towards Judaism, as indeed both Mr. Voysey and Mr. Stopford Brooke have practically shown. Now, however much we may differ as to what Judaism is, and of recent years we have agreed to differ exceedingly, there is one point on which we are all agreed. Judaism is differentiated from Unitarianism by an additional element, which may be called either racial or historical. The practical recognition of God in history, and of a divine mission for Israel, is a necessary part of Judaism according to all schools, however much they may differ as to the mode of operation of the Divine Spirit in men's affairs, or as to the exact character of the function Israel is to play in order to fulfil the designs of that Spirit. It is this quality that makes Judaism, which, at first sight, seems so akin to Unitarianism, on closer investigation turn out to show a closer kinship with the Roman Catholic Church, as is after all only natural, as their historical relationship is really that of mother and daughter.

The Broad Church is singularly unsusceptible to the claims of history and of development in religion, and Browning shares in this quality of his school. Indeed, he extends this unsympathy with the conception of history as a divine process so far as to limit very much his general poetic treatment of historic subjects. For a poet who dealt so much with the past as he did, there is singularly little of the nationalist point of view of treating history—I mean the conception that nations, just as religions, have their main function in the creation of specific types of human character. Considering that he lived so much in Italy when her noblest elements were most deeply imbued with this conception, considering also that Mrs. Browning had the deepest sympathy with it, it is curious how very little there is in Browning that strikes the patriotic or nationalist note. Here, again, he chimes in with the general sentiments of his school of religious thought, who have been cosmopolitan to a fault.

Perhaps the most distinctive point in Browning's teaching is the view which I have elsewhere ventured to sum up in the formula "Aspiration is achievement" (*Athenæum*, December 21, 1889, p. 859). This, as applied to theology, would perhaps lead to one of the most striking doctrines of the Broad Church in one of its more recent developments. I refer to Dr. Abbot's remarkable view of the religious use of illusion as leading on to higher forms of truth. From a Jewish point of view, this is of interest, as chiming in with Maimonides' conception of Christianity and Islam being two forms of useful illusion that will lead on to Judaism. But there is no evidence that Browning shared Dr. Abbot's view, and for this reason I have affiliated him with the school of Stanley.

Hitherto in regarding Browning as a theologian of the Broad Church School we have been dealing rather with the points in which he and his school, or rather his school and he, differ from the Jewish way of looking at things religious. But there remains one other point besides the tendency to Unitarianism wherein the Broad Church approaches Judaism, as Jews have every reason to know and be thankful for. With all its vagueness of doctrine and attenuation of dogma, the Broad School has been ever honourably distinguished by its toleration, both in theory and practice. Both in eschatology and in the doctrine of sin, Judaism and the Broad Church are at one in declaring a man's deeds, and not his creed, to be the criterion of his claims to the higher life, both here and hereafter. Here universalism and nationalism are at one.

It is here, of course, that Browning's Jewish poems come in as part of his general theological attitude, and it may be of interest to review those that deal most directly with Jewish subjects. "Holy Cross Day" puts with considerable humour the case against conversion in the form of a Roman Jew's soliloquy while attending, but not listening, to a sermon which the

Jews of the Ghetto were forced to endure once a year.
No Jew could wish to have the *Apologia pro domo suâ*
put with more force than in the ringing lines in which
the poet makes his Rabbi address the Christ :—

> O thou, if that martyr-gash
> Fell on thee coming to take thine own,
> And we gave the Cross, when we owed the Throne—
>
> Thou art the Judge.　We are bruised thus.
> But, the judgment over, join sides with us !
> Thine too is the cause ! and not more thine
> Than ours, is the work of these dogs and swine,
> Whose life laughs through and spits at their creed,
> Who maintain thee in word, and defy thee in deed.
>
> ·　　·　　·　　·　　·　　·
>
> By the torture, prolonged from age to age,
> By the infamy, Israel's heritage,
> By the Ghetto's plague, by the garb's disgrace,
> By the badge of shame, by the felon's place,
> By the branding tool, the bloody whip,
> And the summons to Christian fellowship,—
>
> We boast our proof that at least the Jew
> Would wrest Christ's name from the Devil's crew.

Another less well-known poem of toleration is that
entitled "Filippo Baldunecci on the Privilege of
Burial," telling how a petty-minded painter annoyed
the Jews by putting up a picture of the Virgin overlooking their graveyard, and when he had agreed to
remove it for a consideration, replacing it by one of
the Crucifixion.　At last the Jews buy both pictures,
on the plea that they may have them in their possession, just as a Christian would not scruple to have
one of Venus or of Zeus.　The scorn of the Jews at
Baldunecci's action, and the meanness shown by it,

is heightened by their dignified and lofty rebuke at
being plagued even in their graves.

> Death's luxury we now rehearse
> While, living, through your streets we fare,
> And take your hatred! nothing worse
> Have we, once dead and safe, to bear.

Another slight poem of Browning's, never printed,
I believe, in any of his works—it appeared in *The
Keepsake*, 1856—expands a well-known saying of the
"Ethics of the Fathers":—

BEN KARSHOOK'S WISDOM.

I.

> Would a man 'scape the rod,
>   Rabbi Ben Karshook saith,
> "See that he turn to God
>   The day before his death."
>
> "Ay, could a man inquire
>   When it shall come?" I say,
> The Rabbi's eye shoots fire,
>   "Then let him turn to-day!"

II.

> Quoth a young Sadducee,
>   "Reader of many rolls,
> Is it so certain we
>   Have, as they tell us, souls?"
>
> "Son, there is no reply!"
>   The Rabbi bit his beard,
> "Certain, a soul have *I*—
>   *We* may have none," he sneered.
>
> Thus Karshook, the Hiram's Hammer
>   The Right-hand Temple-column
> Taught babes in grace their grammar
>   And struck the simple, solemn.

Browning's toleration is shown in even a higher way than in these direct attacks on intolerance. It cannot have been by accident that he chose to give two of the most important summaries of his *Weltweisheit* by means of Jewish speakers. "Rabbi Ben Ezra" and "Jochanan Hakkadosh." "Rabbi Ben Ezra" is by many considered Browning's most striking poem, and certainly it yields to none of his in dignity and lucidity. It is of peculiar interest to English Jews as the eponymous hero is Abraham ibn Ezra, who was himself in England, "the island of the corner of the earth" (a pun on Angle terre), as he calls it, in the spring and summer of 1158. It is scarcely likely that Browning knew more of him than that he was a distinguished Rabbi of the Middle Ages. Certainly the poem has none of those satiric touches with which Abraham ibn Ezra's name is associated in the mind of the student of Jewish literature. Nothing can be more dignified and stoical than the soliloquy of the old Rabbi reviewing life, and seeing that it is very good, both in youth, with its pleasure, and in age, with its experience. The image of the Potter and the Wheel, hackneyed as it has been by the homilists, has never been more finely utilised than in the concluding lines of the poem. Man as clay in the making is thus addressed—

> What though the earlier grooves
> Which ran the laughing loves
> Around thy base, no longer pause and press?
> What though, about thy rim,
> Skull-things in order grim
> Grow out, in graver mood, obey the sterner stress?
>
> Look thou not down, but up!
> To uses of a cup,
> The festal board, lamp's flash and trumpet's peal,

The new wine's foaming flow,
    The Master's lips a-glow!
Thou, heaven's consummate cup, what need'st thou with
        earth's wheel?

But I need, now as then,
    Thee, God, who mouldest men!
And since, not even while the whirl was worst,
        Did I, to the wheel of life
        With shapes and colours rife,
Bound dizzily—mistake my end, to slake Thy thirst.

So, take and use Thy work,
    Amend what flaws may lurk,
What strain o' the stuff, what warpings past the aim!
        My times be in Thy hand!
        Perfect the cup as planned!
Let age approve of youth, and death complete the same!

There remain a number of poems which go even
further than toleration of the Jewish life and creed.
They imply a certain sympathy with Jewish ways of
thought and fancy, and a certain acquaintance, though
not a very profound one, with Rabbinic literature.
These are chiefly contained in the volume called
Jocoseria. This contains one of the Midrashic legends
of the Queen of Sheba, though diluted through Arabic
sources, as is indicated by the title, "Solomon and
Balkis." It is scarcely more than a *jeu d'esprit.*

The most important of these poems is, however, the
legend of "Jochanan Hakkadosh," a sort of Rabbinic
Hagada on the theme "Unless ye be as little children,
ye shall not enter the kingdom of heaven." The great
Rabbi Jochanan, on the point of dying, has a year of
additional life granted him by the expedient of certain
younger men giving up three months of their lives to
the venerated sage. He lives their life, and thus at
the height of his wisdom is enabled to judge of the
value of their various occupations. "Vanity of Vanity"

is the refrain four times in succession, as his disciple Tsaddik visited Jochanan, after he had lived three months the life of a married lover, a warrior, a poet, and a statesman. But by accident some little child had also pressed upon the sage three months of its life, and this additional experience harmonises all the discrepancies of the others, and allows the sage to depart in peace, and assured that life is not vain.

Attached to "Jochanan Hakkadosh" are three sonnets on the well-known Talmudic *Lügenmärchen*, to use the folklore term, of the legend of Og's bones and bedstead. They are said to be from a work משך של רבים בדים which I need scarcely say neither exists nor could exist under such a title. Much headbreaking has been caused by the bad Hebrew of the title, but Browning would probably have given the Johnsonian explanation of "Ignorance, madam, ignorance." As some indication of the slightness of his acquaintance with Hebrew idiom, I may mention that he was going to call his Jochanan "Hakkadosh Jochanan" (= John Saint). Through a common friend I pointed out the error to the poet, and the adjective was put in its proper position. The fact seems to be that Browning could read his Hebrew Bible, and that was about the extent of his Hebrew learning, though it was a foible of his to give an impression of recondite learning.

But it is not in the minutiæ of Hebrew scholarship that we are to look for Browning's sympathy with the Jewish spirit. This comes out in the lines I have been quoting and in his poems of toleration. That this sympathy was not due to any agreement with the characteristic features of Jewish faith is, I think, undoubted. All the more honour to the poet who could rise above differences of creed, and pierce to the human nature

which is common to Christian and Jew, because it is
the gift of a Common Father.

NOTE.—The following passages in some recently published correspon-
dence of Browning throw interesting light on his attitude to Jewish questions :—" The two Hebrew quotations (put in to give a grave look to what
is mere fun and invention) being translated amount to—first, ' A Collection
of many lies ' ; and the second is an old saying, ' From Moses to Moses arose
none like Moses.' . . . The Hebrew quotations are put in for a purpose,
as a direct acknowledgment that certain doctrines may be found in the
Old Book, which the Concocters of Novel Schemes of Morality put forth
as discoveries of their own."

THE TRUE, THE ONLY, AND THE COMPLETE
SOLUTION OF THE JEWISH QUESTION

(*From " The Jewish Chronicle," October* 5, 1883)

SIR,—Last Tuesday night week, meditating on the past glories and present miseries of our race, I thought out, alone and unaided, the true, the only, and the complete solution of the Jewish Question which has been for many years past agitating and disquieting the world. I hasten to communicate it to you and your readers, and speaking to them and to all Israel, I say : *Make fools of your children!*

I know this requires some explanation. Permit me to explain by placing before you the line of thought which led me to this conclusion. Looking around me I find that Jews are getting themselves disliked, as the saying goes, in all the lands of civilisation. Now unless all the world, except the Jews, is both mad and bad, there must be something dislikeable in Jews to cause this universal dislike. What can it be, thought I to myself. Are the Jews too good? The world does not like perfection, as witness Aristides and Socrates, not to speak of examples nearer home. No, Jews are not perfect, I had to allow to myself, and hastened on to ask : Is it a matter of religious antipathy? That can scarcely be, answered my other self, for the world is getting more tolerant and, to speak truly, more indifferent about religion every day. Is it our wealth? I seemed to be getting warmer in the game of hide

and seek I was playing. The world envies wealth, and
Jews, or some of them, are undoubtedly wealthy. But
I had to grant that the feeling evinced by anti-Semites
was more like hatred than envy, and that it was displayed as much against poor Jews as rich ones. Then
there is our success—but the world worships success,
and it does not worship us.

Disappointed in these directions, I turned to think
of Jews rather than of their possessions, of our character
and qualities rather than of our wealth and honours.
I reviewed the long roll of Jewish virtues, and the
short list of Jewish vices. Charity, love of home,
sobriety—here I stopped a moment, for the world
rather likes one who "indulges," but, on the other
hand, it cannot be said to hate the temperate—our
cosmopolitanism (but the world rather admires Matthew
Arnold and Max Müller), our clannishness.—Here I
began to see light, or darkness as I thought, and reflected. Jews hold together and aloof from others, it
is true ; but Quakers and Scotchmen are also clannish,
and yet they are not disliked overmuch. Then again,
Jews have been getting less clannish just in the years
when opposition has been waxing more and more.

I turned impatiently to our vices. We play cards—
but only among ourselves. Our wives and daughters
dress showily, but then they dress badly, and we are
saved. Our *chutzpah* (there is no other word for it)
may make our neighbours wince at the ill-breeding of
it, but after all it is redeemed by a touch of wit now
and then. Our vanity? The world may laugh at it,
but hatred cannot coexist with a hearty laugh. I
began to despair, and had almost given up my search,
when I remembered that I had broken off suddenly in
enumerating our virtues. So I went back to these,
and recalling to mind the many speeches I have heard

on prize-days and at inaugurations, I luckily bethought myself of the special qualities on which we all pride ourselves—our intelligence, our energy, our patience. First I thought of them one by one, then I thought of them two by two, and then I summoned up all my powers of abstract thinking, and combined the whole three into one. At that moment the inspiration came upon me, and I would have cried "Eureka," but that I never thought of that word till long afterwards.

Here you must allow me to digress for a moment. Have you ever reflected, sir, on all that is meant and implied by that expressive phrase, "a Jew's eye?" I cannot help thinking that the outer world associates with it an ever-watchful gaze, keen to perceive, ever on the move, never relaxing its intensity. Here, then, we have a most appropriate symbol of intelligence, energy, and patience rolled into one. Now, admirable as such an eye and the qualities which it represents and typifies are in the battle of life, and necessary as it must have been in the past for a race that lived in arms, "the Jew's eye" becomes a rather inconvenient and objectionable organ in the pauses of the struggle. Life is not all battle, and he that tries to make it so will not be liked by his more peaceful neighbour. Putting one's self in the place of a *Goy*, it must be somewhat exasperating to think that in whatever relation you meet the Jew, his eye is for ever unslaked in brilliancy, and his soul ready for the conflict, and as a necessary condition of conflict, ready and desirous to get the better of the fight. To have that eye upon you at all times, even in moments of relaxation, is enough to goad the *Goy* into perpetual irritation. Thus it was in the combination of our three chief virtues, as symbolised in "the Jew's eye," that I found the irritant which has caused such ill-will. To drop symbolism, it is because our intelligence is combined with energy, and is therefore combative, and because these two qualities are combined with patience, so that our combative intelligence is never at rest, that the world dislikes us.   Such was my conclusion as to the cause of our being disliked by the world.

So far, so good.   I had found the cause, as I thought; now to seek for a remedy.   The essence of the world's opinion of us I took to be that a Jew is never to be found unarmed.   "You can never best a Jew," is the feeling of *les autres*.   And not alone is the Jew not to be bested, but he is certain to be the conqueror in any struggle, not so much by superiority of power, as by the persistent use of it.   And this is not all.   The Jew carries on the conflict of life into affairs where there should be no conflict.   He converses on politics, the theatre, a friend's character, or what not; he is never content unless he comes off victor, or at least has the last word.   "If you want to stop a Jew's talk," a friend once said to me, "agree with all he says; without the stimulus of conflict he cannot continue."   All this leaves an unpleasant flavour with it; there is no repose in the relations of Jews to others. Thus thinking, I saw my way to a remedy.   We must change all this.   Let us now and then give way.   Let us be content to be at times second best in a bargain, a competition, or a conversation; or, still better, let us cease at times to bargain, compete, or polemicise at all.   We have waged the fight long and bravely; let us put aside our arms for a while and meet our whilom enemies in friendly converse.   I thought of proposing a new festival, a kind of All Fools' Day for Judaism (say *Arav Tischa b'Ab*), on which every Jew should try as hard to lose some prize in the battle of life as he now does to win it.   The experiences of a

few anniversaries would convince Jews of the wisdom
of my advice, and the solution of the Jewish Question
seemed at hand.

And then a vision rose before me of the Reign of
Peace between Jew and Gentile. I saw the Jewish
tradesman content (mark you, *content*) to make a bad
bargain, or, if that were too much to hope, only a good
bargain, and not the very best bargain that could possibly be made. I saw the Jewish lawyer satisfied now
and then to take an adverse verdict without straining
every technicality of quibble and appeal to wrest a final
victory. I saw the Jewish scholar or scientist turn
aside to some bypath of speculation which would not
tell on the work of his life. I saw the Jewish publicist
refrain from pressing to its last consequences some slight
advantage he had gained in debate. I saw Jews re-
fusing to take advantage of some slight "opening,"
and ceasing to place the obtrusive elbow therein. My
mental eye brought before me a vision of the idol of
Tachlith deposed from its pedestal, and, in the height
of my enthusiasm, I thought that for a moment by its
side I had caught a Jew asleep.

But this beatific vision vanished the moment I turned
the critical rays of reason upon it. How could I expect
a Jew not to take advantage, and that a fair one, when
he sees his way to it? Everything in him, everything
about him, tells him that success is the be-all and end-
all of life. From our earliest moment we regard success
as not alone the most desirable thing for ourselves, but
our teachers never cease to point out how we raise our
brethren by succeeding. I saw, then, that what I was
aiming at was that Jews should be satisfied to be made
fools of now and again, and to acquiesce in the operation. Every Jewish instinct would rise in rebellion and
cry "Perish the thought!" What! we who pride our-

selves on our cleverness to allow the world at odd times to laugh at our folly in good-humoured fellow-ship. One might as well ask a man of clear vision to wish a cataract to come over his eye because its brilliance was too overpowering. I saw that I was asking no less than that Jews should make fools of themselves ; and the hopelessness of any such project stared me in the face. It was then that I turned, like all ardent reformers, to the coming generation ; and you may now perhaps understand what I mean when I declare my honest conviction that the only way for Jews to remove the world's dislike, and by so doing to solve the Jewish Question, is to make fools of their children.

Let us Jewish fathers of families set about the task. We must first of all change the motto of our training. We have perverted Kingsley's line—

"Be good, sweet maid, and let who will be clever,"

into the unmetrical version—

"Be clever, my son, and let who will be good,"

not because we love goodness less, but because we prize cleverness more. This must cease. We must give up praising our little ones for every act or word of " sharpness " we observe in them. We must check, rather than encourage, *chutzpah* and forwardness in them. We must make our sons foolish enough to think that there are other ends in life besides success, and that it is well at times to act without any definite aim at all. We must teach our daughters to be so foolish as to regard culture and comfort, rather than splendour and "respectability," as the ideal of home. Let us rejoice, rather than feel shame, when we find some of our children dull but kindly, and even encourage the amiable weakness. Before their eyes let us hold up as an ideal life the pursuits of those engaged in art and science where one man's victory is all men's gain, and let us even encourage them to be foolish enough to enter such careers, even though they show no transcendent genius for them. Let us smile approvingly when we see young men spending a goodly part of the years of their youth in pleasures and frolics, being "taken in" and "taken down" after the manner of their kind; and let us frown on those who scorn delights and live laborious days solely to raise a competence into a fortune. I am sure most Jewish fathers and mothers will agree with me that if they take my advice they will be making fools of their children.

But enough. I have explained my plan sufficiently. I am not saying that the game is worth the candle; but the Jewish public now know how they can solve the Jewish Question, if they choose to adopt the remedy. I enclose my card as a guarantee of good faith, but I must beg that you will make no use of my name. Sensible as I am convinced my plan is, I know Jews too well to have much hope of its early application. I should lose my reputation as a "practical" and "able" man if my congregation knew of my connection with this proposal, and even my friends would write me down a fool, though I am only a

MARSHALLIK.

[The "Marshallik" is the licensed wit of the Galician *ghetti*.]

JEHUDA HALEVI, POET AND PILGRIM [1]

THERE are some few men in the world's history whose thoughts and lives seem to rise above the bounds of space and time, and pass over into the world of ideals that ever lives anew in the souls of those coming after. In them the nation that produces them recognises its best self, in them it sees embodied its typical excellences. Their memory is preserved among their people with something of the ardour of personal affection, and with reason; for it is these men that give a people its rank in the hierarchy of nations. For when a race or a nation is arraigned at the bar of History and asked what are its claims to the recognition of humanity, the answer must be in the last resort that it has produced men such as these. And when that question is asked of Jews, no one will deny that among the representative men of Israel must be numbered the name of Jehuda Halevi.

When we look into the lives of these men of whom I have spoken, we find, I think, that they owe their proud position to a sort of artistic unity in their lives. Their inner thoughts and outward acts form a harmonious whole that puts to shame the petty inconsistencies and unfulfilled aspirations that distract the lives of most of us. Their lives are so rounded off that they seem to possess a kind of plot which we can follow with all the interest of a drama. Each act and word of theirs seem linked together by a bond of consis-

---

[1] A paper read before the Jews' College Literary Society, March 13, 1887.

tency, so that, though we cannot anticipate what they
will do, yet when it is done it seems just the thing we
should have expected them to do. Thus it is that their
lives for the most part are found to be dominated by
one inspiring idea, with which their names are for ever
associated. St. Louis and saintliness, St. Francis and
tenderness, Bayard and chivalry, Nelson and valour,
Gordon and duty, are almost synonymous. And so
with Jehuda Halevi there is a word that gives the
dominant chord which harmonises the music of his
life, and that word is—Jerusalem. I shall best achieve
my task of explaining the magical attraction with
which the name of Jehuda Halevi is connected in the
minds of Jewish scholars if I group what I have to say
about this dominant motive of his life. Much will
have to be left unsaid that might well be worth the
saying, but the best way to show the man Jehuda
Halevi as he was and felt, is to trace the rise and
growth of the master-passion of his life, his love for
the discrowned capital of Judah, and to say how he expressed his love in beautiful words and inspiring deeds.

Let us, however, begin at the beginning and say
something about the clime and time that saw our
hero's birth. Jehuda ben Samuel Halevi, or, as his
Arabic fellow-countrymen knew him, Abu'l Hassan ibn
Hallâwi, was born in Toledo about the year 1085,
fourteen years before the First Crusade. He thus
comes in point of time in the centre of the finest
group of men that Israel has produced since Bible
times. Ibn Gebirol, the poet and philosopher, Rashi,
the exegete, and Alfasi, the jurist, were of the preceding generation; and Moses ibn Ezra, the sweet singer,
and Abraham ibn Ezra, astronomer, wit, rover, and
commentator, were his contemporaries. Maimonides,
the great eagle, and Charisi, the rhymester, came soon

after him, and then the great ones ceased. It was by
no mere accident that all but one of these names were
connected with Arabic Spain. The culture of Islam
was in some respects superior to that of Christendom,
and especially in the tolerance accorded to Jews—that
barometer of civilisation. And there were special
reasons why the Jews of Spain enjoyed an exceptional
share of toleration, not alone from the Moors, but even
from the Christians of the country. For they held a
position there somewhat analogous to that which they
now hold in the dual empire of Austro-Hungary. In
the conflict of races, their influence, though not para-
mount owing to their small numbers, was yet considerable enough to extort consideration from both sides in
the struggle that was now going on between the Cres-
cent and the Cross in the Peninsula. The struggle had
reached its turning point just at the birth of Jehuda,
the period of the Cid, Rodrigo Diaz, with whose name
is connected the onward movement of the Christian
hosts from the Pyrenees to the Mediterranean, which
never ceased from his days to the final downfall of the
Moors in 1492.

The very city of Jehuda's birth, Toledo, had been
captured by Christian valour about the year when he
was born, 1085, and remained during his lifetime at
once the outpost and the capital of Christian Spain.
It was a fit cradle for a poet's youth, the spot where
Orient and Occident met, where Christian scholars,
like Michael Scot, came to study the learning of the
East, including the black art. There were learned
those Arabic numerals which the Arabs had brought
with them from India. There a college of translators,
many of them Jews, helped to bring philosophy and
science within the reach of Christendom. There, too,
lived descendants of the Khozars, who were to give

the historic basis of Jehuda's greatest work. We can imagine the boy's wonder at these strangers from the outlandish Crimea, who had brought with them memories of the remarkable Jewish kingdom that had flourished for two centuries on the northern shores of the Black Sea.

Of the lad's education we know little except by the results of it to be found in his work. But we have plenty of contemporary evidences of the wide spread that liberal education took among the Jews of Arabic Spain. Thus Samuel ibn Abbas gives the following course of study as usual in his days:—Hebrew grammar, the Torah and its commentaries, engaged a boy's attention till the age of thirteen, then in the fourteenth year came Indian arithmetic and astronomy, to be followed by medicine, Greek mathematics, geometry and algebra, and the whole curriculum was crowned by the study of the Talmud, which seemed to have begun at the age of fifteen. We find traces of these studies in the *Kusari*, and may take it that Jehuda's education was somewhat on these very broad lines. Nowhere north of the Tagus could such a liberal education have been obtained at that period.

In this enumeration of his studies one important branch has been omitted. Verse-making was a favourite amusement of Arabic cultured society, and the fashion had been taken up by the Jews of Moslem countries and applied to the holy tongue, so that a whole art of rhythm had been developed with elaborate rules founded on the laws of Arabic versification. Hebrew poetry thus became one of the branches of Jewish education in Spain, and it was clearly the part of Jehuda's education which most attracted him. He early obtained proficiency in the art, and his fame soon spread. The earliest glimpse we catch of him gives perhaps the occasion which brought him to the notice of the learned circles of Jewish Spain. He had gone, about 1100, to Lucena, near Granada, then the centre of Talmudic study. There he seems to have relieved the monotony of halachic disputations with some swallow-flights of song. To whom should he send these if not to Moses ibn Ezra at Granada, the chief literary authority of the time, and one of Israel's sweetest singers of all time? The elder poet received the youth's attempts most graciously, and in his reply, which alone has reached us, expresses his wonder at Jehuda's early proficiency, in the following words :—

> " How can a boy so young in years
> Bear such a weight of wisdom sage,
> Nor 'mongst the greybeards find his peers
> While still in the very bloom of age ? "

This interchange of civilities was followed by a close friendship, which lasted for many years till Moses ibn Ezra's death in 1139. Indeed, Jehuda seems to have possessed in a special degree the gift of attractiveness, and his friends include all the most distinguished Jews of Spain. Joseph ibn Migash at Lucena, Judah ben Gayath at Granada, the two Jewish viziers, Samuel Almollam at Seville, and Meir ibn Kamnial at Saragossa, as well as the philosopher Joseph ibn Zaddik at Cordova, all fell under the charm of his personality. In this respect he contrasts strongly with Solomon ibn Gebirol, who seems to have been of a somewhat churlish disposition. Jehuda, on the other hand, seems to have possessed an almost magnetic attraction, due to his bright affectionate nature, that shines forth in all his poems of his early period, and is echoed in the poems addressed to him.

He soon became poet-laureate of the Jews of Southern

Spain. No festive occasion was considered complete that was not celebrated by Jehuda's muse. We have still extant no less than forty-three marriage odes, written by our poet with much grace of feeling and skill in adapting appropriate Biblical passages. If a distinguished Rabbi was appointed to an important post, the ceremony of reception would include an ode of Jehuda. And on more solemn occasions, when Jews had to mourn the loss of some distinguished man, the general sorrow found a voice in Jehuda Halevi. Thus when Alfasi, the great codifier of Jewish law, died, Jehuda expressed in the hyperboles of the following lines, the conviction that a second Moses had passed away from among men :—

> On Sinai's day the mountains bowed before thee,
> Angels of the Lord came forth to greet thee.
> Upon the tablets of thy heart they wrote the Law,
> Upon thy head they placed the crown of glory.
> Even sages cannot learn to stand upright
> Unless they have sought for wisdom from thee.

Besides these official epithalamia and epitaphs, Jehuda contributed to the social gatherings of which he formed part many short and witty poems, containing riddles, which were then the fashion. A couple of these may serve as specimens of these elegant trifles :—

> What is it that's blind with an eye in its head
>   But the race of mankind its use cannot spare ;
> Spends all its life in clothing the dead,
>   But always itself is naked and bare ?

[A NEEDLE]

> Happy lovers, learn our law,
>   Be joined in one, as we ;
> Aught that parts us through we saw,
>   And again are one, you see.

[PAIR OF SCISSORS]

'Tis dead and scattered on the earth,
  And men bury it all bare ;
Yet in the grave to children gives birth,
  That start full clothed from their lair.

[AN EAR OF CORN]

He seems also to have been much in request by
lovers, for many of his poems deal with the tender
passion, whether on his own behalf or for others is
difficult to say. The following quatrain forms a not
ungraceful *motif* for

A SERENADE.

Awake, dear one, from thy slumber arise,
  The sight of thee will ease my pain ;
If thou dream'st of one that is kissing thine eyes,
  Awake, and soon the dream I'll explain.

Or again, another quatrain expresses a pretty fancy.

Once I nursed Love on my knee.
  He saw his likeness in my eye,
  He kissed the lids so tenderly,
'Twas his image he kissed, the rogue, not me.

A note of deeper passion is struck in a poem on
separation, which you will be glad to have from the
more skilful hands of Miss Emma Lazarus (" Songs of
a Semite," p. 73), though diluted through Geiger's
German version.

SEPARATION.

And so we twain must part ! Oh, linger yet,
  Let me still feed my glance upon thine eyes.
Forget not, love, the days of our delight,
  And I our nights of bliss shall ever prize.
In dreams thy shadowy image I shall see,
Oh, even in my dream be kind to me !

Though I were dead, I none the less would hear
  Thy step, thy garment rustling on the sand ;

And if thou waft me greetings from the grave,
   I shall drink deep the breath of that cold land.
Take thou my days, command this life of mine,
If it can lengthen out the space of thine.

No voice I hear from lips death-pale and chill,
   Yet deep within my heart it echoes still.
My frame remains—my soul to thee yearns forth.
   A shadow I must tarry still on earth.
Back to the body dwelling here in pain,
Return, my soul, make haste and come again!

Or, as a last specimen of the poet's earlier manner, we may take a literal prose version of a description of Spring which, at any rate in the original, marks the highest tide-mark of Jehuda Halevi's powers as a poet of the *salons* of Granada.

SPRING.

Yestreen the earth, like a suckling babe, drained the breasts of the
   wintry clouds;
Or, like a bride with soul shut up, yearning for the time of love;
Yearned for the summer of its love when its weary heart is healed;
Or, like a dainty girl, blushing in her new donned robes,
In garments all of golden flowers and broidered work of lilies,
The earth each day its robes renews and wins fresh beauty,
Changing here from lily white to rosy red, and there to emerald
   green,
Now turns pale, and now it blushes like a bride kissing her lover.
The beauty of the flowers was surely stolen from the starry skies.
To-day we sought this Paradise with wine that kindles the fire of
   love,
Though cold as snow when held in cup, it burns like fire within.
As we pour it into the jewelled beaker, it rises like the sun above
   the earthern brim.
Then walk we with Spring as she laughs at the showers;
She rejoices, the raindrops are like tears on her cheek, like jewels
   from a broken necklet;
To her the cry of the crane is as new wine, and to the cooing dove
   she keeps sweet accord;
She exults amidst the budding leaves like a damsel dancing and
   skipping in her new robes.

My soul seeks the morning breeze as she scatters her fragrance
around the beloved.

The breeze rustles the myrtle, and its scent is dispersed to join
lovers that are parted.

How, then, one might ask, did Halevi gain such
general fame if his powers only reached the ears of the
learned, as must have been the case with poems written
in Hebrew? A curious anecdote, discovered by the
omniscient Steinschneider, transcribed by the obliging
Neubauer, and published by the indefatigable Kaufmann
(Graetz, *Monatsschrift*, Feb. 1887), gives us an insight
into the cultured life of the time, and explains in a
measure how Halevi gained his renown. It occurs in an
Arabic commentary of Joseph ibn Aknim on Canticles,
who says : " I will mention a fine anecdote of our poet-
philosopher, Jehuda Halevi, that bears upon our text.
One of the sages of Granada has told us that he used
to meet him at conversaziones and in circles in which
a company of friends, and among them Jehuda Halevi,
used to meet for friendly discussions in one of the most
splendid palaces of the town. ' Once when we were
all praising the wisdom of the Creator, there came in a
lady whose beauty was equalled by the elegance of her
toilet. We all began to admire her beauty, and to
praise God for the perfection of His creatures. Just as
we were noticing her fine features and stately carriage,
she happened to address one of her acquaintances.
Then we observed what a harsh voice she had, and how
badly she spoke. And when Jehuda Halevi noticed
this, he said, "The mouth that caused [the charm] has
broken it." This witty application of the words of the
Mishna (Kethuboth, ii. 1) caused the whole company
the most lively amusement.' " Some of the liveliness
of the amusement has vanished for us with the lapse
of centuries, but the whole story gives us at least a

lively insight into the mingled pedantry, poetry, and piety that reigned in the Jewish *salons* of Granada some eight centuries ago.

I have perhaps now said enough to leave with you some impression of the poet's personality in the early years of his life. Bright, witty, the soul of every circle he visited, surrounded by bright smiles and gay glances, we see him enter upon manhood's years under the most delightful auspices. Yet those are not the conditions that are likely to make a great poet; and we shall soon see that Jehuda Halevi, like others, had to learn in suffering what he taught in song. And here it seems convenient to discuss for a moment the question which has been raised in Germany by Professor Lagarde as to the poetic merits of Jehuda Halevi. Was he really a great poet? To answer that question, I must ask you to make with me a distinction between poetic force and poetic form—a distinction which I can best illustrate by examples. Thus Mr. Browning has great poetic force, but little poetic form; Mr. Swinburne great poetic form, but only slight poetic force. So, too, in German, Professor Lagarde's friend Rückert has considerable poetic form, but only moderate poetic force. Or again, consider how great an amount of poetic force there is in many of the old ballads, combined with how poor a quality of poetic form. We all of us have some poetic force, or else we could not appreciate poetry—the poetry of deeds as well as that of words; but too few of us, as I am myself painfully aware, have any power of poetic form. And so I think we can answer Professor Lagarde's question by saying that Jehuda Halevi had great poetic force, but that he worked in a medium that did not admit of great poetic form. Or if you prefer to put it shorter, we may say he was a great poet, though his poems are not great. It is necessary to recognise

this, because otherwise we shall be adopting a pro-
vincial standpoint in judging of New Hebrew poetry.
Jehuda Halevi was the greatest New Hebrew poet,
but New Hebrew poetry was not, could not be, great.
It was essentially a literature of reminiscence, over-
shadowed by the past, and is thus exactly analogous
to the New Latin poetry of the Middle Ages. This is
especially the case with the religious poetry of New
Hebrew literature. Here the Jewish poet had before
him the Psalms, the grandest religious lyrics of the
world's literature, judging them merely from the literary
standpoint. It was impossible for him to hope to rival
them on their own lines, equally impossible for him to
depart altogether from those lines. Hence the *Piyutim*
are full of quotations, popular or otherwise, and most
of them ought to be printed in inverted commas.
Hence the greatest point of skill a Paitan could show
was to wrest a Bible verse out of its true sense, somewhat in the same way as Jehuda Halevi made a new
application of the Mishna text in the anecdote we have
just read. I have had to say this, as I have found it
impossible to present to you any of Jehuda Halevi's
religious poetry which would not lose all point in translation, except the greatest of them all, the *Zionide*.
Any one that has read the weary, dreary versions given
in the "Treasures of Oxford" will remember how every
other line depends for its effect on the ingenuity with
which 2 Samuel, chapter so and so, verse so and so, had
been misapplied to mean something it could not possibly mean in its own context. That effect cannot be
reproduced in translation.

And there is another quality of New Hebrew poetry
which weakens it in my opinion. The *Paitanim* bor-
rowed from Arabic poetry a fatal facility of rhyming,
which gives a jingling sound to their verses. And in

adopting rhyme from the Arabs, the Jewish poets
adapted it to a language much less fitted for it.   You
can understand how easy rhyming is in an inflexional
language ; it would not be difficult to run off any number of Latin lines ending in *is*, or Greek ones finishing
with *ai*.   Now, Hebrew being philologically a younger
language than Arabic, has retained many fewer of the
primitive inflections than the sister tongue.   It thus
happens that three-fourths of the Hebrew rhymes are
furnished by the endings וֹ (*Yigdal* preserves this rhyme
throughout)—ד—יֹם and וֹת.   And when poets, to carry
out the Arabic practice, used one of these rhymes right
through a poem of ever so many lines, the result produces a tickling sensation to a Western ear.   The only
English poem that I can think of with the same artifice
is Southey's " How the waters come down at Lodore."
It is all very ingenious, I know, but the very ingenuity
produces an air of artificiality that disturbs the impres-
siveness of the poem.   We could not, ior example,
imagine a Psalm written in that style.   I do not know
whether it was this to which he was referring, but
towards the end of his life Jehuda Halevi is said to
have regretted that he had followed Arabic models in
his poetry.   At any rate, the reasons I have given will
be sufficient to explain the inadequate medium which
New Hebrew verse gave for the expression of Jehuda
Halevi's great poetic force.

For by universal consent he was the greatest of the
poets who chose that means of clothing their burning
thoughts.   Charisi, critic as well as poet, has expressed
the general opinion of our hero's ability in some lines
of rhymed prose, which I may venture to quote for their
felicity of expression, as well as for the illustration they
give of the inadequate nature of New Hebrew rhyme in
point of form.   " Three read verses—the simple , the first

is—thinker the second, poet the third—he knows the might of the word—Thus poets are simple sometimes—the everyday man enjoys their rhymes—again they are deep and profound—only philosophers their meaning can sound—or their metre is full of surprises—such as only a poet surmises. So different poems are for different people—some they attract and some they repel. But a poem has these qualities three—is surely the highest that high can be—and so is Jehuda's poetry—simple, deep, yet full of fire—with verse that poets can admire —Solomon ibn Gebirol's song—is very profound and very long—Moses ibn Ezra is the poet's poet—he knows his art and how to show it" (*Tach*, ed. Lagarde, xviii. 4, 46 *seq.*). Moses ibn Ezra refers to him as "the pearl diver and lord of most rare jewels and brilliants in song." It is thus universally agreed that Jehuda Halevi is the greatest Jewish poet of the Middle Ages. Yet Professor Lagarde may ask, "If that be so, how is it that there is no complete edition of his poems?" And I fear that no satisfactory answer could be given to him. It is with a mixture of shame and irritation that I reflect upon the unedited condition of Jehuda Halevi's poems. While the most trumpery supercommentary on any indifferent commentary is reproduced with all the honours of further comment, the finest products of the Jewish spirit are allowed to moulder unedited in the dust of the Bodleian. There was some excuse while Luzzato lived and contemplated an edition, but Luzzato has been dead these twenty years, and an edition of Jehuda Halevi's poems seems as far off as ever. You will all join with me in the hope that this reproach to Jewish taste and Jewish scholarship will be speedily removed.

We have been so long occupied with Halevi's poetry that we may well imagine Halevi himself to have

passed through manhood to middle age in the interim.
Of the outward events of his life we know little. He
married and had an only daughter, who did *not* marry
Abraham ibn Ezra, as the well-known legend tells,
but who gave him a grandson also named Judah. If
the following epigram were to be taken literally, we
might assume that he had suffered some loss of fortune.
But the epigram was probably only written for the
puns, which form its chief merit. I have endeavoured,
as far as possible, to reproduce them.

> As went my money, my man he went with it
> With scorn in his looks, saying " To leave thee I'm ready."
> Then I asked, " But what is my sin, my son ? "
> "Thou art naughty, since thou hast naught," said he.

The same kind of wit is shown in another epigram,
which records a professional experience of Jehuda's.
He was a doctor, and, it would seem, had a very good
practice. It was once his fortune to be called in to
visit some lady patients in a harem. He laughingly
confesses his disappointment that he was only received
on a strictly professional footing :—

> They called me in, but did not call me.
> Though among them, I was not of them.
> I paid them a visit, though not a visitor.
> They desired my art, and not my heart.

It is right for a man to take the pleasures of life
as they pass before him, provided they be innocent
pleasures, and we have seen Jehuda taking the joys
of life with all the zest of youth. But life has duties
as well as joys, and these duties with the nobler spirits
are connected with wider issues than the merely personal lot. There were circumstances of the time that
made Jehuda Halevi feel acutely the lot of his people.
His was the age of the Crusades ; Islam and Chris-

tendom were meeting in the struggle which was to decide the religious future of civilisation for many long centuries. In the clash of creeds, religious animosities, the most irritable of human passions, rose to fever heat, and the Jews, who were a kind of buffer between the two opposing hosts, were among the first victims. It is usually assumed that the lot of Jews in Moslem countries was free from the intolerance that characterised Christian usage. But as a matter of fact, fanaticism on the part of the Christian induced fanaticism on the part of the Moslem, and from the beginning of the twelfth century there was little to choose between the followers of ˉthe two creeds. As early as 1107 an attempt was made at forcible conversion at Lucena, where the Israelites of that "Jew-town," as the Arabs called it, were asked to don the turban. Jehuda Halevi was clear-sighted enough to see that neither of the two opposing forces was really tolerant. In one of his poems he says :—

> A curse on Edom and on Kedar ;
> Whichever conquers or is conquered,
> Always woe is with my people.

If anything, his sympathy was with Christendom. Perhaps he was influenced by memories of Alphonso VI. of Castile, who was so favourable to the Jews that he was called "The King of the Two Creeds," and is said to have refused to fight on Saturday for the sake of the Jewish contingent among his forces. But though he recognised the failings of Roman Christianity—

> They change the Creator of the earth into an image—

yet he was the first to recognise the propædeutic value both of Christianity and of Islam in a passage of his great philosophical dialogue, part of which I will venture to quote, as it strikes me as one of the most remarkable passages of that work; the spirit of lofty toleration was certainly unique in that age of conflicting creeds. The King of the Khosars points out to the master that Christians and Moslems had passed through contempt and persecution, but with a triumphant result in the end. To what purpose had Israel gone through all the travail of the ages? The master replies, "You are right to reproach us with the fact that our banishment has yet borne no fruit. But I think of the meanest among us who could shake off this slavery and contempt by a word easily spoken, and yet speak it not because they wish to remain true to their faith. . . . The wise providence of God towards us may be compared to the planting of a seed of corn. It is placed in the earth, where it seems to be changed into soil and water and filth, and is no more to be recognised. But in very truth it is the seed that has changed the earth and water into its own nature and then raises itself from one stage to another, transforms the elements, and assuming its own form, throws out shoots and leaves. . . . So, too, the Law of Moses changes them who come in contact with it, even though it seems to be cast aside by them. These peoples are the preparation and preface to the Messiah we expect, who is the fruit Himself, and whose fruit they all will be when they acknowledge Him and all become one mighty tree" (*Kus.* iv. 23). Remember that these words were spoken when Israel was being persecuted by both branches of the tree, and its noble tolerance cannot fail to strike you.

Other points might be given in which Jehuda's thought shows a certain affinity to Christianity. He seems to set up an infallible Synagogue against the infallible Church. Geiger notices that the divine development in one line postulated by the *Kusari* is a counterpart of the Christian doctrine of hereditary sin. But it was chiefly the crusading spirit of Christendom that found a sympathetic echo in our poet's soul. The first Crusade took place when he was fourteen or fifteen years old, and we can imagine how the news of the fall of Jerusalem came to an impressionable lad of his temperament. He must have felt like the rightful heir when his patrimony is being disputed for by two other relatives whose claims are not so close as his, yet he has not the means, or, worse still, has not the courage to assert his rights.

The Crusades, I have said, worsened the condition of the Jews both in Christian and in Moslem countries. In many of Jehuda's poems we see the depression brought upon him by the changed condition of his people, in which he himself shared. At times he bursts forth in a sort of savage pride in persecution. "Men insult me," he cries:

> Men insult me; fools, they know not
> That insults borne for Thy sake are an honour.

At other times he would seem to have withdrawn from all communion with his fellows in proud isolation of self-communion.

> They say to me, "Canst thou delight thyself without a brother?"
> I answer: "I have that within my soul to delight me;
> Thoughts delight my soul within me;
> My thoughts form an Eden in my heart."

For he had likewise much to sadden him within his community as without. On looking back on the past we catch sight chiefly of the more ardent spirits, and attribute to an age what is special to its choicer minds. Indifference to religious duty is no prerogative of the nineteenth century. On one occasion Jehuda has to complain of what we may term an American laxity on the part of his co-religionists; in Christian Spain many kept their Sabbath on the Sunday, in Moslem Spain there were several who kept it on Friday. With oppression without and indifference within, there was enough to make an ardent soul sink. Even the resources of his art failed him; he lost for a time the gift of song; the sweet bells were jangled and out of tune. In the bitterness of his soul he said, Even this is vanity.

> Wisdom is like the mighty sea,
> Song but the foam on its surface.

When all else fails a man in moments like these, the daily call of duty is the last solace, the mechanic iteration dulling pain. Yet even this last comfort was denied to our poet if we may judge from a letter written about 1130 to one David ben Joseph of Narbonne, who had asked him for a solution of a mathematical problem. In apologising for not giving it (it was afterwards solved by Abraham ibn Ezra), he writes as follows :—

"And besides, I am very busy almost every hour of the day and night in the vanities of the art of healing which has no power to heal. The city is large and its inhabitants imperious, and they are hard masters. And how can the slave please his masters except by spending all his days in serving their will and by consuming his years in healing their infirmities! · 'We would have healed Babylon and she is not healed'" (Jer. i. 9). Then he bursts out with, "I have sought from my God and asked Him to find a good opportunity, for He has many, to hasten the redemption, to call forth liberty out of captivity, to grant me rest, and remove me to the fount of living waters."

That last outburst is characteristic of the man. It is natural that in times of oppression the oppressed should look for, long for, the time of deliverance. And the promises of redemption for Israel form as integral a part of Judaism as the Law itself. Judaism is a discipline, but it is also a hope. The Bible contains the Prophets as well as the Law, though both friends and foes to-day too often forget the fact. And Jehuda's significance in the history of Israel rests on the fact that he carries on the work of the Prophets as other Rabbis like Alfasi and Maimonides and Joseph Karo carried on the work of the Law. Not that there need be any antagonism between the two. Jehuda Halevi is the most orthodox of the orthodox in his theological treatise, and he has put into some fine verses the sentiment which Berthold Auerbach so finely expressed in prose when he spoke of a man being *Frei und eins mit dem Gesetz*, " in free subjection to the Law." Jehuda's lines run :—

> The servants of Time are servants of servants,
> The servant of the Lord is alone free,
> When each man seeks his lot in life
> My soul exclaims, " The Lord is my lot."

But combined with this willing subjection to the yoke of the Law, Jehuda has a passionate faith in the promises of the Prophets. It finds expression on every occasion. We have just seen it burst from him in a letter to a stranger. At the end of one of his marriage-songs, the happy union of the lovers is connected with a wish for the happy union of Israel and the land of Israel. In speaking of the blessings of the Sabbath the same wish escapes him, and the passion for redemption, not of his own soul, but of his own people, shines out at every opportunity.

He was not alone in this passionate desire, though

he was alone in the power with which he gave expression to it. The Jews of the time listened with burning feelings of mingled dismay and hope to the clash of Christian sword and Moslem scimitar contending for the possession of the land that they had never ceased to regard as theirs, for the city which remained the symbol of all that was holy for them. And some went further than mere thoughts about the matter. Maimonides, in his letter to Yemen, in 1172, says: "Forty-five years ago (*i.e.*, in 1127) a man rose in Fez, who gave himself out as the herald of the Messiah, pretending that the latter would appear in the same year; his words, however, were not fulfilled, and the Jews only suffered fresh sorrows. About ten years before that a man had arisen in Spain at Cordova, who represented himself as the Messiah, and it wanted but little that this did not produce the ruin of the Jews." It is probable that Jehuda was for a time caught by the enthusiasm for this Jewish Mahdi. For in one of his poems addressed to the Dove of Israel, a frequent expression of his for the Synagogue, he looks forward to the return as something near at hand.

> Rouse thyself to return to the land of beauty,
> And to sadden the plain of Edom and of Ishmael,
> Lay waste in wrath the house of the robbers,
> And throw open the house of love to thy lovers.

If Akiba could have been misled by Bar Cochba, if we can call it being misled to attempt to free one's own land of foreign conquerors, so we can imagine the fervent zeal of Jehuda Halevi roused by the unknown enthusiast of 1117. Thirteen years later, in a powerful poem, spoilt only by the inverted commatisms of its concluding lines (which I omit), he gives a vision of the downfall of Islam in the year 1130 corresponding

to the eight hundred and ninetieth year of the fifth
thousand since the Creation (4890).

> " Thou has slept and dreamt. Why rise up trembling?
>   What is this dream that thou hast dreamt?
> Perchance thy vision made thy foe appear
>   As poor and low while thou wert raised?"
> " Say ye to the son of Hagar: Remove thy proud hand
>   From the son of thy mistress whom thou hast subjected;
> I saw thee in dreams fallen and abject:
>   Perchance on awakening I shall find thee desolate,
> And the year 890 will see thy pride broken
>   And all thy plans put to shame and confounded."

The wish was clearly father to the thought, but neither
thought nor wish were to be realised in Jehuda's days,
which rather saw a revival of Saracen zeal in the Almo-
hades, who brought all the fierce fanaticism of the
Koran into Spain.

But fulfilled or not, Jehuda's aspirations were not
daunted by failure, however long continued. And his
longings for the redemption of the land of Israel concentrated themselves at last in a mighty love that
overcame every other feeling of his soul. It was an
age for such passionate devotion. In Provence the
knights and troubadours held courts of love, in which
minutiæ of the tender passion were settled by quasi-
halachic rules. Knights devoted themselves for years
for the honour of a fair dame whom they had scarcely
seen. Love for love's sake, without the hope of possession, became the ideal of chivalric affection. It was
such a love that now seized Jehuda Halevi. It
was Heine that suggested the analogy, let him carry
it out.

> " And the hero whom we sing,
>   Judah ben Halevy, too,
> Had also his own lady love,
>   But one of especial sort.

She was not like the Laura
Whose eyes of mortal fire,
Kindled in the Minster
That world-renowned flame

No Chatelaine was she,
In the bloom and crown of youth,
Presiding at the tourney,
Awarding the victor's crown.

No graduate of science gay,
No lady doctrinaire,
Lecturing in the Colleges
Of the courts of Love.

She whom the Rabbi worshipped
Was a woe-begone poor darling,
Desolation's very image,
And her name—Jerusalem."

Heine was somewhat of an authority on the kind of love to which he alludes, but I should myself have compared Jehuda Halevi's passion as something more akin to the thinker's love for his own ideals, or better still, to the passionate devotion of a saint to his creed. For Jerusalem was to Jehudah a symbol and a type of all that was distinctive of the history of his race. It was an incarnation of its glorious past, a constant reminder of its woe-begone present; it spurred him on continually to hopes of a more glorious future. It was the stirring of the historic consciousness within him that was at the root of his love for Jerusalem. And after all, it is that sentiment of the historic continuity of the race which has given much of its vitality and all its romantic colouring to the varied fate of Israel. Of course, I know it has not gone alone : the religious ideal has been of even greater force. But the religious ideal has ever gone hand in hand with the political, and the connection has all the authority of the Prophets on its side. It was the spirit of the Prophets revived again within him that caused Jehuda Halevi's love for Jerusalem, and the same spirit still inspires millions of Jews who find themselves in oppression as he did. For man ever seeks to embody his ideal in outward symbol, and the stern repression of all image-making in Israel has only intensified the tendency to give a local habitation and a name to Israel's prophetic ideal. Thus Jerusalem has been for ages the personi-fication of Jewish history, and must continue to be so while Jewish hearts still beat and care for aught beyond the needs of the present and the self.

Jehuda Halevi's love for Jerusalem thus becomes typical, and gives his figure an epic grandeur that transcends the significance of any other mediæval Jew. Lawgivers, commentators, philosophers, give way to the claims of the poet in whom his people instinctively felt that the Prophets lived anew. He gave voice to the dimly felt longings of his people. This is the great-ness of the poet. The lawgiver controls our action, the thinker interprets our thoughts, but the poet gives expression to our selves, to what is innermost and deepest within us. This merit had Jehuda Halevi, and so his claim to be a true poet is established. Whether he was a great one, is perhaps for others to say ; for that is, in fact, the question, whether the Jews of the Middle Ages, whose voice he was, were a great people. And from this point of view, we may put in some defence for the choice of poetic form which tech-nically was so much in his way. For it was the same historic instinct which led him to put his thoughts into the language of his fathers, which almost ceases to be a dead tongue in his hands.

But it is time to let the poet give expression to the feeling of longing. At one time he accounts for his depression in the following lines :—

My heart is in the East, but I in the depths of the West;
　　How can I care for the details of our lives ;
How perform my vows, though the Lord's behest,
　　While Zion's still in Edom's snares, and I in Arab gyves?
All the beauty of this land of Spain is but vanity at best,
　　Whilst e'en the very dust of the ruined fane survives.

There is a tone of sincerity about these lines that gives
them almost as much force as the passionate outburst
of the Psalmist, "If I forget thee, O Jerusalem! may
my right hand forget her cunning," words that might
well stand as the motto of Jehuda's life, and were ap-
propriately prefixed by Heine to his *Romanzero*. At
another time our poet passionately asks :—

> Who will give me wings of a dove
> That I may fly and dwell there?
> I would abandon both north and south
> To drink in the air of Zion.

The poet was soon to show that this was no mere
empty rhetoric. The longing overcame him, and he
determined on his celebrated pilgrimage to Zion, which
gave him his fame, and showed, at any rate, that his
idealism could survive the test of practice. His child
was settled with her husband and child; his wife, of
whom we hear nothing, was probably dead; his best
friend, Moses ibn Ezra, had died in 1139; and about
the following year Jehuda Halevi left his native land
and sought the object of his desire—Jerusalem.

But before he left, he had written as a sort of testament his philosophical masterpiece, the *Kusari*. It
is beyond the scope of this paper to deal with this
philosophical dialogue after the manner of Plato or
"Iflatun," as the Arabs called him. The historical
groundwork is the conversion of the King of the
Kosars in the Crimea in the eighth century, which
placed a Jewish kingdom in what is now Southern

Russia for over two centuries. Lady Magnus, in her
charming paper on our poet, showed unusual scepticism
about the reality of this Jewish kingdom ; but we have
plenty of evidence from independent observers, such as
Arabic geographers and Greek monks, as to its existence. And plenty of scope is left to the imagination
as to the course of history, and of Jewish history, if
Russia had become Jewish instead of Christian. The
King of the Kosars seeks in turn a philosopher, a
Christian, and a Mohammedan, who each gives an abstract of his creed—and Halevi's abstracts are models
of fairness—and claims superiority over other faiths.
But as all of them grant that while their own creed is
the best, the Jewish faith is the next best, the king
summons a Jewish master, who goes through the whole
of Jewish theology, and at last converts the king. The
fable points to one great strength of mediæval Judaism,
which must have aided greatly in its hold on the minds
of Jews. For there was a consensus of civilisation as
to the claims of Judaism ; every Jew could feel that
both Christian and Mohammedan allowed he was right
so far as he went. The arguments of the book do not
seem very convincing nowadays ; our standpoint has
changed, and the perplexities of our times are different.
But the feeling underlying the argument has not become obsolete : thus the polemic against the Karaites
is based on the feeling of historic continuity which is
still powerful among some of us. And it was only one
who was both poet and philosopher who could have
given utterance to that finest of aphorisms :

ISRAEL IS AMONGST THE NATIONS AS THE HEART
AMONG THE LIMBS.

And thus, too, the abstract arguments of the book are
often influenced by the master feeling of the poet-

philosopher; *e.g.*, he strains all his powers of dialectic to prove even against Talmudic authority that prophecy was only possible in the Holy Land, or, as he has to modify it, about the Holy Land, and he introduces a couple of dramatic touches which bear upon our immediate subject. When the master expatiates on the excellences of Palestine, the King of the Khozars very pertinently asks him why he and all Jews did not go there. The master answers, "Thou hast shamed me, O King. Yes, that is why we have not had a complete fulfilment of the prophecies." Later on, at the end of the book, the master shows he has been touched by the reproof of the king, and announces his intention to go there, though at the risk of his life, giving many quaint reasons why it was worth losing one's life in order to set foot on the land of the glories of old. The reasons are quaint, but the feeling that inspired them was not so. Even the greatest of poets and profoundest of philosophers may fail to account for our deepest feelings.

What he represented the master as doing, the poet did himself. He was literally at the extreme end of the then known world; Jerusalem was in the hands of the Christians, who had murdered every Jew as they entered; the sea had its own peculiar terrors—yet the poet made up his mind to dare all in order to fulfil his longing. This determination roused the greatest possible enthusiasm among his fellow Jews. The whole of Israel rose at him, to use a theatrical expression. The man who was known to all of them as the greatest poet of his time, who had recently added to this the renown of being its greatest philosopher, was about to dare what they all wished to have the courage to dare. He was, as it were, each Jew's best self putting each man's ideal into practice. There were not wanting some friends who urged the dangers, and these he answered in tones of earnest conviction, "Shall a body of clay stop a soul urged by eagle's wings?" he asked. He passed through Cordova, exchanging civilities with Joseph ibn Zaddik, passed on to Granada, and then took ship for Alexandria. A wondrous calm had fallen on him: he writes with a dignity and force that is often missing in his earlier poems. His muse took a higher flight, and I may venture to give here a couple of sea-pictures probably written during the voyage. The first is the sea in storm, and in my version I have endeavoured to give as nearly as possible the metre, or at least the rhyme system, of the original. Its technical name is *Mowashech*, or "Girdle rhyme," so called because the last syllable of each stanza in the poem remains the same, and so forms a girdle for it.

THE STORM.

The waters roar
As their wheels roll o'er,
Becoming less and more
    On the face of the sea.

The waters grow black,
Grim lowers the rack,
The breakers rear back
    Till the depths you can see.

The cauldron boils o'er
With a hiss and a roar,
And none can restore
    Its tranquillity.

And brave men must fear
As the waves disappear,
And a mountain is here,
    And there a valley.

I

> The ship turns like a vane,
> Bows and rises again ;
> And the eye asks in vain,
>   Where, pilots, are ye ?
>
> And my heart then stands still,
> But bows down to His will
> Who to Moses gave skill
>   To divide the Red Sea.
>
> To the Lord I would call,
> But to sin I've been thrall,
> And I fear to recall
>   The punishment due.

The last syllable rhymes with other stanzas, and thus gives a girdle for the whole poem, which has five stanzas of the same length, each beginning with one of the letters of the poet's name, so as to form an acrostic. Even the faultiness of my version cannot hide the poetic power of the picture, which is certainly remarkable in a mediæval poet. As a companion picture in a simpler metre, as is appropriate, we may take

A CALM NIGHT AT SEA.

And when the sun retires to the mansions of the skies,
Where all the hosts of heaven their general await,
The night comes on, an Ethiop queen, her garment all of gold,
Comes here decked with azure and there with pearls ornate.
And the constellations wander through the centre of the sea,
Like pilgrims doomed to linger far from all that's consecrate ;
Their twinkling forms and figures their likeness reproduce
In ocean's mirror, and images of flaming fire create.
The visage of the ocean and of the heavens mingle here,
And gather sharp and bright in a pattern complicate.
And the ocean and the firmament commingle in their hue
And form but two oceans that now communicate,
And in the very midst of them my heart another sea contains
With the echoes of its passion—the billows of its fate.

I have selected these two specimens of his muse at this time, because they seem to me to have least of the deficiencies of New Hebrew poetry, the naturalness of the emotion produced by the sea, that fit cradle of poetic feeling, overcoming the artificiality of the medium in which they are written.

Arrived in Egypt, the poet was received with no less enthusiasm than in his native home. The best houses of Egypt welcomed the famous poet and philosopher with open arms, nor was he unwelcome to the daughters of these houses. The temptation which assailed the youth in "Excelsior," assailed the man of middle age in Egypt. But after a short stay, broken by a visit to Arabia, he took up again his pilgrim's staff and landed at Tyre, and made his way to Damascus, there to seek a favourable opportunity for approaching Zion, for the poet did not wish to commit a needless suicide. It was at Damascus, almost at the gates of the Paradise for which he yearned, that he is said to have written the far-famed *Zionide*, in which all the passion of that yearning is expressed.

THE ZIONIDE.

Zion, wilt thou not send a greeting to thy captives,
    Who greet thee as the remnant of thy flocks?
From West to East, from North to South, a greeting,
    From far and near, take thou on all thy sides.
A greeting sends the captive of desire, who sheds his tears
    Like dew on Hermon; would they might fall on thy hills.

When I bewail thy affliction my voice is as the jackal's:
    When I dream of thy freedom, I am as a harp for thy songs.
My heart is sorely troubled for Bethel and Peniel,
    For Mahanaim, and all the meetings of thy saints.
There the holy Presence is present to thee and thy Maker,
    Over 'gainst the gates of Heaven ever opes thy gates.

The glory of the Lord is thy sole light; nor hast thou
     Sun nor moon nor stars for thy illumination.
I desire that my soul be poured out in the place where
     God's spirit was poured out unto thy saints.
Thou wert house of kings and throne of God! how comes it then
     That slaves ascend the thrones where sat thy rulers?

Who will grant me to wander around the spots where
     Appeared the angels to thy sight and to thy envoys?
Who will make me wings that I may fly and cause
     The ruins of my heart to move amidst thy ruins?
I will bend my face to thy soil, and I'll hold dear
     Thy very stones, and be tender to thy dust.

And then, when I stand at the graves of my fathers,
     And at Hebron admire the choicest of thy tombs,
I will pass through thy fields and thy forests and stand
     On Gilead and gaze at thy Mountain Abarim,
At Mount Abarim and Mount Hor, where are
     The two great luminaries, thy lighters and thy leaders.

Life of the soul is the air of thy earth, and pure myrrh
     The grains of thy dust, and honey of the comb thy streams:
It would rejoice my soul to go, even naked and barefoot,
     Towards the ruins where once were thy fanes;
To the place where the Ark was treasured, and the spot where
     The Cherubim dwelt in the innermost recesses.

I rend and cast hence the beauty of my locks, and curse fate
     That in earth contaminate, defiles thy Nazarites.
How can I care for meat or for drink at a time
     When I see curs devour the whelps of thy lions?
Or how can the light of the day be a joy to my eyes
     When I see in the maw of the raven the flesh of thy eagles

Cup of sorrow, away! and cease for a while; for laden
     Heavily are my loins and my soul with thy bitterness:
At the hour that I call to mind Ohola I taste of thy poison,
     And when I remember Oholiba I drain all thy dregs.

O Zion, perfect of beauty, thou combinest love and grace
     From of old and in thee unite the souls of thy companions:

They rejoice in thy prosperity, they are pained
 At thy desertion, and they are weeping for thy ruin.
From the depths of the captivity they are longingfor thy presence ;
 Each from his place is bowing towards thy gates.

The flocks of thy own host, that are exiled and are spread
 Over mountain and o'er plain, yet do not forget thy folds :
They are clinging to the fringes of thy garments, and they hasten
 To rise up and to seize the branches of thy palms.

Shinar and Patmos, can they near thee with all their greatness ?
 Nay, vanities are they compared with thy Light and thy Right :
To what compare thy anointed, and to what thy seers,
 And to what compare thy Levites and thy singers ?
Mutable and transient is the sov'ranty of idols,
 Thy power eternal, from age to age thy crown.

Thy God desires thee for His dwelling, and blessed the man
 He has chosen to be brought near to dwell in thy court.
Blessed is he that awaits and draws near and sees the rising
 Of thy lights and upon him breaks forth thy dawn,
And that sees the welfare of thy saints, and exults in
 Thy joy and thy return to the old ways of thy youth.

The poem has the defects of want of concentration and over-elaboration, but under the old-world phrases you can hear the human heart-throbs that are of all time. In power of compressed emotion it comes nearer to the Psalms than any of the new Hebrew poems. It is a fitting swan's song for the " captive of desire," as he calls himself, the lover of Jerusalem.

For at Damascus history loses sight of him. There are some indications that he was not spared the last pathos of a disappointment. A poem headed " After he had seen the Holy City," speaks in terms of disenchantment, but the heading is uncertain, and history leaves him at Damascus. But if history fails us, legend supplies the gap, and you all know the story of the grey-haired poet, pierced with the lance of a passing

Arab, just as his longing eyes had caught sight of the
walls of Jerusalem, and he was reciting the *Zionide*.
The legend is probably false, as the only authority for
it is Gedalya's "Chain of Tradition," which has been
irreverently but truthfully called "The Chain of Lies."
But the myth may be true, though the fact is not, for
it embodies the thoughts of men as to how such a
man should die. And so having lived an ideal life,
he dies in legend a death that is also ideal. It is this
union of idea and act, of inner conviction and outward
deed, that gives the dramatic unity to Halevi's life,
and makes him, of mediæval Jews, the typical figure
to which men of Jewish blood still look back with
something akin to personal affection and enthusiastic
reverence. For in all time men will regard those who,
like Jehuda Halevi, have dared greatly because they
loved much, as the patterns and exemplars of human
excellence.

JEWISH DIFFUSION OF FOLK-TALES [1]

THE post-biblical history of the Jews may be divided into two main divisions; the internal development of Jewish thought and feeling, and the mutual relation of Jews and their neighbours in all the lands of civilisation. The outlines of the former are gradually becoming clear to us, thanks in large measure to the masterly treatment of Professor Graetz. But the other branch of Jewish history—the influence of the national culture of their native country on the Jews of various lands, and their reaction upon this—is only as yet in its beginnings. We are only just commencing to know something of the way in which Hellenistic, Roman, French, German, Italian, Moslem, or English culture affected the Jews who came under their influence in early times, and the light of dawn is scarcely visible in the even more complicated question, How far did the Jews influence their neighbours in the Middle Ages apart from affording them the materials for an occasional massacre or a perpetual feast of scorn? I propose this evening to treat one of the more definite side-issues of this problem, and to discuss the influence of the mediæval Jews in helping to spread popular tales among the hearths and homes of the common folk of European lands. We shall not esteem it a slight thing, I hope, if it be proved that Jews have done something on their part to brighten

---

[1] A Lecture delivered before the Jews' College Literary Society, May 27, 1888.

the lives of those who have done the hard work of the world.

If we were to trust some writers on this subject, our hands would be more than full with materials. Attempts have been made at various times to show that all, or nearly all, folk-tales and fables, all the phantasmagoria of popular fancy, can be traced to Jewish sources. I have a lurking sympathy with such views, as I trust I have with all that is youthful and enthusiastic. I was young myself in this sense not so many years ago, and had a tendency to cry " Cherchez le juif" in all investigations into origins. To see in all philosophy only the influence of Philo, Ibn Gebirol, Maimonides, and Spinoza, to trace all mysticism to the Kabbala, to see in mediæval science only the work of the Jewish translators, and in mediæval exegesis only the influence of Philo, Rashi, Ibn Ezra, and Kimchi— these are the temptations which assail the young Jewish investigator when he first comes to appreciate the solid contributions to human knowledge and insight which must for ever be associated with these names. But soberer thoughts come with wider knowledge, and we learn to look upon Jews not as monopolists, but as co-operators in the grand work of building the mighty fabric of human knowledge.

Scientific caution is especially necessary in the particular branch with which we are at present concerned. At first sight it seems only natural, when we find a popular tale or superstition first mentioned in a Jewish source, to trace all other occurrences of it to this. But both the Jewish and the other may have been derived from a third and earlier source, and we may be mistaking the relation of cousinship for that of paternal affiliation. Thus to take a familiar example. In Mr. Halliwell's collection of " Nursery Rhymes and

Tales" the history of "The House that Jack built" is gravely traced back to the familiar "Chad Gadya" of the Haggada Service, and Mr. Clouston follows his lead in his recently issued "Popular Tales and Fictions," calling the Haggada a part of the Talmud. Yet it is well known that the "Chad Gadya" itself was derived from a German "Volklied," and only appears in later MSS. of the Haggada. Similarly, Dr. Landsberger several years ago attempted to prove that Judæa was the original home of the fable, and that the collection known by the name of Æsop was derived from Jewish sources, and he could point to a large number of beast-fables related in the Talmud and a still larger number referred to, R. Meir being credited with no less than 300 fables on the cunning of Brer Fox, to use "Uncle Remus'" expression. But beast-fables are found before Talmudic times, or even before Biblical times, in Egypt and Assyria, and there is even a probability that some of the Talmudic ones could be traced to India, which has been the most prolific home of these apologues.

We have then to be very careful in tracing any popular tale to Jewish sources as its original, and even when we have, there is always a presumption against the Jewish being the original origin, if we may so be tautological. For how are such stories spread? In friendly chat by the fireside, in convivial gatherings, on occasions of family rejoicing and the like? Alas! there have been but few periods or places in Jewish history where Jews could join in these gatherings, and contribute their quota of instruction and amusement. Our oral tradition has been almost entirely amongst ourselves, and in seeking for any traditions which Jews may have handed on to their neighbours we must look to books. Though common folk avoided Jewish society throughout the Middle Ages, scholars and students always had a hankering after the "wisdom of the Hebrews," and in each age some sate at the feet of the Rabbis. But they chiefly sought them for instruction in theology, and the only folk-tales likely to have spread in this way were those about the Old Testament characters. It was, of course, in this direction that Jewish imagination took its main flight, and many, if not most, of the legends about Old Testament characters can be traced directly or indirectly to the Midrashim. In particular, all the Biblical legends of Mohammed can be traced to this source, as many scholars have shown.

If we reflect a little, we shall see why Jews must have had but few folk-tales of their own apart from the Hagadic elements of the Talmud, dealing for the most part with Biblical characters. The school of Tylor and Lang have proved almost to certainty, in my opinion, that the bizarre elements of folk and fairy tales—the transformation of men into beasts, the speaking birds, the cannibal ogres, and the like—are "survivals" of savage and idolatrous practices and beliefs involving the grossest and crassest superstition. Now it is the proud boast of Israel that the practices that degraded the other nations of antiquity in this respect were stamped out for ever by the majestic utterances of the prophets, and died away utterly after the exile. Folk-tales could not, therefore, flourish in an atmosphere denuded of nearly all the superstitious material out of which they are formed.

I may seem to have cut the ground from under my feet in asserting that Jews, speaking broadly, had no folk-tales of their own, and if they had any, as the lawyers say, they had no opportunities of transmitting them to their neighbours in social intercourse. Yet though Jews may have had none of their own, comparatively speaking, except Biblical stories, they may have adopted such of their neighbours' as they could get access to in literary form. For Jews have always taken readily to the literature of the countries in which they lived, and have adapted and translated in the sacred tongue such things as took their fancy. And as regards their transmitting these to the peoples around them, though they may not have done this in social intercourse, their books, when written in the vernacular, would have their fair chance in the struggle for literary existence. In short, it is in the translating activity of the mediæval Jews that we can look for any influence of theirs on folk-tales, and it is, in fact, certain Jewish translations of popular tales to which I propose mainly to direct your attention.

This subject of Jewish translation is a very wide one, and forms an important element in the second division of Jewish history to which I referred at the beginning. The Jews being scattered everywhere, have translated from and into every tongue of civilised lands. To master this enormous territory of literature has been given to only one man, my good friend Dr. Moritz Steinschneider, and we are all awaiting with impatience the appearance of the crowning work of his life on the Jewish translators of the Middle Ages. You will all join with me in expressing the hope that it may be given to this illustrious scholar to see the end of his laborious years crowned with success. I have referred to Dr. Steinschneider, as for much of what I shall have to say I am indebted to his *Manna* and *Volks Literatur der Juden*, though I hope that I have managed to pick up a few unconsidered trifles that have escaped even his omniscient eye.

Turning, then, to the Jewish translations of popular

tales to which we have now narrowed our inquiry we
must distinguish between what I would term, in rail-
way parlance, "termini" and "junctions." When a
collection of folk-tales, after passing through many
hands, comes into those of Jews and is translated by
them, but never emerges again from Hebrew or Jüdisch-
Deutsch, I call such cases "termini." Permit me to
refer to two or three instances of what I mean, though
one could easily fill a whole lecture with examples.
One of the most interesting holy legends of the Middle
Ages was that of Barlaam the sage and Josaphat the
prince. Liebrecht proved that Josaphat was no less
than the great Indian religious reformer Buddha or the
Bodisat, and he showed that owing to this legend
Buddha had been canonised and been made a saint of
the Catholic Church. Well, Steinschneider had shown
that Abraham ibn Chisdai's בן המלך והנזיר ("Prince and
Dervish") is no other than a poetic version of the
Josaphat legend. But it did not pass from the Hebrew
to any other language (till a few years ago, when Dr.
Meisels translated it into German), so that we cannot
attribute to it any influence in spreading the legend
from India to Iceland. It got into Hebrew, and there
it stopped, and for that reason I call it a "terminus."
Or take a case nearer home : one of the best known of
the English romances is that of "Sir Bevis of Southampton," which passed into French, and thence into
Italian, where it was called *Bovo d' Ancona*. This
was translated into Jewish-German as the *Bovobuch*,
and became food for the imagination of Jewish young
ladies in Germany. But it passed no further; it had
reached a "terminus" on that line. Neither of these
cases, nor the many like them, can be adduced as instances of the Jewish diffusion of folk-tales. For that
purpose we must turn finally after these long and, I

fear, wearisome preliminaries to the instances of what I term "junctions," when the train of tradition passes through the Jewish station, carrying a few extra passengers perhaps, but practically the same train that started from the original "terminus." So far as I can ascertain, these Jewish "junctions" consist of five books—(1) Petrus Alphonsi's *Disciplina Clericalis;* (2) Simeon Seth's translation of the Alexandreid, if this "find" of mine be substantiated; (3) the various Jewish versions of the fables of Bidpai, known by the name of *Kalila and Dimna;* (4) R. Joel's *Mishle Sendabar;* and (5) Pauli's *Schimpf und Ernst.* The "junction" character of two of these is rather doubtful; the first is not very long, and the last is somewhat late. But the fables of Bidpai are undoubtedly a Jewish "junction;" they are equally, without doubt, very important, one school of folk-lorists even tracing the whole *corpus* of European tales to them.

I have recently been engaged in preparing an edition of Sir Thomas North's version of Bidpai's Fables, which will shortly appear, and I may, therefore, be excused if I devote the greater part of my attention to this collection : its importance deserves it quite apart from my personal interest in the matter. But I propose dealing with the others, taking the five books in the order I have just mentioned.

(1.) First, as to Petrus Alphonsi's *Disciplina Clericalis.* Petrus Alphonsi was the Christian name of a Jew named Moses Sephardi, who changed his name when he changed his religion in 1106 under the auspices of Alphonso VI., whose godson he was. He wrote, like other renegades, against his former co-religionists, but he interests us here as the author of a collection of thirty-three tales, entitled "A Training School for the Clergy." The book had remarkable popu-

larity : it was utilised by clergymen for their sermons,
though it is difficult to understand how they could do
so if there were any ladies among the audience.   Most
of the stories were adopted into the *Gesta Romanorum*,
one of the most popular of mediæval story-books, which
includes others from the remaining " junctions," so that
it might almost be called the *Gesta Judæorum*.   It was
also translated into French, and by a curious chance I
recently discovered that some of the stories formed
part of one of the earliest books. printed in England.
Happening to look at Caxton's translation of the fables
of Æsop, I found at the end thirteen " Fables of
Alfonce," as they were called, and, looking into them a
little more closely, I found that these were a selection
from the *Disciplina Clericalis*.   As I have before hinted,
few of them will bear repetition " in the presence of
Mrs. Boffin," to use a phrase of Dickens, but I found
one which is quite harmless, and you would perhaps
like to have it in Caxton's own words :—

" The v. Fable is of the faith of three fellowes.

" Oft it happeth yt. the euyl which is procured to other cometh to
him which procureth it, as it appareth by three felowes of the which
twayne were Burgeys and the thirde a Labourer the which assembled
them togither for to goe to ye holy Sepulture, these thre felowes
made so greate prouision of floure to make their pilgrimage in suche
wise that it was al chaufed and consumed, except onely for to make
one lofe.   And when the Burgeys sawe the end of their floure,
they said togither, If we find not the maner and cautele to begile this
Uilayne bicause that he is a right great galaunt we shal dye for
hunger, wherefore we must fynde the maner and facion that we may
have the Lofe which shall be made of al our flour, and therfore they
concluded togither and sayde when the Lofe shal be put in the ouen
we shall goe and lay us for to slepe and he that shall dreme best the
Lofe shal be his.   And bicause that wee both be subtill and wise, he
shall not now dreme as wel as we shal, wherfore the Lofe shal be
ours, whereof all they three were well content and all beganne to
sleepe.   But when the Labourer knewe and perceyved all their fallace

and sawe that his two felowes were a sleepe he went and drew the
Lofe out of the ouen and eate it, and after he fayned to be a sleepe
and then one of the Burgeyses rose up and sayd to his felowes, I
have dreamed a wonderful dreame, for two Aungelles have taken and
borne me with greate ioye before the deuyne maiestie. And the
other Burgeys his felowe awoke and sayde, Thy dreame is wonderfull
but I suppose that myne is fairer then thyne is. For I have dreamed
that two Aungelles drew me one hard grounde for to leade me in to
hell, and after they did doo awake, the Uilayne which as dreadfull
sayde, who is there, and they answered we be thy felowes. And he
said to them howe be ye so soon retourned, we departed not yet fro hens.
And he sayd to the, by my faith I have dreamed that the Aungelles
had leade one of you into paradise or heaven and the other into hell.
Wherefore I suppose yt. ye should never have come againe and therfore I arose me fro sleepe and bicause I was hungrie I went and drew
out of the oven the lofe and eate it, for oft it happeth that he which
supposeth to begyle some other is himselve begyled."

The story is also to be found in the *Gesta Romanorum*, whence it passed into many others quarters (see
Oesterley, *Gesta Rom.* 106).   It is not a very startling
one, and would scarcely be received nowadays in any
of the comic newspapers.   But laughs were raised more
easily in the Middle Ages, and the story may interest
us by its antiquity if not for its comicality.   At any rate,
it will serve as a specimen of the *Disciplina Clericalis*.

(2.) We pass on to Simeon Seth's Greek translation
of the Alexandreid from the Persian, if it is his translation, if it is from the Persian, and if it really was the
source of the later European versions.   Simeon Seth
was a Jewish physician practising at the Byzantine
Court toward the close of the eleventh century.   Both
Warton and Weber state that his Greek version of the
Alexander legend was the source of all the other versions, and if this were so, we should have arrived at a
very important " junction " indeed.   For the Alexander
legend was one of the most popular of the mediæval
romances, and, being one of the earliest, it had great

influence on the rest. The French version was written in twelve-syllabled lines, which are called Alexandrines to this day. You remember Pope's lines—

" A needless Alexandrine ends the song,
  Which like a wounded snake drags its slow length along."

But I fear there must be some misunderstanding in Warton's account, as Zacher traces the Pseudo-Calisthenes back much earlier than Seth. Yet Seth's versions might have been an adaptation, and he would still be the immediate source in that case. My principal reason for doubt, however, is that I cannot think that this fact would have escaped the notice of Dr. Steinschneider or of M. Israel Levi, the latter of whom has written very learnedly on the subject, and has edited a Hebrew text of the Alexandreid (which is another case of a " terminus "). Still I have thought it right to mention the claims of Simeon Seth here as, if substantiated, they would add very considerably to the proved influence of Jews on the diffusion of folk-tales. Simeon Seth was, at any rate, certainly connected with the Greek translation of the fables of Bidpai, to which we may now turn.

(3.) Before entering into the Jewish details as to the fables of Bidpai, I think it desirable to give you some idea of the character of the book itself, and of the very wide extension it has had in the East and in Europe. As regards the latter, the bare description of the particular version I have been editing will indicate how wide a traveller it has been. For it is the English version of an Italian adaptation of a Spanish translation of a Latin version of a Hebrew translation of an Arabic adaptation of the Pehlevi version of the Indian original. In that bridge of traditions there are two keystones, the Latin and the Hebrew versions, and both were made by Jews. This is only one of the many lines of tradition. I have drawn up a bibliographical pedigree of the Bidpai literature, from which it appears that the book has been translated into thirty-eight languages, in 112 different versions, which have passed into over 180 editions since the invention of printing. Only the Bible itself surpasses that record among books. Having sufficiently whetted your curiosity about the fables of Bidpai, I propose to satisfy it by picking out a specimen of the stories it contains. But before doing so, we had better settle by what name we are to call this much translated book. We might refer to it as the *Pantschatantra* or the *Morall Philosophie of Doni*, or the *Exemplario contra los enganos*, or the *Homayun Namah*, or the *Hitopadesa*, or *Stephanites kai Ichnilates*, or any of the many names which the stories have borne during their long travels. My own edition I have entitled the "Fables of Bidpai," because that is the name by which the stories are best known from Galland's French translation of the Turkish version. But speaking before a Jewish audience, I prefer to speak of them by the name of *Calila w' Dimna*, the title of the Hebrew version, of the seventh chapter of which I now propose to read to you from M. Derenbourg's admirable edition. I can feel some confidence in the accuracy of my version, as I have been able to check myself by M. Derenbourg's elegant French translation, though our English tongue, I fancy, permits me to reproduce the Hebrew turns of expression more closely.

CHAPTER SEVEN

AND THIS IS THE CHAPTER OF THE NAZARITE

The king said to the philosopher: "I have understood all that thou hast told me, how things are lost when their owner knows not how to preserve them; and now tell me, I pray thee, of him that is hasty in his acts and does not reflect on them or foresee their results, and tell me a story thereon." Then said the wise Sendebar: "Every one who acts as thou sayest and does not foresee consequences, fails in what he does and repents too late. And it happens to him as it happened to the Nazarite who killed the dog that had done no harm, because he did not examine the matter and knew not of it." And the king said, "How was that?" The sage replied: "Once upon a time there was a city of the isles of the sea, and in it lived many good and upright men, among them a Nazarite good and God-fearing, and his wife was childless. And after many years she gave promise of bearing a child, whereat the Nazarite rejoiced and said unto her, 'Rejoice and be glad, for thou wilt bear a son who will rejoice our souls and please our hearts, and I'll give him a lucky name and a good education. And God will exalt my name in him, and he will cause my memory to endure after my death.' The woman said, 'Alas, speak not of what thou knowest nought and what beseems thee not. How knowest thou that all will go well with me, or whether the child will be a boy or a girl, or if it will live, or if its character and conduct will be good? Let such things alone, and trust in God, who will give thee according to His will. For a sensible man does not speak of things he knows not of, and does not prejudge the acts of the Lord. "There are many devices in a man's heart, nevertheless the counsel of the Lord, that shall stand" (Prov. xix. 21). For it haps to him that presumes to speak like thee, what happened to the Nazarite, on whom fell the pot of honey.' He said unto her, 'And how was that?'

"His wife said to him, 'Once upon a time a Nazarite lived near a king, who gave him for his daily sustenance a cake and a little pot of honey. He used to eat the cake, and put the honey away in a little cruse hanging over his head until the vessel became full. And honey was very dear in those days, and one day, lying on his bed, he raised his eyes to the cruse of honey and thought how dear it was, and said to himself, "When the vessel is full, I will sell the honey for a piece of gold. And then I will buy ten sheep, and each of them will have

a lamb, and there will be twenty. After that the flock will increase,
till in less than four years there will be four hundred. I will then
buy a cow and a bull [for every four sheep] as well as a piece of land,
and the cows will give me calves, and I will take the males and work
with them the piece of ground I have bought, and, besides, the
heifers will give me milk. Scarce five years will have passed before
all this will have multiplied, and I shall have a grand fortune in
cattle and grain, and I will build me a great and goodly house, and
buy man-servants and maid-servants, and I will take as wife a beautiful and well-born damsel. And soon she will give me a fine hand-
some boy, born under a lucky star, and in a propitious hour ; he will
be a blessing, and preserve my memory after my death. I will give
him an auspicious name, and will care for his education. Ah ! if he
doesn't obey me, won't I thwack him with this stick !" And with
these words he raised the stick as if he were going to beat him, and
struck the cruse of honey, which broke and poured its contents over
the head and body of the Nazarite.

   " ' I have told thee this story, so that thou mayst not speak of what
thou knowest not. And long ago it was said, " Boast not thyself of
to-morrow; for thou knowest not what a day may bring forth " '
(Prov. xxvii. 1).

   " The Nazarite hearing these words was silent and stood corrected.
And when her time came she brought forth a fine child, a charming
boy, who caused great joy to the Nazarite. And when the days of
purification were over, she said to her husband, 'Stop with thy son,
I will go purify myself.' And when the father had sat by the cradle
a little while, behold, the king's messenger came after him. He closed
the house and went to the Palace. And there was in the house a dog,
and it saw a serpent come out of a hole and go to kill the child. The
dog seized and killed it, and so soiled its jaws with the blood.

FIGURE OF THE CHILD, AND THE DOG KILLING THE SERPENT

   " The Nazarite returned quickly from the Palace, and when he
opened the door, the dog came out to meet him. Seeing his jaws
stained with blood, the Nazarite thought the dog had killed the child,
and he slew it with his stick, without thinking of what he was doing.
But as soon as he entered his room he saw his child alive and the
serpent dead. Then he repented and was sad and mournful, saying,
' Would to God the child had not been born, then I would not have
slain this dog, for I have acted like an ungrateful wretch who does
not recognise the good he has received.' When his wife returned

and saw the dog and the serpent slain, she asked the reason of this from her husband, and he told her what had passed. Then she said, 'See the reward of those who act precipitately, without seeing how things really are. After such deeds you repent and regret in vain, and without lessening your grief.'"

After this, Sendebar the Wise said to the king, "Wise and thoughtful men, thanks to thought and reflection, succeed where passionate men fail that act hastily. The prudent man ought to reflect, to observe, and then to act slowly and gently, so as to mark the object he aims at."

(END OF THE CHAPTER OF THE NAZARITE).

That chapter will give you some idea of the kind of book *Calila w' Dimna* is. And at the same time, it will give you some impression of the very great influence of the book in providing materials for popular literature. For the story of the Nazarite who breaks the pot of honey is the origin of La Fontaine's Perrette, who counted her chickens before they were hatched, as Benfey showed in the introduction to his *Pantschatantra*, and as Professor Max Müller explained in his charming lecture on the "Migration of Fables," which was almost entirely devoted to *Calila w' Dimna*. And the main story of the chapter is no less than the original of the far-famed one of Llewellyn and his dog Gellert, which has likewise been traced all over the world by Benfey, and after him by Mr. Clouston. I will not deny that I have been cunning enough to pick out the chapter which best exemplifies the enormous spread of the stories contained in the book. But almost all its stories have had some voyage, and many have had quite as much as Perrette or Gellert. And even more influential has been the form in which the stories have been put. You know the method by which, in the "Arabian Nights," story is introduced into story much the same way as those Chinese balls of ivory which have other balls within them, while those have others, so that at last you wonder how they got there.. Well, that idea of a frame to hold a number of stories which is found in Boccacio's "Decameron," and from there in Chaucer's "Canterbury Tales," and in innumerable other collections, came originally from the *Calila w' Dimna*. And in tracing the origin of this very important idea of a frame, we begin a story which is much more interesting, to my mind, than that of Perrette or Gellert or any of the others—and that is the story of the book itself, in which, as will be seen, Jews have played so large a part.

The idea of a frame to hold the stories and many of the stories themselves can be traced back to the great Indian sage and saint Gautama Sakyamuni, the Buddha, whom we have already met with in the והנמיר בן המלך. Soon after his death, which has been fixed about 453 B.C., a number of the moral apologues he had told, and doubtless a number which he had not told, were collected together as the Jatakas, or Buddhist Birth Stories. These are tales supposed to be told by the Buddha, and to be in each case experiences undergone by him, or witnessed by him, during one of his former manifestations on earth. These manifestations of the Buddha were supposed to be sometimes in the form of animals, and thus many beast fables occur in the "Jatakas" which are undoubtedly the source of some of the fables that go by the name of Æsop, and of all Æsop's fables according to the opinion of some. It is obvious that this idea of including all the experiences of the Buddha in all his manifestations was a most ingenious way of combining any number of stories, and the 500 Jatakas are supposed to contain nearly 2000 stories, and it is not surprising that some folk-lorists wish to trace all popular tales back to the Jatakas. Among them is one that interests us, as it

contains an exact analogue of the Judgment of Solomon,
with Buddha as the Solomon, and a Raksha or female
demon as the false mother. Now I think it not impossible that the story was carried out to Ophir by
Solomon's vessels, and thus it would be the earliest
instance of Jewish diffusion of folk-tales, that a Bible
story has thus become part of the Buddha-legend. On
the other hand, when we find Rab declaring that the
false mother must have been a demon in disguise, we
cannot help suspecting that the Indian version had
somehow percolated to Babylon and influenced the
Talmudic doctor. This story has by a curious fate
been translated back into Hebrew (from the English
version of a Cingalese translation of the Pali) ten years
ago, and may be found in Jellinek's *Beth Hamidrash*,
Bnd. vi.

The Jatakas were held to be so sacred, that many
of them were sculptured round the sacred Buddhist
shrines, a fact not without importance for the future
inquiry. Some of them from Amaravati may be seen
on the walls of the grand staircase of the British
Museum. And many of the stories can be traced in
the *Calila w' Dimna*, and must have been in its
Indian original, which was probably named "Karataka
and Damanka." As they are there divorced from all
connection with Buddha, our book must have been
composed when Buddhism was on the wane in India,
say about 300 A.D., and in Brahman circles who substituted the sage Bidpai for the saintly Buddha. Unfortunately, the Indian original is lost, and is only
represented by later excerpts, as in the *Pantschatantra*
or *Pentateuch*, containing five of the original thirteen
books, or the *Hitopadesa*, which has four of these.

The moment the stories start on their travels from
the Indian peninsula their Jewish interest begins.

The ordinary account given in most versions of the book itself is that they were first translated into Pehlevi or old Persian by order of Khosru Nurshirvan (Chosroes the Great) about 550 A.D. Yet if M. Halévy is to be trusted, the name *Calila w' Dimna* occurs in the Talmud in the mouth of Rava, who flourished under the Sassanide Sapor II. about 350 A.D., or 200 years before the ordinarily accepted date. In a discussion contained in the Babylonian Talmud (Sanhedrin, 74b) the question is raised how far a Jew may legitimately have anything to do even with the ceremonial of idolatry. Rava lays down the general principle that a Jew need not suffer martyrdom for merely accidental connection with idolatrous ceremonies. "For if it were so," he continues, "how could we give fire to קוזקי ודימונקי," as it is written in the editions, or קורקי ודימוניקי, in the MSS. of Carlsruhe and Munich, or, as M. Halévy would amend it, קרדקי ודמנקי, which is sufficiently near the names Karataka and Damanaka of the original Sanskrit. Yet what meaning can we give to the sentence if we are to adopt this emendation? Jewish tradition connects the words with sacrificial fire-irons which M. Halévy connects with our story-book by the following links. Karataka and Damanka are the names of two jackals which figure in the first chapter of the book. The Jews, according to M. Halévy, called the Zoroastrians jackals, which has thus come to signify fire-snatchers, and then were applied to fire-dogs and so to fire-irons. All this is very ingenious—M. Halévy is never anything but ingenious—but it is not very convincing, and I fear I must add that M. Halévy is generally anything but convincing. The fact of dates is dead against him in this instance. Rava lived about 350 A.D., and Persian tradition, and the text of the book itself, unanimously attribute its

entrance into Persia under Chosroes about 550 A.D.
Firdausi, the great Persian epic poet, thought the
event so important, that he devotes a number of his
precious lines to the subject in his poetical annals of
Persia when he comes to treat of the reign of Khosru
Nurshirvan. We must, therefore, reject M. Halévy's
subtleties and allow קווקי ודימנוקי to remain an unknown
quantity till M. Darmesteter or some other Zend scholar
solves the riddle for us.[1]

From the Pehlevi the fables passed almost immediately into Syriac, in a version which was discovered
under romantic circumstances a few years ago ; and
about 750 A.D. the Pehlevi version was translated into
Arabic by Abdullah ibn Almokaffa, a Zoroastrian converted to Islam. But there is another account how
the book got into Arabic which especially interests us.
Dr. Steinschneider published some years ago in the
Zeitschrift der deutschen morgenländischen Gesellschaft
an extract from one of Abraham ibn Ezra's astronomical tracts, which I will shortly give you. The learned
doctor was for the time more interested in the astronomical points raised in the quotation, but we need only
take that part of it which relates to *Calila w' Dimna*.
This runs as follows :—

" In olden times there was neither science nor religion among the
sons of Ishmael that dwell in tents till the [author of the] Koran
arose and gave them a new code of religion after his desire . . . till
the great king in Ishmael, by name Es-'Saffa'h [fl. 750 A.D.], arose,
who heard that there were many sciences to be found in India . . .
and there came men saying that there was in India a very mighty book
on the secrets of government, in the form of a fable placed in the
mouths of dumb beasts, and in it many illustrations, for the book was

---

[1] The suggestion of Dr. Jastrow that they are corruptions of the Greek
and Latin names of Sunday, *Kuriake* and *Dominica*, is equally unconvinc-
ing (*Revue*, viii. 277).—J. J.

greatly honoured in the eyes of the reader, and the name of the book was *Kalila and Dimna,* that is, the Lion and the Ox, because the story in the first chapter of the book is about them. The aforesaid king fasted therefore forty days, so that he might perchance see the Angel of dreams, who might allow him to have the book translated in the Ishmaelitish tongue. And he saw in his dream according to his wish. Thereupon he sent for a Jew who knew both languages, and ordered him to translate this book, for he feared that if an Ishmaelite versed in both tongues were to translate it he might die. And when he saw that the contents of the book were extraordinary—as indeed they are—he desired to know the sciences. He therefore gave a large sum to the Jew who had translated the above-named book to go to the city Arin [in Ceylon] which lies under the equator . . . perhaps he might succeed in bringing one of their sages to the king. The Jew went, and used many artifices till one of the wise men of Arin determined for a great sum of money to come to the king. . . . Thereupon the wise man, whose name was Kankah, was brought to the king, and *taught the Ishmaelites the principles of number, which consist of nine figures.*"

You will observe that according to this account it was by the mediation of a Jew that the figures which we call "Arabic numbers," but the Arabs themselves "Indian signs," were first brought into use in the West. But what we are more intimately concerned with is the statement of Ibn Ezra's, that the Jew translated the *Calila w' Dimna* direct from the Indian. All the Arabic sources, and most of the MSS., attribute the translation to Almokaffa, and state that it was made from the Pehlevi or old Persian. At first sight it might seem that we could reconcile the two statements by assuming that Almokaffa employed the Jew as a "ghost" or "devil," and it would only be natural to receive two different accounts from the two sides. But this would negative any direct translation from the Sanskrit, which is the important point in Ibn Ezra's account. I fancy I can show that there is some plausibility in the tradition reported by Ibn Ezra, and as the question is of vital importance in the Bidpai literature,

you will perhaps allow me to dilate upon it. The state
of the Arabic text is very unsatisfactory; the partial
edition of Schulten's and De Sacy's complete one were
both made from very poor MSS., as Guidi and Nöldeke
have shown. But it is quite clear from these editions,
and the extracts printed by Guidi, that there are two
distinct families of MSS. Does not this point to two
distinct translations, and so far confirm Ibn Ezra's
account? Again, Benfey is continually pointing that
the Latin translation of John of Capua, and therefore
the Hebrew version of R. Joel, and consequently the
Arabic version from which this was undoubtedly made,
comes much nearer to the Indian original than the
other family of Arabic MSS. represented by De Sacy's
text. On one occasion he even shows that the Latin
text alone of all the versions preserves one of the verses
of the Indian original. Does not this say something for
the other contention of Ibn Ezra's account, that one of
the Arabic versions was derived directly from the Sanskrit? To test this remarkable hypothesis requires
more linguistic resources than I am able to command.
I have small Arabic and less Sanskrit, and it would
require a master of both to decide authoritatively on the
point. But I trust I have shown enough to cause the
problem to be taken up by competent Orientalists. M.
Derenbourg has given us the best edition of the Hebrew,
he is giving us the best edition of the Latin. I trust
he may still be spared to us to give us an adequate
edition of the Arabic version, and in so doing decide
the question whether our Arabic version was not made
by a Jew directly from the Sanskrit, as Abraham ibn
Ezra relates.

And in deciding this question I fancy I have discovered a test of crucial value which will enable
Arabists to determine with ease the affiliation of MSS.

I refer to the illustrations which, as we have seen, Ibn Ezra declared to exist in the Indian text, and was there probably derived from some such sculptures of the Jatakas as may now be seen in the British Museum. Three of De Sacy's MSS. have illustrations, and two have places where the illustrations ought to be, but are only mentioned.   Now a remarkable discovery which I have made with regard to the Hebrew text renders it probable that the illustrations were considered as integral parts of the text, and were passed on from a MS. of one language into that of another.   The unique MS. of the Hebrew text now at Paris has no illustrations, unfortunately, but it indicates on almost every page the place where illustrations ought to be, as you will remember in the chapter that I read to you.   We have definite proof that there were illustrations in other copies, for Isaac ibn Sacula, who composed in 1283 a goody-goody collection of stories, משל הקדמוני, expressly as a rival to *Calila w' Dimna*, put in illustrations so that his book should be equally attractive.   Well, the Hebrew MS. of the *Calila w' Dimna* had illustrations, and on comparing the illustrations referred to in M. Derenbourg's edition with those actually given in the *editio princeps* of the Latin, I become convinced that John of Capua must have taken into his Latin translation the illustrations of the Hebrews, or at least copies of them.   You will become equally convinced, I think, if you will allow me to run through for two or three chapters the two lists of the illustrations referred to in the Hebrew, and given in the Latin, German, and Spanish, who all have the same illustrations, the two former from the same blocks.

CHAP. VI

Referred to in *Hebrew*.	Given in *Lat., Germ., Span.*
Ape on tree and reptile in water.	Ape on tree, reptile in water.
Animals in water.	Ape and reptile in water.
Ape on tree and reptile in water.	
Lion and ass running away.	Lion, ass, man, ape.
Lion seizing ass and fox looking on.	Lion seizing ass, ape above.

CHAP. VII

	Ascetic striking pot of honey [= La Perrette].
Child and dog killing serpent.	Child, dog killing serpent [= Gellert].

CHAP. VIII

Cat in net, bird on tree, dog and mouse.	Cat in net, bird on tree, dog and man.
Mouse gnawing net.	Mouse gnawing net.
Mouse, net, cat in tree, and hunter going away.	Mouse, net, cat in tree, and hunter going away.

CHAP. IX

Child killing little bird.	Child killing little bird.
Pinza taking child's eyes out.	Bird like a gryphon [= Pinza] taking child's eyes out.
King calling Pinza on a mountain.	King calling Pinza on a mountain.

As the Latin took its illustrations from the Hebrew, so the Hebrew in all probability took them from the Arabic ; and we ought to be able to see in the Arabic illustrations which are still intact, some trace of Indian influences, if Ibn Ezra's account is correct. If that turns out to be the fact, the same remarkable history that applies to these stories applies to their illustrations, which can thus also be traced from India to Spain.

But whether any Jew had any hand in bringing the fables from India, there is no doubt that it was chiefly by their instrumentality that *Calila w' Dimna* was

brought to Europe.   There are four chief channels by
which the Arabic version was brought into Christendom
—the Persian, the Greek, the Hebrew, and the Old
Spanish.   Now, the Persian only came to be known in
Europe at the beginning of the last century, and does
not count for much as regards popular diffusion.   And
all the other three channels are Jewish; that is certain
for two of them, and I think I can prove it for the third.
The Greek was done about 1080 by Simeon Seth, whom
we have met previously; from this were derived old
Slavonic and Croat versions.   The Hebrew was, of
course, by a Jew, whose name was said to have been
Joel.   This was translated in Latin about 1270 by a
converted Italian Jew named John of Capua, and from
the Latin version were derived German, Spanish, Dutch,
Danish, and Italian versions, and from the last the
English version I have been editing.   There was
another Hebrew translation by R. Eleazer ben Jacob,
discovered by Steinschneider, and also edited by M.
Derenbourg.   This seems to be fragmentary and had
no offshoots, in fact, was what we have termed a "terminus."   The third offshoot of the Arabic which influenced Europe was the Old Spanish, which was translated
in 1251.   Now the colophon of this reads: "Here
endeth the book of *Calyla and Digna*, and was done
into Latin from the Arabic and romanced [*i.e.*, put into
Spanish] by command of the Infanta Don Alforso, son
of the very noble King Don Fernando."   Now this was
exactly the way in which the Jewish translators used
to work, and we know that this very Alfonso established
a college of Jewish translators at Toledo just about this
time.   I therefore suggested some years ago that this
Old Spanish version, from which Raymond of Béziers
made a Latin poem, was, like the other chief offshoots
of the Arabic, the work of a Jewish translator.

Not alone have Jewish translators done most for the spread of *Calila w' Dimna;* Jewish scholars in this century have done most for the critical investigation of that spread. The introduction of Benfey to his translation of the *Pantschatantra* is a marvel of erudition, even judging it from a German standpoint. And at the present moment the great master of the *Calila* literature is M. Derenbourg. I think if this book could be claimed by any nation besides the one that gave it birth, we might venture to call *Calila w' Dimna* a characteristic Jewish book, and one of the glories of Jewish literature.

And the book in itself deserves all the attention that Jews have bestowed upon it. We should find it, perhaps, dull compared with the sensational novels of the day. But its appeal to the mediæval mind is shown by the large number of translations it went through. Indeed, there is a tendency in some quarters to trace all folk-tales, and especially all beast-fables, to this book. I have examined these claims with some care and at some length in my introduction to the English version, and come to the following results :—As regards folk-tales, about one-tenth of the European collections can be traced to this source. And as regards beast fables, many of the so-called fables of Æsop are derived from these, and even those of Babrius and Phædrus were influenced by the "Jatakas" in the point of putting a "moral" at the end of the fables, which is a distinctive Buddhistic feature. I have already pointed out the influence of the book in the literary device of a framework to hold the stories, which is again Buddhistic, and I sum up my conclusions as to the origin and influence of the book by stating roundly that the fables of Bidpai are the fables of Buddha. The book has indeed had the unique fate of appealing to all the great religions of the world. Originating in Buddhism, it was adopted by Brahmanism, and passed on to Zoroastrianism, Islam, and Christendom, chiefly by the mediation of Jews.

(4.) We pass now to the fourth of our "junctions," which is known by the name of משלי סנדבר, or "the Seven Sages." This has passed through much the same history as *Calila w' Dimna*, and is, like that, also a framework story. I fear I cannot explain the story before a mixed audience, as it is practically a variant of the "Mrs. Potiphar formula," as folk-lorists would say. Nor can I give you an example of the tales, for the same reason; the few that are not coarse are dull. Nor am I so certain that the *Mishle Sendabar* forms a "junction" in the train of tradition. It is usually stated that the Latin version which forms the source of the European variety was derived from this, but I have seen no very definite proof of this. Dr. Paulus Cassel has recently produced an elaborate edition of the book, but he does not enter into this point, and is chiefly concerned in discovering the highly moral tendency of what seem, to the unsophisticated eye, very immoral stories.

There is a point of connection between the *Mishle Sendabar* and the *Calila w' Dimna* which may detain us a moment. Both books (in Hebrew) have been attributed to a rabbi named Joel, and it is likely enough that the same person should have translated both. If that is so, we can understand how the name of Bidpai occurs in *Calila* as "Sendebar." For the Arabic form is Baidaba, and as the difference between B and Th and I and N only depend on diacritical points, Joel probably read this as Thindaba, which he thought a misprint for Sindabar, which in itself is a misreading for Sindibad. Confusion has often been caused between the two books by this mistake, and I thought it worth while to draw your attention to it.

(5.) Finally, we have Pauli's *Schimpf und Ernst*, the work of a converted Jew at the beginning of the sixteenth century. It was the Joe Miller of Germany, and passed through over thirty editions. Oesterley had edited it with elaborate notes showing its wide influence, and among his references I note some of the Elizabethan jest-books, so that some of Pauli's jokes may have tickled Shakespeare. But his collection is more of sharp answers than of folk-tales, and this notice of him must suffice. I would, however, remark that the fact of so many converts being concerned in the diffusion of folk-tales confirms what I have said as to the unlikelihood of Jews in general coming sufficiently in contact with their neighbours to transmit to them their own stories.

We have arrived at the last of our "junctions," and may now make up the way-bill. The importance of the *Calila* overshadows all the rest, and the influence of Jews upon it was so marked, that we might almost sum up its influences as the total. But that amount is a very large one, amounting, as we have seen, to one-tenth of the whole *corpus* of European folk-tales. Of the remaining nine-tenths of folk-tales the origin is very obscure; and whenever we can trace direct borrowing from one nation to another it is almost invariably from the Bidpai cycle, so that we may say that, so far as the European nations share their folk-tales with one another, they owe this fact to Jewish diffusion.

To some persons this will not seem any great thing to boast of. They will feel tempted to call all such inquiries as this by some vigorous name not exactly expressing admiration. They consider nothing of Jewish interest unless it touches upon Jewish theology. In Jewish history they have only a care for the inner development of Judaism, not for the human relations between Jews and others to which most

Jewish historical students are nowadays devoting their attention. That was the defence in principle of the Anglo-Jewish Exhibition of last year with which I had something to do. We looked upon English Jews as men and not merely as theologians, while recognising that their theology has had a determining influence on their relations to their fellow-men. To look upon Jews merely as theologians and not as men is, I will not say one-sided, but is bad theology. It has been said that he who knows only the Bible does not know the Bible, and similarly, we may say that he who is only a theologian is a bad theologian.

I think that to a wider conception of theology there is even a point of view from which the subject we have been studying has its theological interest. I know no more humanising thought than the idea of all the workers of the world laughing at the same jokes, and of little children all over the world repeating the same stories, the thought that little Hindoos are prattling to their nurses the same tales as little English men and women. It is one of those touches of nature which make the whole world kin. These folk-tales form a bond not alone between the ages, but between many races who think they have nothing in common. We have the highest authority that " out of the mouths of babes and sucklings has the Lord established strength," and surely of all the influences for good in the world, none is comparable to the lily souls of little children. That Jews, by their diffusion of folk-tales, have furnished so large an amount of material to the childish imagination of the civilised world is, to my mind, no slight thing for Jews to be proud of. It is one of the conceptions that make real to us the idea of the Brotherhood of Man, which, in Jewish minds, is for ever associated with the Fatherhood of God.

L

THE LONDON JEWRY, 1290

(*From "Papers of the Anglo-Jewish Exhibition"*)

In the plan[1] accompanying this paper I have endeavoured to restore the ground plan of the London Jewry
as it was when the Jews of England were expelled by
the harsh decree of Edward I. in 1290. My aim has
been to do this with as much exactitude as a surveyor
laying out an estate; and, in fact, as will be seen, the
basis of my reconstruction is the Ordnance Survey of
the City, which is accurate to inches. The method I
have been able to employ is, I believe, novel, and the
ground plan, if successfully plotted out, will be the
first which has ever been drawn with such claims to
accuracy after the lapse of six hundred years without
actual excavations.

I have been enabled to do this owing to the fact that
the boundaries of the City parishes were fixed just
about the time the Jews were expelled. Some time
between the years 1273 and 1294 the boundaries of
the City parishes were settled as we have them at
present marked out on the Ordnance maps. Now, it
is known that the parish boundaries followed the outline of the backs of the houses, and a cursory glance
at the map will show that, in many instances, the
various plots of ground adjoining the boundaries can
be reconstructed. The fronts of the houses are, of
course, given by the lines of the streets, and between
the two we can, I think, restore the outlines of the

---

[1] Reproduced by kind permission of the editor of the *Jewish Chronicle*,
where it first appeared.

THE LONDON JEWRY, 1290

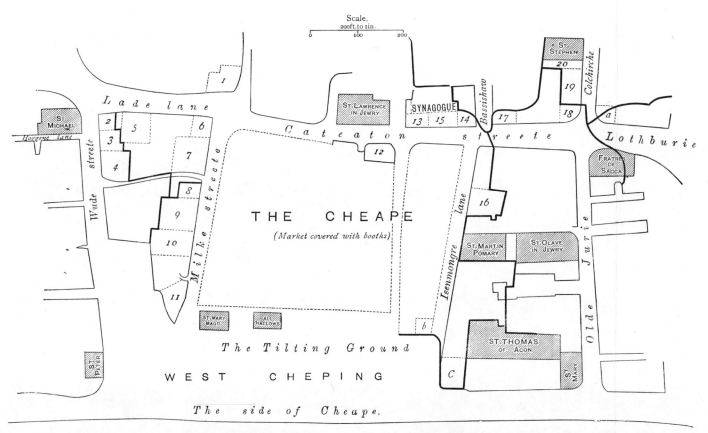

Scale.
200ft. to 1in.
0   100   200

Dark lines indicate Parish Boundaries.
Plots with Numbers belonged to Jews at the Expulsion.

Shadowed buildings represent Churches.
Plots marked by Letters were owned by Jews previous to the Expulsion.

1. Sara Diei.
2. Mosse fil. Elie.
3. Community.
4. Gamaliel de Oxon.
5. Bateman f. Cresse.

6. Roes' Anteman.
7. Mosseus Crispin.
8. Benedict f. Jacob.
9. Jacob f. Bonami.
10. Muriel f. Cresse.

11. Roesia Truyte.
12. Thippe vid. Isaac.
13. Benedict f. Hagin.
14. Manser f. Aaron.
15. Antera vid. Vives.

16. Leo f. Cresse.
17. Elie Fraunceys.
18. Aaron f. Slemme.
19. Jorvin Sackerel.
20. Elie f. Mosse.

a. Earl of Derby, formerly Isaac of Norwich (1214).   b. Earl of Essex, formerly Abraham f. Muriel, formerly Abraham f. Rabbi (1214).
C. Earl of Lancaster, formerly belonging to a Jew, temp. Ric. I.

plots of ground on which London houses stood when
parish boundaries were fixed.   Thus, to take an example, the peculiar configuration of the parish boundary of St. Michael's, Wood Street, at the corner of
Wood Street, can only be explained by supposing it to
be formed of the backs of three houses—two in Wood
Street itself, and the third in the adjoining street,
called Lad Lane at the time of our inquiry, but now
known as part of Gresham Street.   Similarly, the
former configuration of the Hospital of St. Thomas of
Acon is partly defined by the boundary of the parish
of St. Mary Colechurch.

Applying, then, this method, we can obtain, with a
very great degree of certainty, the outline of London
houses about 1290.   The further step remains of identifying the owners; and this, in the case of the expelled Jews, was not, after all, such a difficult task.
For their houses escheated to the king on their expulsion, and he immediately issued writs for inquisition
into their value and position, and then proceeded to
distribute them among his faithful followers.   The
letters patent containing these grants, with the names
of the Jewish owners and of the Christian grantees,
and indications of the position and value of the houses,
are still extant in the MSS. Department of the British
Museum (Lansd., 860).   From this I derive the names
of twenty-two Jewish owners of London property, as in
the accompanying table, and of these I can localise with
some tolerable degree of certainty the exact position
of their holdings.   From other sources I have obtained
two other names and localities (Nos. 11 and 17).

The positions of these holdings are not laid down
with any great precision; in many cases merely the
street, in some only the parish, is given, but by an
application of the processes of exhaustion we can get

Jewish Owner.	Locality.	No. in Plan.	Rental.	Christian Grantee.
			£ s. d.	
Leo. f. Cresse f. Mag. Elie	St. Martin Pomeroy, Ironmonger Lane	16	2 14 8	Isabella, widow of Adam de St. Albans.
Abraham Matron	St. Lawrence	...	2 6 8	Will. le King de Hatton.
Benedict f. Mayre	Catte Street	20	0 6 8	Galfries de Norton Clericus.
Elie f. Mossei	"Placea," Colchirche	10	2 10 0	Robert de Basinges.
Muriel f. Cresse f. Gente	St. Mary Magd, Milk Street	18	2 0 0	Alan le Cordwainer.
Aaron f. Slemme	St. Olave Jewry, Colchirche Street	8	0 6 6	Guidoferre.
Benedict f. Jacobi Clerici	St. Mary Magd, Milk Street	3	0 8 8	John de Lanfare.
Communitas	"Placea," Wood Street	12	0 6 8	Adam de Horsham.
Thippe vid. Isaac de Southwark	St. Lawrence, Catte Street	19	3 18 8	Alan de Hommade.
Jorvin Sackerel	St. Olave, Colchirche	13	6 17 4	Benedict de Shoreditch.
		6		Prior de Chicksand.
Elie le Evesk	Sporier Street	...		
Benedict f. Hagin	St. Lawrence, Catte Street	1	1 2 8	Edmund de London.
Roes' Anteman	Corner Milk Street			
Sarra Diei	St. Lawrence, corner Aldermanbury	2	2 18 8	William de Leyre.
Mosse f. Mr. Elie	Corner Wood Street	15	2 14 6	Isabella, widow of John de Vescy.
Antera, vid. Vives f. Mossei de Ironmonger Lane		14	12 17 0	John de Butterleye.
Manser f. Aaron	Catte Street		6 13 4	
Elie Baggard	......	7	...	Isabella de Vesey. Martin, servant of Queen Eleanor.
Mosseus Crispin	Milk Street	9	3 19 0	Henry de Enfield.
Jacobus f. Bonami de Ebor	Milk Street	4	3 0 0	
Gamaliel de Oxon	Wood Street	5	2 10 0	Matilda de Kellenden.
Bateman f. Cresse	Lade Street		7 10 0	Will. de Ideshale.
Sarra de Oxon		...	...	
Sepultura	Lyrestowe extra Cripelgate			......

some sort of precision out of them. Thus, in three
cases, the houses are at the corners of the streets,
Mosse f. Mag. Elie, at the corner of Wood Street (2),
the house which is so clearly defined by the parish
boundary; Sarra Diei (Dyaye it is elsewhere spelt)
at the corner of Aldermanbury (1), and Roesa Anteman
at the corner of Milk Street (6). In the last case
there might be a doubt as to which corner, but I have
found elsewhere ("Hist. MSS. Report," iv. p. 449) that
the south corner was held by another Roesia Truyte,
who is distinctly mentioned as residing "opposite
the church." We have thus both corners of Milk
Street accounted for. In the case of Aaron fil.
Slemme, whose tenement was in the parish of St.
Olave and in Colechurch Street, the parish boundary
forces us to locate him near the south-west corner of
that street. But there is another tenement, that of
Jorvin Sackerel, with the same description; how can
we determine the relative positions of the two ? Here
another criterion comes in, that of the rental : Aaron's
house let for £2 per annum, Jorvin's for no less a
sum than £3, 18s. 8d., which can only be because
it was on the larger plot. Similarly, Mosseus Crispin's
house in Milk Street must have been a large one,
as his rental was £3, 10s., against Roes' Anteman's
of only 11s. 4d., so that will justify us in allotting him
the plot No. 6 in our plan. The relative positions of
other owners is sometimes given by our knowledge
of the previous history of the houses. Thus taking
Milk Street again, we learn from a Patent Roll of 4
Ed. I., 1276, that Cresse and Elias, sons of Magister
Mosse, were allowed to inherit the house their father
formerly held in Milk Street, and which lay between
the house of Henry de Trowyk on the south, and that
of Bonamy of York on the north. Now, sixteen years

afterwards, the date of our plan, we find Muriel, the
daughter of Cresse and Jacob, the son of Bonamy,
holding houses in the same street; and we cannot be
far out in assuming that these were the same houses
that their fathers had held, and therefore we are
justified in placing these two names side by side, with
the Yorkshire Jew to the north of the London Jewess
(9 and 10). In two cases the positions are given
precisely in a document giving the limits of the parish
of St. Stephen, Coleman Street, to which my attention
was called by Mr. C. T. Martin. This enables us to
locate Manser fil. Aaron at the south-west corner of
Basinghall Street (15), and one Elie Fraunceys at the
opposite house (17); and we learn incidentally that
the same house had been previously held by Elie his
father (of whom he was probably a posthumous child),
and by Simon his grandfather, who had clearly come
from France. Nor are these the only cases where one
can trace the previous history of the houses vacated
at the Expulsion. The block of buildings in Catte
Street, to the east of the church of St. Lawrence, is
especially interesting from this point of view, as well
as from others. We find in 1207 that Isaac the Cyro-
grapher, or keeper of the chest in which the *Shetaroth*
were preserved, was enfeoffed before the Justices of the
Jews of lands in St. Lawrence Jewry which had belonged to Josce de Ebor and Samuel Hoppercol, and
had escheated to the king (Mag. Rot. 7 Joh. 1b).
This Josce of York was the father of Aaron of York,
and the lay head of the York community, and as such
had the honour of being killed last in the magnificent
scene at Clifford's Tower at York in 1190, where
500 Jews and Jewesses preferred death to change of
faith. Yet his houses escheated to the king because
of his death. In 1220 one Hugo de Nevil sues

Sampson, son of Isaac, for ten years' rent of houses in St. Lawrence Jewry, and the said Sampson declares that Hugo had freed his father Isaac for one pound of cummin seed (Cole "Documents," p. 293). In 1227 the same Sampson fil. Isaac pays half a mark for having inscribed on the Great Roll of the Exchequer that he has given to Abraham his son, and the son of Malke his wife, the land which he holds in St. Lawrence Jewry, which land lies between the property which was¡ Abraham's fil. Avegaye, on the east, and Judah of Warwick's, on the west, and extends in length from the highway to the *Synagogue* (Brit. Mus. MSS. Add., 4542).

Here, then, is a hitherto unknown synagogue in the parish of St. Lawrence, in a street running east and west, which can only be Catte Street, now Gresham Street. There is a curious confirmation of this in old Stow's " Survey of London," which enables us to identify the house, and what is more, to obtain a sketch of part of it. In speaking of Basinghall Ward, Stow remarks (p. 108, Ed. Thoms), " On the west side, almost at the south end thereof, is Bakewell Hall, corruptly called Blakewell Hall, concerning the original whereof I have heard divers opinions, which I overpass as fables without colour of proof. . . . In mine opinion, the foundation thereof was first laid since the conquest of William, Duke of Normandy, for the same was built upon vaults of stone. . . . But that this house hath been a temple or Jewish synagogue (as some have fantasied), I allow not, seeing it had no such form of roundness or other likeness." In his last remark Stow is referring to the general opinion that the only Jews' synagogues were round, as tradition declares the round Norman churches at Cambridge and Nottingham to have been synagogues.

Now we have seen a record of a synagogue exactly in
this neighbourhood, given in the document I have
just referred to, and here we have Stow reporting a
tradition of Bakewell Hall having been a synagogue.
The conclusion is almost forced upon us that Bakewell
Hall was once a synagogue or public building of the
London Jews. And if so, I think I can explain its
somewhat enigmatic name. Bakewell Hall is in all
probability a corruption of Bathwell Hall, the bathing-
place or *Mikveh* of the London Jewesses, where they
used to perform the ritual lavations prescribed by

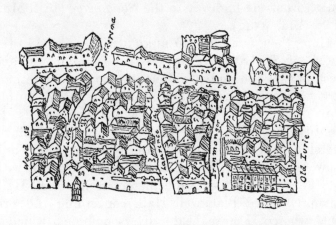

Rabbinic law. I find exactly the same change of
name in a Derbyshire village now termed Bakewell,
but in the thirteenth century, Bathquell (Palmer,
"Folk Etymology," *sub voce*). Bakewell Hall stands
clearly in Ralph Aggas' map of London, 1560, and if
my conjecture is right, we have in it a sketch of a
Jewish synagogue of 1290, the latest of them, and
yet one of the earliest we can trace, and the only one
that remained throughout in Jewish hands.

The history of the successive fates of the London
synagogues is typical of the history of the community.

St. Stephen's Church was once a synagogue (Stow),
and so was probably St. Mary Colechurch. These
were confiscated, and devoted to the all-devouring
Church. In 1232 the synagogue was given to the
Friars of St. Anthony, and became afterwards St.
Anthony's Hospital, on the site of the present City
Bank. In 1262 another synagogue was defaced and
partly destroyed; and ten years later the synagogue
at the north-east corner of Old Jewry was given to
the newly founded order of Sackcloth Friars (Fratres
de Saccâ), because the howling (*ululatio*) of the Jews
at prayer disturbed the worthy friars. The building
must have been a fine one, as it subsequently became
the residence of two Lord Mayors of the fifteenth
century. It ultimately subsided into a tavern, the
memory of which is still preserved by Windmill passage. (Seymour, "London," p. 556.)

But, reverting to our synagogue facing St. Lawrence
Church in no friendly fashion, how can we explain
that it is not mentioned as such in the list of buildings escheated to the king. At Lincoln, Norwich,
Canterbury, Nottingham, and Northampton, we find
a "schola" mentioned among the tenements left vacant
by the Jews, and the "schola" was a synagogue, and is
strangely similar to the familiar word "shool" for synagogue, still in common use among English Jews. But
there is not even a "schola" mentioned in the London
Jewry. How is this? The explanation is simple:
Synagogues had been forbidden by Bishop Peckham in
1283 (see Mr. Martin's edition of his Letters, vol. iii.
p. xiv.) to be opened or used publicly anywhere in his
diocese. Yet the question remains whether the synagogue remained in the possession of the London Jews
down to the Expulsion, seven years after Peckham had
issued his decree. We should have supposed that a

synagogue would be communal property.   But that was
not necessarily so, as we find mention of a synagogue in
St. Mary Colechurch, held by Abraham fil. Rabbi, about
the beginning of the thirteenth century, and a synagogue in Catte Street, probably the very one we are
discussing, belonged to Aaron fil. Vives in 1281.   If,
then, we are to find any trace of the synagogue, it
could only appear in the ownership of a private person,
and without any name of synagogue or "schola," as
that would be against Peckham's decree.   Now, the
average rental of the Jews' houses is about £3 per
annum, equal, probably, to about £120 a year nowadays; but one of them has the practically enormous
rental of £12, 17s., equal to about £500 a year; and
this house is in Catte Street, and was in the possession
of Auntlera, the widow of Vives fil. Mossei of Ironmonger Lane.   She was probably the mother of Aaron,
the son of Vives, who had settled the property on his
mother, and we are thus enabled, I think, to identify
both the synagogue and the owner of it at the time of
the Expulsion.   At present the site of Bakewell Hall
is occupied by Gresham College, which has even to the
present day connection with English Jews, for it is the
headquarters of one who in old days would have been
called Philippus fil. Magni, Judæus, but is now known
to us all as Sir Philip Magnus.

These details will perhaps be sufficient to convince
you that, in allocating the different plots to various
owners, different lines of reasoning have to be adopted.
In rebuilding the Old Jewry I have had ·to collect my
bricks from all possible quarters, and it is possible that
in some cases I have merely been "jerrymandering,"
and the whole structure may come down over my head
under the critical assaults of antiquarians better versed
than I in the minutiæ of London topography.   I can

only say that I have had some reason in every case for fixing upon any particular plot as being inhabited. And even in the three or four cases where some indication of locality has been given without my being able to fix it definitely, I have had reasons for not fixing. Thus Benedict Mayre had a tenement in Catte Street, and there is a tempting location just opposite St. Lawrence which would fit the case well, but that I happen to know that it was inhabited by Michael the Arblaster in 1290. So we must leave Ben. Mayre and two or three others without a home for the present. The plot next to it (No. 12) has some historic interest from its connection with John Wyclif, the great Reformer, who, as Master of Balliol, had possession of it, but was attacked in the Law Courts for wrongful possession. In the pleadings it came out that the house had been built by Thippe, the widow of Isaac of Southwark, one of the most important financiers of the time, by whose means the original St. Thomas' Hospital was built.

I spoke just now of rebuilding Old Jewry, but that is just what I have *not* been doing, as must have occurred to any of you who is in the slightest degree acquainted with the ordinary ideas about early London topography. Jewish houses are conspicuous by their absence in the street which is now called Old Jewry, and is generally supposed to have been the early home of the London *Ghetto*. It has come to me as the greatest surprise of my researches to find not a single house that can be definitely located in Old Jewry, and belonging to a Jew in 1290, when they left. A little reflection and research, however, has enlightened me on the subject. Jews lived no longer in the Old Jewry in 1290 because their lands and houses there had been, under one pretext or another, taken away from them during the preceding century. Thus, at the south-west of Old Jewry was the house where Thomas Beket was born, and, after he was canonised, his family established a monastery of St. Thomas of Acon on the ground now covered by Mercers' Hall and Chapel. In doing this, two Jews were displaced—one named Moses of Canterbury, who had to make way for Thomas of Canterbury.[1] What with this monastery, St. Mary Colechurch near it, St. Olave's in the centre, with St. Martin Pomary at the back, and the Penitentiary Friars at the north-east corner, the space of the Old Jewry was crowded out with churches. The Church, indeed, seems to have been specially careful in providing the Old Jewry with spiritual weapons against the unbeliever. There was once a synagogue in St. Mary Colechurch, in Ironmonger Lane. This had become the property of the Earl of Gloucester, after having been that of Abraham f. Muriel, and previously belonging to Abraham f. Rabbi.[2] The corner house of Ironmonger Lane was purchased by the Earl of Lancaster as early as Richard I. (*Notes and Queries*, Sixth Series, vi. p. 138) from a Jew. These two houses were convenient to these great nobles because of their proximity to the tilting ground, where all the jousts were held. At the opposite corner of Old Jewry a house at the corner of Lothbury, belonging to Isaac of Norwich, was granted by John, in 1214, to the Earl of Derby.[3] It is clear from these instances that the houses of the Jews were of exceptional grandeur, and they have always had the credit of being the first to build houses entirely of stone, nearly the earliest instance of such houses used for domestic purposes still extant being the Jews' house at Lincoln.[4]

---

[1] Loftie, i. p. 114.
[2] Brit. Mus. Harl. Ch. 43, A. 56.
[3] Maitland's "London," p. 438b.
[4] H. Turner's "Domestic Architecture," vol. i.

The characteristic feature of this is the rich tracery of
the window, which is of two lights with shaft between,
the fireplace on the first floor, with a corbelled chimney
running up the side of the room nearest the street.
The dwelling-room would thus seem to have been on
the first floor, and at Moyses' Hall, Edmondsbury, there
is no window at all on the ground floor.[1] This was
possibly for security.

Though the houses were grand, the inmates had
little certainty of retaining them in their families.
Besides the instances I have already given, there are
several others where Jews' houses were given by the
king to others.   Thus, one Bonevie Miltrun, in 1227,
had several houses and much land in no less than three
parishes, almost all the land now surrounding the Guildhall on the south belonging to him.   Yet it was all given
away at his death to clients of the king, except one house
in Bassishaw, given to Joce, the priest and bishop.[2]
When Joce died, in 1252, he left no less than nine
houses, four in the parish of Bassishaw, three in that
of St. Olave's, and two in Coleman Street.   These came
into the possession chiefly of his daughter Henna, only
one house in Bassishaw falling to his son Isaac.   An
inquisition was made into his property by a mixed jury
of Jews and Christians, and the record of their verdict
is still extant in the Record Office.   (Inq. p. m., 36
Hen. III., No. 49.)   From this we can gather something of the selling price of property.   Thus Isaac's
house had a rental of £2, and the Christian jury ad-
judged its value at £40, taking twenty years as the
selling price.   The Jews, on the other hand, considered
it worth £53, 13s. 4d .,or nearly seven years longer.
This discrepancy occurs throughout the document, for

[1] H. Turner's "Domestic Architecture," vol. i.
[2] Stow, p. 105.

what reason I am unable to conjecture. There is another inquisition of a similar kind, consequent on the death of Jacob Crispin, in 1240, who leaves four houses in Wood Street to his sons Isaac and Mosse, and three in Ironmonger Lane to his son-in-law, Abraham Cokeman. He was probably an ancestor of the Moses Crispin who held a house in Milk Street (No. 7 in our plan) at the time of the Expulsion. In these and similar cases the houses once belonging to the Jews had evidently gone out of their hands by the time of the Expulsion, and a third inquisition throws light on the reason. On the death of Cress, the son of Moses, in 1270, an inquisition was held on his property, and it was decided that the king had no right to his chattels or lands, as he had never transgressed the laws, but had always acted as a good Jew.[1] It follows from this that if any offence could be proved against a Jew, his property escheated to the king on his death, and thus a premium was put upon indicting a Jew for any crime. It was the direct interest of the king's officials to obtain any sort of conviction against a Jew, as this would cause him to forfeit his property at his death. It was, doubtless, by some such means as these that the Jews were gradually ousted out of Old Jewry. Indeed, there are long lists in the Record Office of Jews whose property had thus escheated to the king.

And this leads me to discuss for a moment the tenure by which Jews could hold land. We here see them in possession of land in the most valuable part of the City, and yet it is generally asserted that Jews could not hold land. A note of Madox, the historian of the Exchequer, which I found in his MS. collections at the British Museum,[2] will throw some light to the initiated, though it is couched in language not easily compre-

---

[1] Tovey, p. 127.   [2] Add. MSS. 4542.

hended of the vulgar: "When Jews were seised of lands," he says, "they were not seised of them in the same manner as the king's subjects or homagers were; the Jews did no homage for theirs *pro homagio et servitiis*, for a Jew was incapable of being a homager. He was, therefore, only seised of it as a Gaige gaiged to him in simple seisin at king's will. They were king's villeins or serfs." That is, I take it, that if a man owed a Jew money, he could gaige or pledge his land to him till he repaid it, during which time the Jew held the land at the king's pleasure. And this is so far confirmed, that, though I have found many commissions for an assize of novel disseisin between Jew and Christian, I have never found one of *mort d'ancestor* between Jew and Jew, which would imply that a Jew succeeded by right to his parents' land, whereas the other would merely imply that he succeeded to the debt owed his father, for which the land was a pledge. A Jew could not be a homager, for paying homage was a distinctly religious ceremonial, in which both suzerain and vassal could join, and often implied spiritual benefices. Nor could any one hold as a homager to a Jew, for the same reason. One of the most striking incidents in the history of the London Jewry was when the Jews petitioned, in 1270, for liberty to have the custody of Christian heirs and the advowson of Christian livings. The Franciscans stormed and raved against such a proposal, and one of them "manfully faced the Council," as the chronicle puts it, and managed to prevent Jews succeeding to the spiritual rights of land ownership, which were then of such importance.[1]

We can now understand how the Jews gradually lost hold of their possessions in the Old Jewry, which

[1] *De Antiquis Legibus,* p. 234, seq.

they held simply at the pleasure of the king. And I would venture the suggestion that the place was known as the Old Jewry even before the Expulsion, for in the Latin document giving the limits of the parish of St. Stephen's, to which I have before referred, there is a reference to "veteri Judaismo." This at once does away with the usual assertion of the historians of London that the Old Jewry was so named about 1660, to contrast it with the New Jewry, near Aldgate, where the Jews settled on their readmission.[1] The name Jewry may perhaps legitimately detain us a moment. It is a French collective term, and reminds us that the London "Jewry" is a daughter of the Rouen "Juifverie." It is sometimes spelt Giwerie, Latinised variously as "Judearia" and "Judaismus," whence we find a Cambridge parish "in the Judeism," and a purely English collective is sometimes used, "Juhede." It does not necessarily imply a place at all, but merely a community of persons who were all responsible for each, as the Jews actually were under old English law. There is yet another compound of Jew still preserved in a London street, viz., Jewin Street, near Cripplegate. This was formerly known as Jewyn Garden, and was the burial-place of the London Jewry, and indeed up to 1177 of all the Jews of England. In the document giving the list of the Jews' houses escheated at the Expulsion, which forms the basis of our work, it is termed Lyrestowe, a term I cannot explain. The word "Jewin" is really an old plural,[2] similar to that in "oxen," "children," "brethren," and "rosen," still used in country places for "roses." Many of the gravestones of Jewin Garden

---

[1] Knight's "London," vi., "Old Jewry."
[2] An over-ingenious friend suggests that it is an old dative plural = *Jewina*. He forgets that Middle English did not have this inflexion.

were taken in 1215 by the barons to repair Ludgate with, and one of them was found in Stow's time with the inscription, מצב[ת] ר׳ משה בן הרב ר׳ יצחק ח׳ ו׳.[1]

There is said to be yet another Jewry in London previous to the Expulsion. In 1238 we read of a Jew, Joce, and his wife, Henne, being slain in the Jewry of the Tower; and in 1279 a writ was issued to the Lord Mayor to arrest certain apostates from the Catholic Faith who turned out to be "in Judeism," and so under the jurisdiction of the Constable of the Tower. It is not quite clear whether these were converts to Judaism, though we have several instances mentioned in the records. But we seem here to have evidences of a Jewry somewhere near the Tower—tradition says, in St. Catherine's, to the east of the Tower.[2] Some historians of London have conjured out of this fact the idea of a double Jewish colony in London, one brought over from Normandy, and residing near the Tower; the other already here, in Anglo-Saxon times, residing near the Cheape. But there is absolutely no evidence of Jews in England before the Conquest, except in the eyes of crotchet-mongers; and the presence of an asylum for Jews near the Tower is sufficiently explained by their frequent need of protection. The chief resort of the Jews of London in olden times was where they were most wanted, near the great market of the City, West Cheape. You will observe that I have placed no Jews' or other houses between Ironmonger Lane and Milk Street. That was because there were no houses there,

---

[1] Stow, p. 15. There can be little doubt that this was the tombstone of R. Moses b. Isaac, the author of the *Sepher Hassoham*, the most considerable literary production of English Jews before the Expulsion. He must, therefore, have died before 1215.

[2] Knight's "London," vi. ("Old Jewry"). Dr. Gross doubts any such Jewry, regarding the above phrases as having regard to jurisdiction of the Constable of the Tower.

M

but only booths or sheds, just like a Continental market.
There was the Cheape, or selling-place (*cf.* the German
Kauf and our "cheapen"), where the various merchants
exposed their wares, after which some of the streets of
the neighbourhood are called Milk Street, Wood Street,
Bread Street, Ironmonger Lane, and the like. We
know that this remained an open place at least up to
1274. One of the most brilliant chapters of Mr.
Loftie's "History of London" deals with an interesting
struggle between the Corporation and the traders as
to their right to keep their booths fixed. "Cheapside"
is usually interpreted to mean "the side of the Cheap;"
but there is another suggestion that the word means
the "shid or shed of Cheap," the grand stand that
used to be erected to see the jousts that were performed
in the Tilting Ground, which filled the southern part
of Cheap.

Here, in the centre of London's busiest life, the
Jews settled for a time in lordly houses and in general
luxury, varied only by occasional massacres. They
probably did not do so till close upon the end of the
twelfth century; for in 1135 the street of the Jews was
in Haco's Ward—for wards were then named after their
aldermen, a remnant of which practice still remains in
the wards of Farringdon and Basinghall.[1] The ward
of Haco seems to have been in Broad Street, and the
westward movement of the Jewry may be said to have
continued ever since, with an interruption of some four
centuries, till at present the "Jewries" are as far west
as South Kensington.

The position of the Jewry near the chief market
seems so natural as scarcely to need explanation, and
almost all the English Jewries are so situated. In
York, it was near the Guildhall, as in London, for the

[1] Loftie, "London" ("Historic Towns"), p. 98.

mayor was the natural protector in both cases.   In
Lincoln, the synagogue adjoined the market ; at Oxford,
the Jewry was just in the centre of the town at Carfax
(or *Quatre voies*) ; at Cambridge, at first near the
castle, but afterwards near the market ; and the same
holds good of Warwick, Gloucester, and Winchester ;
and if at Bristol and Southampton the Jewries were by
the chief quays, it was for the same reason.   The only
exceptions to the rule of their being near the market
are at Canterbury and Leicester.

As we are now comparing the various Jewries, we
may attempt some estimate of their comparative importance.   We can do this at two dates, about 100
years apart from one another.   The names of those who
paid towards the ransom of Richard I. in 1195, when
there are 31 London Jews among 360—a twelfth—and
the houses escheated to the king at the expulsion in
1290, when there are 23 London houses out of 138—
a seventh.   In wealth these were out of all proportion.
In 1250 they paid nearly a third of a tallage of £1000
imposed on all the Jews in England.   Making the
best estimate I can, I should reckon that in 1290 the
London Jews were about one-eighth of the Jews
scattered among some 120 towns and villages of the
country.   The exact number of Jews expelled is given
at 15,060, a number on which some reliance can be
placed, as exact registers of Jews' names had to be
kept for tallage purposes, especially since 1274, when
a charge of 3d. per head per annum was charged on
every Jew over twelve.   This would make the London
Jews number some 2000, which is exactly the number
mentioned by a Jewish historian, Salomon ibn Vergas.[1]
It is, however, impossible to believe that these were
lodged in some twenty-five houses, eighty in a house,

[1] *Shevet Jehuda*, ed. Wiener, § 19.   Cf. *Emek Habacha*, p. 41.

though thirty is by no means an unusual proportion in foreign *Ghetii*. We must, therefore, conclude that large numbers of the Jews lived in hired houses. On the other hand, the plots of ground in one place would easily hold more than one house, and in one or two instances I have found a reference to three houses joined into one.[1] Again, our list may not exhaust the number of houses held by Jews, for the simple reason that the king did not give them all away, but may have kept some for himself. Thus there is little doubt that the plot of land between Old Jewry and Ironmonger Lane, in Gresham Street, was inhabited by Jews, and that the king built his Wardrobe on the site of their houses, where it remained till the time of Henry VI. This is expressly mentioned by Stow (p. 106). Our plan cannot, therefore, claim to give all the houses held or inhabited by Jews at the time of the Expulsion.

We have perhaps lingered long enough over the mere outside of the London Jewry, and may now venture to say something as to its inhabitants and their varied fortunes during their stay in England. We can put this in the shortest, though not, perhaps, the most elegant form, in the shape of annals.

1070. Came from Rouen at the invitation of the Conqueror. They can, therefore, boast they came over with the Conqueror.

1130. We first hear of the London Jews on occasion of their being fined £2000, an enormous sum = £80,000, for killing a sick man. Probably some charge of magic is involved in the brief record.

1136. Great fire of London did not spare the Jews' quarter.

1158. A visit from Abraham ibn Ezra, the celebrated Spanish Jewish commentator, poet, philosopher, and traveller. He composed here his Epistle on the Sabbath, and a philosophical work, *Yesod Moreh*.

---

[1] *E.g.*, in the inquisition into the property of Joce the priest, already referred to.

1168. A fine of 5000 marks was imposed on them.

1177. The London Jews were freed from the necessity of keeping a single graveyard for all the Jews of England, who were allowed to have ground wherever they had license to settle. This was a very important concession from a feudal stand-point, because a graveyard must be in absolute possession.

1187. They were fined a quarter of their chattels.

1188. Tallage of 60,000 marks, or £40,000. In estimating the value of these sums we should probably have to multiply by 50, and, at any rate, we should remember that the king's income was only £65,000.

1189. The massacre at Richard's coronation, September 3rd, due probably to the rise of the crusading spirit in England.

1195. London Jews contributed £478, 7s. 4d. out of 5000 marks contributed to the king's ransom by the Jews of England. The "Bishops" of the London Jews were Deulesaut, Vives, Abraham.

1204. An attack was made on them by citizens of London, which called forth a sharp rebuke of John, addressed to the mayor.

1210. John imprisoned all the Jews of England, and imposed a tallage of 60,000 marks. Many fled the kingdom.

1211. Joseph b. Baruch visited England, and induced many English Jews to go on a pilgrimage to the Holy Land. While he was in England he commissioned Jehuda b. Kardinal to make a new translation of Jehuda Halévi's *Kusari*.

1215. The barons in revolt against John plundered the London Jewry, and repaired Ludgate with their gravestones.

1218. All Jews ordered to wear a badge on the upper part of their garments. Two tablets of the Law in England.

1220. "Bishops" of Jews—Josce, Isaac, Benedictus.

1226. Tallage of 4000 marks.

1230. Tallage of 6000 marks.

1232. Synagogue given to St. Anthony's Hospital (now City Bank).

1233. Domus Conversorum, for converted Jews, was founded in New Street (now Chancery Lane) on ground belonging to Jews. The site is now occupied by the Rolls Court, which only recently was presided over by an unconverted Jew, Sir George Jessell. The number of converts in residence was never more than thirteen. They seemed to have kept up their old practices, as we find one Nicholas, a convert, pardoned for recurring to his usurious practices in 1275.

1236. Seven Jews of Norwich were brought up to London, and hanged there for circumcising a young lad.

1237. Elyas elected "Episcopus" in place of Aaron of York.

1240. A Jewish parliament was summoned of six of the chief Jews of each Jewry to consult with the king, chiefly on taxation and tallage. Members of Parliament for London—Benedictus Crispin, Jacobus Crispin, Aaron f. Abraham, Aaron le Blund, Elias le Evesk, Leo Blund; Elias Blund was substituted for Eenedictus Crispin.

1241. As a result, a tallage of 20,000 marks was imposed.

1244. A child was found murdered, with marks on his thighs, arms, and breasts, which a Jewish convert declared to be Hebrew letters. The body was buried with much pomp in St. Paul's, and the Jews were mulcted of 60,000 marks (£40,000) on this pretext.

1249. Another tallage of 10,000 marks.

1255. Jews sold to Richard of Cornwall for £5000.

1256. Two hundred and two Jews of Lincoln were lodged in the Tower for being concerned in the murder of Hugh of Lincoln. Eighteen were executed; the rest were saved, it is said, by the intercession of the Franciscans, who otherwise proved the worst enemies of the Jews.

1257. Bishops of London Jews—Elyas, Jacobus, Solomon. Elyas deposed.

1259. London Jews pay Henry III. 500 marks for his passage to France.

1262. A riot against them; 700 killed, and the synagogue defaced.

1263. The Jewry burned, May 10th, by the party of Simon de Montfort.

1264. A tallage of 60,000 marks demanded from them.

1265. King resumes the Jewry recently given to his son.

1267. The council of Vienna orders the horned cap to be worn.

1267-71. Granted freedom from tallage for £1000 per annum.

1269. Jews defended the Tower against Earl of Gloucester and the Disinherited.

1271. Synagogue at north-east of Old Jewry given to Friars "de Saccâ."

1275. Statute against usury passed. Richard of Reading, a monk, converted to Judaism.

1277. Tallage of 25,000 marks. Manser fil. Aaron sues for an inquiry into some tools for clipping found on the roof of his house (No. 14 in our plan).

1278. Six hundred and eighty imprisoned in the Tower, and 267 hanged for clipping, and their houses and chattels escheated to the king.

1279. A boy being found murdered at Northampton, some Jews of that town brought up to London, dragged at horses' tails, and hanged. Three Jews of London—Abraham de Derkinge, Moses de Cantuar, and another—pursue a man down Broad and Catte Streets, and slay him near St. Lawrence's Church.[1]

1283. Synagogues closed by order of Peckham, Bishop of London.

1287. Fined 12,000 lbs. silver. All Jews imprisoned.

1290. Banished the nation by October 9th.

Such are the outward events that constitute the annals of the London Jewry. Plundered and, let us confess, plundering, their lives were buffeted between the passions of the populace and the avarice of the king. For the reasons of this anomalous state of things I may refer you to the introduction to the Catalogue of our Exhibition, with the views of which I fully agree. While the Jews remained faithful to their creed, and the Church refused citizenship to one of another creed, the mediæval status of the Jew could not fail to be anomalous and degrading. Taxation and massacre sum up the outward history.

As regards their social life we know little, since our knowledge depends on legal documents, which rarely afford much insight of this kind. Of their outward appearance, the badge and horned cap were not peculiar to England, but were prescripts of the Church common to all Christendom. Another law of the Church was that Jews should not eat meat in Lent or on Fridays.[2] An inquiry was once ordered by the Lord Mayor into the Jewish way of slaughtering meat, and it was ordered that no Christian should buy meat declared

---

[1] Riley "Memorials," p. 15.
[2] "Richard of Hovedene," p. 124.

unfit by the Jewish butchers who had previously sold
it to the Christians.[1]   The synagogues were used not
only for religious purposes, as writs were issued order-
ing that proclamations should be made in the Jews'
synagogues for two or three Sabbaths, if any Jew or
Jewess had a claim against so-and-so, they might make
it before the Justiciars.   Jews were not so down-
trodden as to lose all spirit.   We find an instance of
a duel fought by a Jew.[2]   I may add that no Jew
could come to London until it was ascertained that he
could contribute to the tallage.   They were, therefore,
not troubled with the destitute alien problem.

From Jewish sources we learn very little.   It is
probable that Jews when "called up" to read the Law
went up uncovered, as their co-religionists in France
did at the time.[3]   On 20th Sivan a fast was held by
the Jews of France, England, and the Rhine, in memory
of the martyrs of Blois in 1171.[4]   Jews came to this
country *viâ* Dieppe, and the vogage took one day.[5]
Education in Hebrew seems to be very general, judging by the many writers of it we meet in the *Shetaroth*.
What other means of culture they possessed we do not
know, but there is evidence that they shared in most
of the luxuries of the time.

As regards Hebrew literature in the London Jewry,
I have discovered, I fancy, that this was almost
entirely confined to a single family, who are in many
ways so interesting, that I must ask you to take the
trouble to follow their genealogy on the following
page.

Before I enter into any details, I must interpose a

---

[1] Riley, "Chron.," p. 177.
[2] Goldschmidt, *Gesch.*, p. 74.
[3] Zunc, Z. G.
[4] Id., *Ritus*, p. 127.
[5] Semag, § 25.

THE HAGIN FAMILY.

[For collaterals and early stages of the family, see *Jews of Angevin England*, p. 414.]

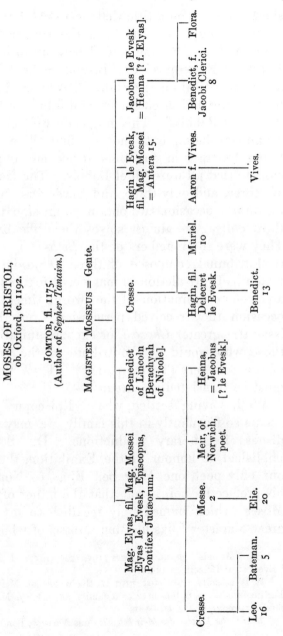

MOSES OF BRISTOL,
ob. Oxford, c. 1192.

JOMTOB, fl. 1175.
(Author of *Sepher Tanaim*.)

MAGISTER MOSSEUS = Gente.

Mag. Elyas, fil. Mag. Mossei
Elyas le Evesk, Episcopus,
Pontifex Judæorum.

Benedict
of Lincoln
[Berachyah
of Nicole].

Cresse.

Hagin le Evesk,
fil. Mag. Mossei
= Antera 15.

Jacobus le Evesk
= Henna [? f. Elyas].

Mosse.
2

Henna,
= Jacobus
[? le Evesk].

Hagin, fil.
Delecret
le Evesk.

Muriel.
10

Aaron f. Vives.

Benedict, f.
Jacobi Clerici.
8

Flora.

Cresse.

Meir, of
Norwich,
poet.

Benedict.
13

Vives.

Leo.
16

Bateman.
5

Elie.
20

short excursus on a title that occurs very frequently in the genealogy, and has been the subject of dispute between Coke, Prynne, and Tovey, as to whether "le Evesk," "Episcopus," or "Bishop of the Jews," meant an ecclesiastical office or not. Tovey decides in favour of its ecclesiastical character, and dubs those who hold it "Chief Rabbis." This might do well enough for a rough translation, but when we find three "Episcopi" living together at one time, it becomes impossible to assume that all were Chief Rabbis. The fact that they are three, and only three, and never less than three— for on one occasion two obtain permission to choose a third colleague—almost solves the difficulty by itself.[1] They were the members of the *Beth-Din*, or ecclesiastical tribunal composed of three *Dayanim* or judges, which had jurisdiction in many civil matters, and made a curious combination of the two at times, as on one occasion they received permission from the king to issue the greater *Cherem*, or excommunication against those who would not contribute to the maintenance of the cemetery (Tovey, p. 127). Thus "Episcopus" must be translated as *Dayan*.[2]

Well, having settled what "Episcopus" is, which occurs so frequently in this family, we may proceed to discuss its literary productions. Dr. Berliner has published, in honour of the Exhibition, the poems of our only poet, one Meir ben Elias, of Norwich.[3] In his preface he points out that the father of Elias was Moses, which immediately recalled to my mind the great Magister Elias fil. Mag. Mosse, of whom we shall

[1] See "Annals," *supra*, in years 1195, 1220, 1257. I find also three "Evesks" at Lincoln in 1240.

[2] It is actually translated חוזה in the poems of Meir of Norwich, Berliner's edit., p. 6, but here as a family name. *Cf.* M. Paris, *Cognomine Episcopus*, p. 824, ed. Wats.

[3] *Hebraische Poesien des Meir ben Elia aus Norwich,* Lond. 1887.

hear more presently. Elias himself wrote responses, and his grandfather, Yomtob, was the author of a legal treatise, now lost, with the title *Sepher Tanaim.* Among the Tosaphists occurs the name of Berachyah of Nicole, who is identical with the Magister Benedictus fil. Mag. Mossei known in the annals of the Lincoln Jewry.[1]

There is a Jacob of London, who translated the *Hagada* into the vernacular for the sake of women and children.[2] I am much mistaken if this is not Jacob le Evesk. Dr. Neubauer has attributed to Hagin le Evesk a Hebrew translation of the *Image du Monde* on very insufficient grounds, as it seems to me;[3] but if true, it only adds one more to the literary members of this family. There remains only one other Anglo-Jewish author of this period, Moses of London, whose "Book of the Onyx," a grammatical treatise of some merit, is the most important product of Anglo-Jewish literature before 1290. One is greatly tempted to identify him with the Moses whose descendants we see here, but unfortunately this is impossible, as the author of the *Sepher Hassoham* quotes that very Moses (p. 37, edit. Collins). But with this exception, important as it is, all the literary products of the London Jewry were produced by this family, which I venture to name, as their discoverer, the Hagin family.

They were not alone authors, but good business men, and their transactions figure very largely in the records. What we are more concerned with at present

[1] On him and his relations, see Mr. M. D. Davis' paper on "The Jews of Lincoln," which would be invaluable but for its being unprovided with authorities. I have omitted Benedict's descendants from the above genealogy, as they all resided at Lincoln. See succeeding Essay.

[2] Zunz, *Ritus,* p. 63.

[3] "Society Heb. Lit. Miscell.," ii. p. 159. The MS. actually gives the name of the translator David b. Moses.

is the traces they have left on the London Jewry. No
less than seven of them held property in the Jewry
at the time of the Expulsion. Leo and Bateman, the
sons of Cresse; Muriel filia Deulecresse; Auntlera,
the widow of Vives or Hagin—for Vives is the French
for Haim, "life," which again is Anglicised as Hagin
—Benedict fil. Hagin and Benedict fil. Jacobi Clerici ;
and last, not least, Elyas le Evesk himself. I have
attached the number of their holdings in my plan to
their names in the genealogy. But the Hagin family
have left much more permanent traces on the London
Jewry than in my plan, unless I am much mistaken.
The whole land between Wood and Milk Streets was
once Cok Aggyn's,[1] who probably got it from his uncle,
Hagin fil. Cresse. Both were *Dayanim*, and had much
of the business of the Jewry to supervise. Their house
at the corner of Wood Street (No. 2) would be frequently
resorted to and well known, and the fact that a Jew of
the name of Hagin was living there would not escape
the notice of even Christian neighbours. Now, the
lane opposite this house is called Huggin Lane to this
day, and the house itself was held by a cousin of
Hagin at the Expulsion. I do not think it too bold an
assertion that this Huggin Lane preserves traces of the
old London Jewry and one of its chief inhabitants.[2]

We must not leave this Hagin family without some

[1] Record Office, "Tower Misc. Rolls," No. 144.
[2] Stow declares, *more suo*, that Huggin Lane was so called after "Hugh
in the lane," *i.e.*, the lane was named after the man, and the man after the
lane. His derivation is, however, of some confirmatory value, as showing
a tradition that the lane was named after some person, though Stow had
no knowledge of Hagin le Eveske or his residence in the vicinity.
Another suggestion has been made, that "Huggin Lane" was named after
hogs. But there are two Huggin Lanes, and it is more probable that they
were named after two Hagins (a common name among Christians as well
as Jews) than that there were two quarters where hogs were sold. Besides,
the shambles and meat market were then situated near Newgate.

account of its chief ornament, Elyas le Evesk, who was elected *Dayan* in 1237, and for nearly forty years was one of the most striking figures on the London Jewry. He was, of course, one of the M.P.'s for London at the Jewish Parliament in 1240. In 1249 he was allowed to have Abraham fil. Aaron as his associate, and three years after he had to elect a third on the *Beth Din*. He early obtained riches, and naturally attracted the notice of the king, who squeezed out of him £10,000, equal to the tallage of all the Jews of England, as well as £100 a year for four years. We can quite understand the energy with which he spoke in 1253, when the king's commissioners tried to get blood out of a stone. I tell the incident in Prynne's quaint translation of Matthew Paris' vigorous description. It is probable enough that the historian was present at the scene :—

"Elyas, therefore, of London, High Priest to the Jews, taking counsel with his companions, answered for them all : ' O noble Lords, we see undoubtedly that our Lord the King purposeth to destroy us from under Heaven. We intreat, for God's sake, that he would give us licence and safe conduct of departing out of his Kingdom, that we may seek and find a mansion in some other place under some Prince who bears some bowels of mercy and some stability of truth and faithfulness. And we will depart, never to return again, leaving here our household stuff and houses behind us. How can he love or spare us, miserable Jews, who destroys his own natural English? He hath people, yea his own merchants, I say not usurers, who by usurious contracts heap up infinite heaps of money. Let the King rely upon them and gape after their emoluments. Verily they have supplanted us and impoverished us. Which the King, however, dissembles to know, exacting from us those things we cannot give him, even though he would put out our eyes or cut our throats when he had first pulled off our skins.' And speaking thus, with sighs and tears hindering his speech, he held his peace, falling almost into an extasy, ready to die. Which when it came to the knowledge of the Magistrates, they permitted them not to depart out of the realm, saying, 'Whither will ye flee, O wretches? Behold, the King of France hateth and persecuteth you, and hath condemned you to perpetual exile. Shunning Charybdis, you desire to be drowned in Scylla.' "

The same year we find a Hebrew response from him in a Rabbinical treatise of Mordecai ben Hillel. Two years afterwards he was cast in prison as a surety for the tallage of the Jews. His prosperity had gone, and in 1257 he was deposed from his office, for what reason we know not. Then comes a tragic incident in his career. In 1259 Elias cognomine Episcopus was "new born in the Spirit," Matthew Paris says, *i.e.*, he was converted, and it was reported that he had confessed strange doings he had done when ecclesiastical chief of the Jews—poisons he had prepared for English nobles, and so on. Fancy what a commotion it must have caused in the London Jewry, this tergiversation of him who had once been their leader. He seems, however, to have recanted his errors, and was again treated as a Jew, for in 1266 the king grants him £50 compensation for losses he had incurred owing to the Barons' War. We hear of him again in 1274 and 1275 as giving or owing money to the king; and in 1277 he was one of the few Jews to whom were granted the privilege of becoming merchants, without becoming members of the Merchants' Guild. And at the Expulsion we find him living still, but gloomily apart, in

Sporier Street near the Tower, the most conspicuous figure in the London Jewry, 1290.[1]

What became of him and his companion-exiles one would like to know. I can only trace two or three of them. In a tallage-roll of the Paris Jewry for 1294 (*Révue des études juives*, No. 1), there are four persons mentioned with the addition of "lenglishe" or "lenglois":—Bonami lenglois, Jovin lenglois, Mosse lenglois et Rose sa femme, and Rose lenglishe. Of these Jovin was in all probability Jorvin Sackerel, the tenant at the corner of Colman Street, and Rose may have been either one of our two Roses at either end of Milk Street.

I have now exhausted all that the time at my disposal will allow me to say about the London Jewry of 1290, its ground plan, its inhabitants, their history and adventures, and subsequent fate.

---

[1] Most of these items about Elyas are given by Prynne, *Demurrer*, Part ii., under the several years. Dr. Gross has pointed out to me evidence of the death of one Elyas le Eveske in 1271, but he was resident at Hereford.

LITTLE ST. HUGH OF LINCOLN [1]

RESEARCHES IN HISTORY, ARCHÆOLOGY, AND LEGEND

> "O yonge Hugh of Lincoln, sleyn also
> With cursed Iewes, as it is notable,
> For it nis but a litel whyle ago ;
> Pray eek for vs, we sinful folk vnstable
> That of His mercy God so merciable
> On vs His grete mercy multiplye,
> For reuerence of His mooder Marye.
> Amen."

THUS sings and prays Chaucer at the end of his "Prioresse's Tale," which is supposed to deal with the *cause célèbre* of Hugh of Lincoln. This is not the fact, since he locates his tale "in Asie in the gret citee." But the invocation to the little Hugh at the end, marked as it is with signs of the most earnest and naïve piety, is even more significant of the general and thorough-going belief in the martyrdom of the little lad of Lincoln. And indeed we know from the widespread and popular ballads devoted to this subject that the case must have made a profound sensation in England, and remained as a standing example in the folk-mind of Jewish cruelty and fanaticism. Such a case as this, therefore, well deserves the attention of the Jewish Historical Society of England. We may be tolerably confident

---

[1] The boy martyr is called little St. Hugh to distinguish him from great St. Hugh of Lincoln, the bishop of that see, who died in 1200, and was curiously enough a friend of the Jews (see Jacobs' "Jews of Angevin England," p. 207).

at the start of our inquiry that we shall not be so easily
convinced of any specific Jewish cruelty and fanaticism
in the case. On the other hand, as Englishmen, we
shall not be too ready to accuse the Englishmen of the
thirteenth century of any deliberate falsification of evidence, or malversation of justice. They were thinking
and acting under the prejudices of their time, and it
will be part of our inquiry to consider the rise of the
said prejudice. Mathematicians are accustomed to
speak of " pretty problems " requiring special ingenuity
or peculiarly elegant methods for their solution. The
history and legend of Hugh of Lincoln presents in this
sense to the historian and folk-lorist a specially " pretty
problem." It might indeed be easily made into an
object-lesson of the modern methods of research in
history, archæology, and legend.

I

Let us take the facts of the case first ; and here we
are especially fortunate in having them stated for us as
they presented themselves to the mind of the time by
Matthew Paris, the greatest historian of mediæval
England. We cannot start our inquiry better than by
giving in English the contents of the Monk Matthew's
by no means inelegant Latinity.[1]

OF THE BOY HUGH OF LINCOLN.

This year, about the feast of the apostles Peter and Paul [July 27],
the Jews of Lincoln stole a boy called Hugh, who was about eight years
old. After shutting him up in a secret chamber, where they fed him
on milk and other childish food, they sent to almost all the cities of
England in which there were Jews, and summoned some of their sect

---

[1] Matthew Paris, *Historia Major*, edit. Luard (Rolls Series), v. pp.
516–18, 522, 543 (?).

N

.from each city to be present at a sacrifice to take place at Lincoln, in contumely and insult of Jesus Christ. For, as they said, they had a boy concealed for the purpose of being crucified; so a great number of them assembled at Lincoln, and then they appointed a Jew of Lincoln judge, to take the place of Pilate, by whose sentence, and with the concurrence of all, the boy was subjected to various tortures. They scourged him till the blood flowed, they crowned him with thorns, mocked him, and spat upon him; each of them also pierced him with a knife, and they made him drink gall, and scoffed at him with blasphemous insults, and kept gnashing their teeth and calling him Jesus, the false prophet. And after tormenting him in divers ways they crucified him, and pierced him to the heart with a spear. When the boy was dead, they took the body down from the cross, and for some reason disembowelled it; it is said for the purpose of their magic arts. The boy's mother, when her son had been missing several days, sought for him diligently, and the neighbours told her that they had last seen him playing with some Jewish boys of his own age, and going into the house of a Jew. So the mother entered the house suddenly and saw the boy's body lying in a well; the bailiffs of the city were then cautiously summoned, the body was found and drawn up. It was a remarkable sight which then presented itself to the people; the mother's cries and lamentations provoked all the citizens assembled there to tears. There was present John of Lexington, a man of learning, wise and prudent, who said, "We have heard sometimes that Jews have dared to attempt such things in insult of our crucified Lord Jesus Christ;" and then addressing the Jew whose house the boy had entered whilst at play, and who, as being for that reason a greater object of suspicion, had been arrested, "Wretched man, dost thou not know that a speedy end awaits thee? All the gold in England would not suffice to ransom or save thee. Yet unworthy though thou art, I will tell thee how thou canst save thy life and limb from destruction. Both of these will I save thee if, without fear or falsehood, thou wilt expose unto me all that has been done in this matter." Then the Jew, whose name was Copin, thinking that he had found a way of escape, answered, "My lord John, if thou wilt repay my words with deeds, I will show wondrous things unto thee." Then when John zealously urged and encouraged him, the Jew continued: "What the Christians say is true. Almost every year the Jews crucify a boy in injury and insult to Jesus. But one is not found every year, for they do this privately and in remote and secret places. This boy, whom they call Hugh, our Jews crucified without mercy, and after he was dead, and they wished to hide his corpse, they could not bury or conceal it. (This they wished to do, as the body of an innocent boy was considered useless for augury, which was the reason for disembowelling it.) In the morning, when they thought it was hidden away, the earth vomited and cast it forth, and there it lay unburied on the ground to the horror of the Jews. At length they threw it into a well, but still they could not hide it, for the mother never wearied in her search, and finding the body, informed the bailiffs." The Jew was kept in chains, and the body given to the canons of Lincoln, who had asked for it, and who, after displaying it to an immense number of people, buried it honourably in the church of Lincoln, as if it had been that of a precious martyr. The king, when he heard what had happened, was angry with John for having promised life and limb to such a wicked being, which he had no right to do; for a blasphemer and murderer such as that man, deserved to die many times over. Then the guilty man said, "My death is imminent, nor can John give me any assistance. I will tell the truth to you all. Nearly all the Jews in England agreed to the death of this boy, and from nearly every English city where Jews live some were chosen to be present at this sacrifice as a Paschal offering." Then he was tied to a horse's tail and dragged to the gallows, where he was delivered body and soul to the cacodœmens of the air. The other Jews who shared in the guilt, to the number of ninety-one, were taken to London, and imprisoned there; and if any Christians pitied them, they were only dry tears which their rivals the Caursines shed.

OF A CERTAIN SCANDAL WHICH AROSE IN LONDON AGAINST THE FRANCISCANS ALTHOUGH THEY WERE INNOCENT.

At the same time certain Jews notorious for the strange death of a boy crucified by them at Lincoln, having been condemned to imprisonment and death on the oaths of twenty-five knights, seventy-one of them were being kept in the Tower of London, and were about to be hanged. But they sent secret messengers to the Franciscans, as the rivals of these latter affirm, that they might intercede for them and rescue them from death and imprisonment, though they deserved a most dishonourable death. And they indeed did rescue those Jews by their prayers and intercessions from the imprisonment and death which they merited, being induced thereto by their money, as all the world believed, if the world can be believed in such a case, or rather, as I prefer to believe, led by a spirit of piety; since as long as any one is on earth because he has free will he can be saved and there is hope for him, but for the devil and the manifestly damned one must not either hope or pray because there is no hope for them; for death and an unavoidable sentence has once for all irrevocably ensnared them. But the above scandal besmirched them although they were innocent. But the common people did not help them as before in their alms, but withheld their hand from them.

JEWS ARE SET FREE WHO WERE DETAINED IN THE TOWER OF LONDON.

The same year, on the Ides of May, ninety-one Jews were set free from the Tower of London who were kept there as criminals, bound hand and foot, for the crucifixion of St. Hugh, the boy of Lincoln. These Jews, I say, were guilty by the assertion of a Jew who had been hanged at Lincoln in the first instance.

In this account it will be seen that all turns on the evidence of Copin, Jew of Lincoln. It was his evidence that gave to the case the character of a ritual murder connived at by all the Jews of England. It is clear that his evidence was, in the first instance, extorted from him by the unveiled threats of John of Lexington. It was Sir John who first suggested that the little boy's body, found in the pit, had been murdered; for all the evidence we have before us the whole case might be one of accident. It was John of Lexington who started the idea that it was a case of mock crucifixion. It may be said at once, as a key to the whole history, that it was the confirmed and prejudiced belief of all England in the practice of mock crucifixion by the Jews that gave rise to the belief in the "martyrdom" of little St. Hugh. We must first trace this belief to its source before proceeding further. England, I regret to say, is the source and origin of the myth concerning the practice of ritual murder of young children by Jews in contempt and derision of crucifixion.[1]

The myth first arose in connection with the death or murder of the boy William of Norwich in 1144. It sprung fully armed from the vile imagination of an apostate Jew of Cambridge, named after his conversion Theobald.[2] He, for reasons which we are at present unable to penetrate, first suggested that Jews were in the habit of sacrificing little children to gratify their hatred of the Christian religion. He seems to have implicated the Jews of the whole world in the crime, since he suggested that lots were cast each year in Europe as to the place in which the next sacrifice should take place. Thus he asserted that the "martyrdom" of William at Norwich had been fixed upon at a council of Jews in Narbonne. Incalculable has been the mischief which Theobald's accursed lies have inflicted upon the Jews. They were published and obtained credence throughout Europe just at the time of the second crusade, when men's religious passions were aroused to fanatical fury, and Jews fell martyrs all along the track of the Crusaders. Ever since his time, whenever a little child has been missing about the Passover, near a Jewish quarter in Europe, it has been but a chance if the terrible suspicion of ritual murder has not again been raised.

---

[1] I speak here, of course, of the "blood accusation" in its modern form. There was no popular belief in it till after the case of William of Norwich. It is referred to as "fama communis" in 1236 (Strack, *Der Blutaberglaube*, p. 154). It is necessary to emphasise this, as the *Athenæum*, in reviewing an earlier form of this paper, referred to the murder of a child by some drunken Jews, mentioned by Socrates, the ecclesiastic historian, as the origin of the myth. But a myth must live in the minds of men, and there is no evidence of such a belief till after the case of William of Norwich.

[2] We are still awaiting the full account of the martyrdom of William of Norwich by Thomas of Monmouth. Short abstracts are given in Jacobs, l.c., pp. 256 58, and Jessopp, *The Nineteenth Century*, May 1893.

I have been surprised to find in conversation with Christian friends, who have not the slightest taint of Anti-Semitism, how general is the impression that there must be something at the bottom of all these charges, and perhaps for their sakes it may be desirable to point out how impossible it is for Jews as Jews to use human blood or human sacrifices in any way as a part of their religious rites. In the first place, contact with a corpse renders a Jew impure from that moment, and incapable of performing any religious rite whatever till he has been purified. For eating any blood or anything compounded with blood there is the stringent Biblical prohibition (Lev. xvii. 14) : " Ye shall eat the blood of no manner of flesh : for the life of all flesh is the blood thereof : whosoever eateth it shall be cut off." Besides this, human sacrifice has been unknown in Israel since at least the time of the Judges, and the Levitical legislation restricted sacrifices of any kind whatever to the Temple. Since the destruction of the Temple, therefore, no sacrifice has been performed by Jews, except by the Samaritans, who still keep up the Paschal sacrifice to the present day. With the fall of Jerusalem the Rabbis laid down the fine principle that Prayer has replaced Sacrifice. From all this it is obvious that no Jews who believe in the Bible or follow the precepts of the Rabbis would ever think of sacrificing even an animal as part of a ceremony which they could consider pleasing to God.

But, my friends rejoin, may it not be possible that some secret sect of Jews exist who disagree with the general opinions of their fellows, and believe in the efficacy of human sacrifice? It is impossible that such a sect should exist without having left some trace of their existence in the vast literature of the Jews. This has been searched by the bitterest enemies of the Jews

in the hope of finding some such evidence, but in vain.[1]
That some Jews may have been murderers of little
children during the long course of Jewish history, no
one for a moment would deny; but that they did so for
any religious reason, there is absolutely not a vestige of
evidence to show, except the "confessions" of Jews
extracted under torture, and the original assertion of
the renegade Theobald, with whom the whole story
arises. There remained only the possibility of certain
Jews having indulged in these crimes for magical purposes, but if they did so they must have learnt their
magic elsewhere than from Judaism, and were equally
bad Jews as they were cruel and wicked men. Similar
charges have been brought against all peoples who
have incurred the distrust or hatred of their fellow-men.
They were brought against the early Christians, against
the Cavaliers, against the Templars, against the Franciscans. A writer named Daumer has written a book,
Geheimnisse des christlichen Alterthums (Hamburg,
1847), to prove that the characteristic of the Christian
religion, from its origin to the end of the Middle Ages,
consisted in human sacrifice and cannibalism, and the
use of human blood. When Thackeray came over
from India, Napoleon was shown to him at St.
Helena; he was told: "That is Bonaparte; he eats
three sheep every day and all the little children he
can put his hands on." The moment a myth of
that kind arises, who can tell to what length it will
be carried?

At Gloucester, in 1168, the disappearance of the boy
Harold was attributed to the guile of the Jews.[2] At

---

[1] On the whole subject see the admirable monograph of Professor
Strack, Protestant Professor of Theology at the University of Berlin, and
the leading Conversionist of Germany, *Der Blutaberglaube*, vierte Auflage
(Munich, 1892).

[2] Jacobs, *l.c.*, pp. 45-47.

Bury St. Edmunds, in 1181, the little boy Robert was made into a martyr by the same prejudice ;[1] and these seeming confirmations of the myth must have deepened the conviction of England as to its truth. We can see in the case of Hugh how the very existence of the myth would lead to further complications of it. The moment the little lad's corpse is found, without any inquiry as to whether the death had not been the result of accident, the legend of ritual murder by the Jews immediately occurs to men's minds, and John of Lexington gives voice to the suspicion by recalling the myth to the memory of his hearers. Mark what he does next without any further inquiry. Trusting practically to the truth of the myth, the Jew in whose house, or probably courtyard, the boy had last been seen to enter is taken into custody and threatened that unless he tells the truth he will be torn to pieces. The " truth " he tells is filled with a mass of impossibilities. The body of the boy, according to his account, was supernaturally endowed with a capacity for escaping from concealment. Buried in the earth, it rises to its surface again. There is one further touch which connects the whole incident with another set of legends connecting this disappearance of children with practices of Jewish magic. Copin asserts that the entrails of the lad had been removed for purposes of " augury." This is again an English tradition, for in 1222 a deacon of the English Church was executed on the charge of having been converted to Judaism, and having been *particeps criminis* in the evisceration of a Christian lad for magical purposes.[2] It would seem as if the accusers of the Jews had a second string to their bow ; if they could not prove them guilty of cruci-

---

[1] Jacobs, *l.c.*, p. 75.
[2] Matt. Paris, *Hist. Major*, iii. 71.

fixion, they would attempt to convict them upon an equally terrible charge of magic by evisceration.

How far the confirmation by Copin of these charges was the result of a mixture of leading questions and violent threats by John of Lexington we are unable to determine from Matthew Paris's rather confused account. Nor does he tell us from what source was derived the further piece of evidence, that the Jews had kept and tortured Hugh ten days before his crucifixion. As to the later evidence of Copin, implicating the whole of the Jews of England in the charge, even Matthew Paris calls this his ravings ("deliramenta"). I fancy there was more method in Copin's madness than might at first sight appear. It was his last frantic effort to get his doom postponed. If he could implicate the whole of the Jews in his guilt, or in the charge with himself, he might hope to be kept alive as the chief witness while a long and protracted inquiry into the matter was being made. The whole of the Jewish influence would also be enlisted on his side by his perfidious trick. Perhaps I am doing poor Copin an injustice, and his motives were less profound and sinister than I have suggested. He may have been literally driven mad by fear. Both his original charge and his final reiteration of it have been but the delirious ravings of a lunatic. Indeed, Matthew Paris, by calling them "deliramenta," seems to favour this interpretation of Copin's action.

There can be little doubt, however, that some confession of some kind must have been extorted, for it is referred to in another contemporary account in the annals of the abbey of Burton-on-Trent.[1] This differs

---

[1] *Annales Monastici*, edit. Luard (Roll Series), i. 340, *seq.* There is another and shorter account in the "Annals of Waverley," *ibid.*, ii. 346. This adds the trait that the body was thrown into a drinking-well.

in several respects from Matthew Paris's account, and on the whole must be regarded as the superior authority. The boy is kept alive for twenty-six, instead of ten, days, with nothing to eat, instead of being pampered on milk food. His death is decreed by a council of Jews, who cut off his nose and crucified him. Suspicion is aroused against the Jews by the large number who had assembled at Lincoln under pretext of attending a grand wedding. The mother starts off to Scotland to petition the king for an inquisition, and the Jews then throw the body into a well. When it is drawn out a blind woman touches it with her hands, and says, "Sweet little Hugh, alas! that so it happened," and rubbed her eyes with the moisture of the body. By this means she recovered her sight. Thereupon the corpse is carried to the Minster, notwithstanding the protests of the parish priest, who would have liked to obtain the great prize of a boy martyr for his own church. The king then arrives at Lincoln and investigates the charges, and orders the Jews to be arrested. Thereupon a riot occurs, and the houses of the Jews are stormed. As in Matthew Paris, John of Lexington promises life to Copin, "the head of the Jews, and their priest," if he confesses—which he does, but fails to save his life. Eighteen more were hanged at London, though the Dominicans (not the Franciscans) tried to save them. Seventy-one others, the richest Jews of the land, were saved by Richard of Cornwall.

II

So far we have treated the subject entirely from the point of view of the materials offered us by the historians. The science of history has nowadays more means at its command for arriving at the truth than its artistic presentment as given by contemporary historians. In England especially we have almost from the earliest times contemporary records of the Kings' Courts and Chancery with regard to such charges as these. When I first commenced my inquiries into this subject, I was hoping that among the mass of records preserved in Fetter Lane we should be able to come across the official account of the trial of the Jews for the murder of Hugh of Lincoln. For days and days I have searched the Records with this hope. I have found much bearing upon the externalities of the trial, but I regret to say have failed to find the record of the trial itself. The records of the king's jurisdiction in Henry III. are still preserved in tolerable fulness. The trial at Lincoln, if there was a trial, must have occurred somewhere about September 1255, in the thirty-ninth year of the king's reign, as we have just heard from the historian, and shall find confirmed by the records I have discovered. A further trial seems to have taken place in London, at the Tower, in November of the same year—*i.e.*, in the fortieth year of the reign. I have, therefore, looked through the Assize Rolls of the Justices Errant in Lincoln, 39 Hen. III., and for the Tower Assize Rolls for 40 Hen. III.; but unfortunately neither of these contain any reference to the *cause célèbre* of the year. I imagine that the record of the Lincoln trial must have been sent up to London for use in the trial at the Tower, and that both that and the record of the London trial and verdict were kept together in a special Roll which has disappeared.

We must, therefore, be content with a few items which occur in the various classes of Rolls. Thus we can trace the journey of the Jews from Lincoln to London by three entries on the Close Roll of 39

Hen. III. The first of these orders the Constable of
Lincoln Castle to deliver the Jews accused of the
crucifixion to the Sheriff of Lincoln, in order that he
may bring them to Westminster.[1] The others give
orders to the Sheriffs of Huntingdon and Hertford to
assist him of Lincoln on his way through their counties. These are dated 14th of October.[2] We then
learn from the legal annals of London that on the
Feast of St. Cecilia—i.e., November 22nd—the Jews,
then imprisoned in the Tower, had been brought to the
number of ninety-two before the king at Westminster,
and eighteen of them had refused to submit themselves
to the verdict of a Christian jury unless there were
Jews upon it.[3] These eighteen were indicted before the
king, and condemned and executed before the close of
the day. Doubtless this condemnation and execution
were legal according to the law of the time, which
regarded refusal to plead as a confession of guilt. But
it was obviously unfair to press this on the present
occasion without at least change of venue, and especially when the charge was practically one of conspiracy,
notoriously one of the most difficult to prove. This
was a severe lesson for the remaining seventy-four,
who, as we shall see, were prepared to submit their
case to a Lincoln jury, notwithstanding the obvious
prejudices which existed against them in the county.
On the 7th of January 1256 the king sends a royal
letter to the Sheriff of Lincoln stating that a certain
number of Jews had thrown themselves upon the
county to take their trial for the alleged murder of
Hugh, son of Beatrice.[4] To my mind this is conclusive

---

[1] Close Roll, 39 Hen. III., m. 2.
[2] Ibid., m. 2.
[3] Liber de Antiquis Legibus (Cam. Soc.), p. 23.
[4] Shirley, "Royal Letters of Henry III." (Rolls Series), ii. 46.

evidence against their guilt. We have no record of the proceedings taken at Lincoln; but two months afterwards, on March 12th, they were released from the Tower, as we learn from Matthew Paris, who attributes their release to the Franciscans, while the Annals of Burton credit the Dominicans with having brought about this act of mercy or of justice.[1] Whether they were all released on that date is somewhat doubtful; for even two years later I find on the Close Rolls an entry commanding the Constable of the Tower and other officials to release all the Jews in their custody, and on the same occasion Haggin and Cresse, Jews of Lincoln, are commanded to make no distress on the Jews till further orders.[2] But to go back to our records for the year 1256, we now come upon several that begin to throw some light on the action of the king in this matter. At the end of May of that year the king orders an inquisition to be made into the value of the houses of the Jews who had been hanged for the crucifixion of Hugh.[3] He had previously ordered the chest of the cyrographers of the Jews of Lincoln to be sent up to Westminster, obviously for the purpose of ascertaining what debts had been due to the condemned Jews, and claiming them for his own.[4] About the same time there is also a significant entry as to a local inquiry to be made as to what Jews were " of the school of Peitevin the Great, who fled for the death of the aforesaid boy." [5] We shall meet with this Peitevin again, but meanwhile I would draw attention to the evidence here given of the existence of a regular school at Lincoln at this date. As it is obviously

---

[1] Matt. Paris, v. 552.
[2] Close Roll, 42 Hen. III., m. 6 d.
[3] *Ibid.*, 40 Hen. III., m. 11 d.
[4] *Ibid.*, 40 Hen. III., m. 16 d.
[5] Tovey, *Anglia Judaica.*

implied that the scholars might possibly be implicated
in the death of Hugh, it would seem that this school
was grown-up people, and was a sort of Jews' College,
or Beth Hamidrash, of the period.

But to return to the king's plunder.　As the result
of the inquisition of May, the king ordered the houses
of Lincoln Jews in London and elsewhere to be sold
on August 20th,[1] while he made his profit even out of
those that were not sold by claiming fines from those
renting the houses.　By this means we learn, from entries in the Fine Rolls, the names of five Jews who had
been the victims of the terrible prejudices of the times.
These are: Elyas fil. Jacob, Isaac fil. Jude de Ballio,
Deulacres de Bedford, Samuel gener Leonis, and
Sampson Levy.[2]　A son of the last-named is mentioned
in the *Shetaroth* published by Mr. M. D. Davis.[3]

To understand what all this means we must go back
a little.　The king had been fleecing his Jews so un-
mercifully that only fifteen months before the alleged
martyrdom Elyas of London, the Arch-Presbyter of the
Jews of all England, had in an indignant speech asked
permission for them to leave England and find a dwelling with some prince who had bowels of compassion.[4]
Next year, in February 1255, they repeated their request
in more pressing and indignant terms.[5]　This the king
refused, but at that date sold all his rights to his brother
Richard in consideration of a sum of 5000 marks.[6]

[1] Patent Roll, 40 Hen. III., m. 2.

[2] *Rotuli Finium.*, edit. Roberts (Rec. com.), ii. 240.　Other names,
Aaron fil. Peytevin and Hacce (*sic*), are given in the *Athenæum* review of
Hume's monograph on Hugh of Lincoln, 1849, p. 1271 ; I know not on
what authority.

[3] M. D. Davis, *Shetaroth*, No. 160, p. 304.

[4] Matt. Paris, *l.c.*, v. 441.

[5] *Ibid.*, v. 487.　This was the striking passage quoted twice in "Papers
of Anglo-Jewish Historical Exhibition," pp. 50, 266.

[6] Matt. Paris, *l.c.*, v. 488.　Patent Roll, 39 Henry III., m. 13.

In other words, just at the time when the accusation is raised at Lincoln against the Jews the king, by his agreement with his brother Richard, had no right to extract any money from them except by escheat from condemned criminals. We can now understand his annoyance with John of Lexington for letting his prey out of his hands, and the reasons for his taking up the case again after it had been dropped by the local courts. Henry, like most weak princes, was cruel to the Jews; his conduct towards them aroused the compassion of even Matthew. Even his very religiousness would predispose to believe aught of ill from the murderers of Christ. There is no doubt that he approached the case prejudiced doubly by personal interest and religious prejudice, even if both motives were unconscious.

You begin to see how vitally important it would be for the king to make out of the disappearance of the boy Hugh a concerted plan of all the Jews, and especially of all the richest Jews of England, to commit a vile and sacrilegious felony. If it had been merely a case of a murder by a single Jew, the king's interest would be confined to the estate of a single individual; but if by any means it could be shown that it was a conspiracy of all the Jews, the king would once more get a terrible hold of them and their purses. His plan was perfectly successful; not alone did he obtain the estates of the eighteen Jews who were hanged, but there can be little doubt that he received ample compensation for the pardon of the rest. I deduce this from the fact that while the Franciscans and Dominicans, who could only appeal to his conscience or his mercy, were unsuccessful in obtaining "pardon" for the Jews, this was granted them at the request of Earl Richard, who had the control of the

purse of the whole Jewry. Thus a close scrutiny of
the historical records, if it does not altogether clear up
the mystery of little Hugh's death or disappearance,
at least enables us to penetrate to the motives which
raised it into a martyrdom, and implicated all the Jews
of England in the alleged sacrilegious crime.

It is worth while inquiring at this point what foundation there was for the statement that most of the
Jews of England had collected together at Lincoln at
this time under the pretext of celebrating a marriage.
It was this fact, combined with Copin's confession,
which lent colour to the supposition that the death of
little Hugh partook of the character of a ritual murder. I think I can suggest an appropriate occasion
for such a gathering at such time. Sixteen years
later, in 1271, we find a deed—perhaps the most interesting one in Mr. Davis' book [1]—in which Belleassez,
daughter of the Rav Berachyah ben Rav Moshe,
betroths her daughter, Judith, to a young man in
Lincoln, the marriage to take place in four years' time,
showing that little Judith was not yet of marriageable
age, and that her mother, Belleassez, was still a comparatively young woman. I suggest that it was to
attend Belleassez's marriage that the chief Jews of
England were in Lincoln at the end of August 1255.

For her father, Rav Berachyah, was by far the
greatest Jewish scholar living in England at the time
of the tragedy. He is frequently mentioned in the
Tosaphists and Halachic works [2] with great respect
as Berachyah of Nicoll or Lincoln. He was in some
way connected with the trial, for there is in Rymer's

---

[1] *Shetaroth*, No. 156, p. 298.
[2] Zunz, *Zur Geschichte.* (Minchat Jehuda f, 89*b*., Mordecai Berachot,
124, Shilte, Aboda Sara, c. 2.) Neubauer-Renan, *Hist. litt. de la France*,
p. 441.

Foedera a document dated 7th January 1256, releasing Magister Benedict fil. Mosse de Londres from the Tower, and declaring his innocence of the alleged crucifixion.[1] If he could account for the festivities in his house as the accompaniment of his daughter's marriage, the suspicion which might attach to the rest who had travelled to attend the marriage did not apply to him, and he was accordingly released two months before the rest.

I think, too, I can suggest where the marriage of Belleassez took place. The Jews' House in Lincoln, at the bottom of the steep hill, is associated with the name of Bellaset of Wallingford, and it has already been suggested by Canon Venables of Lincoln[2] that she is identical with Belleassez, daughter of Rav Berachyah. It was probably Berachyah's house at the time, and became part of Belleassez's dower, or was left to her at her father's death. It would accordingly be at this house—the finest private residence of its period still extant in England[3]—that the chief Jews of England assembled to do honour to their greatest scholar, and their rejoicings were turned to tragic dismay by the discovery of little Hugh's remains.

So much for what history has to say or conjecture as to the fate of Hugh of Lincoln, and the still worse fate of the Jews accused of his death. Let us, if we can, obtain any further light from that handmaid to history, archæology, which deals with the physical remains of man's activity upon the earth. Can we, for example,

---

[1] Rymer, *Foedera*, ed. 1816, i. 346. Patent Roll, 40. Hen. III., m. 19, at top.

[2] E. Venables, "Walks through the Streets of Lincoln," p. 25.

[3] It has been figured several times, *e.g.*, Turner, "Domestic Architecture," i. 40; Gardiner, "School History of England." Details in Pugin, "Specimens of Gothic Architecture," plate 2.

find any signs of the existence of Hugh? For it by no means follows that in a mediæval case of this kind, when a Jew was accused of murder, there should necessarily exist anybody who had been murdered. The late M. Isidore Loeb, whose loss for Jewish history is almost irreparable, studied carefully a Spanish case very analogous to that of Hugh of Lincoln.[1] When I was at Toledo I was struck with a fresco on the cathedral walls, which I was informed dealt with the fate of El Nino de la Guardia. The picture represented a little lad transfixed on a cross, and around him a crowd of scoffing Jews. Well, M. Loeb went carefully into this case, of which the records are very voluminous and detailed, giving an account of the torment and punishment of several open and secret Jews who were implicated in the so-called crime. He came to the conclusion, for which he gives well-founded reasons, that the little lad of la Guardia never existed at all, and that the Jews were accused and punished for the murder of a non-existent corpse.[2] Can this possibly have been the case with Hugh of Lincoln? and can English justice in the thirteenth century have been so hasty and unjust as to punish for crimes without any evidence of a *corpus delicti?* Here archæology comes to our aid, and enables us after a lapse of 650 years to state that little Hugh of Lincoln was a lad of about four feet two inches high, and therefore well grown for his age of eight; that his face was round rather than long; and that if any violence was done to him, at least none of his bones were broken. You may perhaps wonder by what magic archæology can use a time telescope of this description. The answer is very

---

[1] I. Loeb, *Le Saint Enfant de la Guardia in Revue des Etudes juives*, tome xv.

[2] Loeb, *l.c.*, p. 32 of tirage apart.

simple. In 1791 some repairs were being made at
Lincoln Cathedral, and beneath a shrine which had
always been traditionally connected with the boy Hugh
was found a stone coffin containing a skeleton which
was obviously that of a lad, and which, there was no
reason for doubting, was actually that of St. Hugh.[1]
When these bones were thus exhumed, there happened
to be visiting in Lincoln an artist named Grimm, who
took very thorough and accurate drawings of the stone
coffin and its contents for Bishop Kaye, who then held
the see of Lincoln.   Kaye's topographical collections
ultimately came into possession of the British Museum,
which attracts such things to itself like the magnetic
mountain of Sindbad.[2]

During my researches in connection with the Anglo-
Jewish Historical Exhibition of 1887 I came across
these drawings, and thus found that we are practically
able to see with our own eyes the actual bones of the
little martyr.   But dead men tell no tales, and dry
bones cannot speak.   Though this find of mine is of
interest, even if the interest be perhaps a somewhat
gruesome one, it still fails to solve the question of the
guilt or otherwise of the Jews.

It was indeed stated at the time of their discovery
that no dust was found in the coffin, therefore the story
of the evisceration of the little lad was thereby confirmed.   But this is a somewhat imaginative inference
from the facts of the case.   The bones, at any rate,
were intact.   No very extreme violence could have
been used to the boy ; but whether he died by accident
or by malice, by cruelty or by chance, archæology
telleth not.

There is one part of archæology which is nowa-

[1] S. Pegge, "Life of Robert Grosseteste," 1793, p. 2.
[2] The British Museum reference is Kaye, ii. 363.

days being more and more utilised for the purposes of historic elucidation. The study of topography is more and more resorted to in order to throw light on problems like that presented by the disappearance of little St. Hugh. In his case, as we shall see, a study

of the Lincoln Jewry is absolutely necessary for solution of the problem presented by his death. The following plan of the neighbourhood of the Steep Hill of Lincoln, near which the Jews most did congregate in early days, will place the reader in a position to realise the locality of Hugh's death.

The ancient Jewry of Lincoln ranged from Aaron of
Lincoln's House at the top of the Steep Hill to the
end of the Straight, just where it enters High Street;
in earlier days there was a gate here known as St.

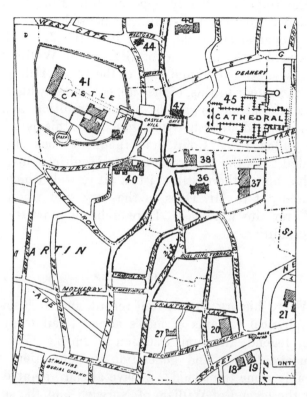

THE JEWISH QUARTER, LINCOLN.

1. Aaron of Lincoln's House.   40. Bishop's Hostel.
2. Jopin's House.   36. St. Michael's.
3. Bellaset's House.   37. Bishop's Palace.

Dunstan's Lock, but previously as Dernestall's Lock:
it was through this lock, tradition states, that little
Hugh went on to his doom. As you may see from the
plan, he had not far to go. Midway up the Straight,

on the left-hand side, are the three houses which local tradition associates with the early Jews of Lincoln.

The open space at the junction of the Straight and the Steep Hill was, there can be little doubt, the scene of the tragedy. Nearly opposite Bull Ring Terrace, so named from the bull-baiting that used to take place in the open space at the end of it, is the Jews' House associated with the name of Bellaset of Wallingford. This is on the left-hand side of the Steep Hill, going up; next door to this, higher up, is a house which, Mr. Haes informs me, is said by popular tradition to have been the old Jewish Synagogue. By this is a lane still called Jews' Court, and the next house is still pointed to as the place where little Hugh met his fate: in this house there still exists a pit or well which was pointed out to Mr. Haes as the very spot where the boy's remains were cast. Here archæology passes over into tradition.

III

Where history, the written record, and archæology, the physical remains of man's activity, fail to give a clue, legend, the oral tradition of men's memories from age to age and generation to generation, may possibly come to our aid. I have already pointed out that the legend of William of Norwich and the super-stition as to the use of human entrails for the purposes of augury by Jews have exercised a shaping influence on the story of St. Hugh from the day his remains were discovered. Besides this, in the case of our little martyr, we are somewhat amply provided with remains of popular tradition of the so-called "martyrdom." There is one French and there are several English and Scotch ballads devoted to the subject. Let us see what contribution they can make to the elucidation of the problem.

The French ballad was published in 1834 by M. Francisque Michel,[1] from a manuscript in the Bibliothèque Nationale. From its diction and metre it was clearly written within a very few years of the martyrdom. It tells how in Nicole, that rich city, the boy Huchon was inveigled away by Peitevin, the Jew, on the eve of the gules of August. His mother sought in vain for him throughout the whole Jewry, and then betook herself to Henry the King, to call for justice on the wicked Jews. This he promises her, but threatens vengeance if her accusation prove untrue. Meanwhile, the richest Jews of England collected together, and the boy was brought before them, bound by a cord, by Jopin, the Jew, who offers him for thirty deniers. Agim, the Jew, buys him for that price from the new Judas, and the boy is then crucified. And when he expires, after being pierced by the knife of Agim, "the dear soul of this infant was borne at once by angels in heaven, chanting together before God all-powerful." The body is buried, but next morning is found again by the Jews upon the surface of the earth, and wherever they attempt to conceal it, it persists in rising to the surface—a fine imaginative touch of the folk-artist who wrote the ballad. They then determine to take it outside Lincoln and place it near a fountain in the neighbourhood. A woman finds it next day and raises the alarm. The body is borne back to Dernestal, the quarter where his mother lived. Then

---

[1] F. Michel, *Hugues de Lincoln, Recueil de ballades Anglo-Normandes et Ecossoises relatives au meurtre de cet enfant commis par les Juifs en MCCLV.*, Paris, 1834, pp. ix.-64. It was reprinted in 1849, with a pseudo-archaic English version by A. Hume. "Sir Hugh of Lincoln ; or, An Examination of a curious Tradition respecting the Jews, with a Notice of the Popular Poetry connected with it." 8vo, 54 pp.

a convert comes along, and seeing the body all be-
smudged with mire and ordure, suggests that it should
be washed with warm water : "I trow that thus we'll
find how the child came to his death." Then became
evident the treason of the Jews. The body is borne
to the cathedral, and the Jews captured, who say,
"We have been betrayed by Falism." Then comes
Jopin, the Jew, who tells again in ballad fashion the
same story, with the addition that all the Jews of
England knew of the crucifixion, and had decided
upon it in common council. For all reward for his
confession, Jopin is condemned to be torn to pieces
by horses. And they hung him at Canewick, a mile
south of Lincoln town.

In this ballad we get in very vivid form the popular
account of the martyrdom which has much in common
with that represented by Matthew Paris, though Copin
here becomes Jopin. We get two other names of
Jews concerned in the misdeed, Peitevin and Agim,
which is obviously the English form of Chayim. You
may remember that I have shown some years ago
that Huggin Lane, in the City of London, derives its
name from a London Jew of the same prenomen.[1]
I think I can identify from Hebrew records both these
new personages. In an undated deed, published by
Mr. Davis in his volume of *Shetaroth*, No. 167, page
309, the Jewish creditor of the abbey of Bardeney
signs himself Peitevin ben Beneit; and as the deed is
also signed by Benedict fil. Mosse, who, as we have
seen above, was implicated in the martyrdom, and
declared innocent by the king, the deed must be about
the date of the martyrdom, and the signatory can
therefore be identified with the Peitevin mentioned in
the French ballad. So, too, in another deed, published

[1] "Papers Anglo-Jewish Historical Exhibition," p. 49.

by Mr. Davis, No. 155, the signature occurs of Chayim de Nicole, who is equally obviously the original of the Agim of the French ballad.[1]   Who Falsim, the convert who betrayed the Jews, was, cannot be at present ascertained.

It is, at any rate, a curious incident that among the Jews imprisoned in the Tower for this crime there was a convert named John, who was pardoned for his share in it, as we learn from Rymer's *Foedera*.[2]   Here, again, we find the sinister presence of a renegade from the faith, always a sign of ill omen in cases of this kind.

Besides this contemporary French ballad there are, as you are doubtless aware, a number of English and Scotch ballads dealing with the legend of St. Hugh. Here the scene is altogether changed, and the historic background fades into the far distance as we can well understand from the late date in which the ballads were collected, none of them being earlier than the last century. Professor Child, in his magnificent work on the English and Scotch ballads,[3] has collected together no less than eighteen versions of it, but decides for the priority of that collected by Jamieson.   In this there is no question of conspiracy of the Jews of England; the tragic interest is deepened by making the crime the work of a female hand.[4]   The Jew's daughter entices little Hugh from his game of football with the allurement of an apple, and leads him through nine dark doors, lays him on a dressing-

---

[1] The French form Agim is nearer to the Hebrew Chayim than the Hagin of the English records.

[2] Ed. 1816, i. 333.

[3] Cambridge (Mass.), 1882, *seq.*, pt. v.   Professor Child has an elaborate and instructive introduction to the ballads, which brings together in a convenient form all that has been hitherto known of the subject from history and tradition.

[4] May we not see here, as Mr. York Powell has suggested to me, some reminiscence of Belleassez ?

table, and sticks him like a swine.[1] She then rolls him in lead and casts him into our Lady's draw-well, fifty fathoms deep. We then follow the fortunes of the poor little lad's mother.

> " When the bells were rung, and mass was sung,
>   And a' the bairns came hame,
> When every lady gat hame her son,
>   The Lady Maisry gat nane."

She searches for him at the Jews' castell, at the Jews' Garden, and at last at the deep draw-well; and at each place she cries—

> " ''Gin ye be there, my sweet Sir Hugh,
>   I pray you to me speak.'
> 'Gae hame, gae hame, my mither dear,
>   Prepare my winding sheet ;
> And, at the back o' merry Lincoln,
>   The morn I will you meet.'
> Now Lady Maisry is gane hame—
>   Made him a winding sheet ;
> And at the back o' merry Lincoln,
>   The dead corpse did her meet.
> And a' the bells o' merry Lincoln,
>   Without men's hands were rung ;
> And a' the books o' merry Lincoln,
>   Were read without man's tongue ;
> And ne'er was such a burial
>   Sin Adam's days begun."

That fine touch of the supernatural ringing of the church bells is only found in Jamieson's version. But fine as it is, the ballad has little instruction to give us on the death of little Hugh, and might celebrate any murder of any child by any wicked woman. Indeed, Mr. Newell, an American folk-lorist, found in the streets of New York a version crooned by a little negress in which the tale is told of Harry Hughes and

---

[1] Qy. reference to the mysterious evisceration mentioned by Matt. Paris?

the Duke's daughter.[1] Thus the prejudices of the Middle Ages have begun to die away even in the memory of the folk. In Lincoln itself, however, the myth is still alive, and inhabitants of that city pointed out to Mr. Haes, after the lapse of 650 years, the very well adjoining Jews' Court into which poor little Hugh was thrown. Other traditions, however, identify it with Grantham's well, outside the old walls of Lincoln.

IV

We have now before us all the materials which history, archæology, and tradition can afford us with regard to the death of the poor little Lincoln lad of the thirteenth century. Do they enable us to arrive at the exact truth of the matter? I fancy they do, and would put forth the following hypothetical account— imaginative, I grant, but I trust not altogether imaginary—of what happened at Lincoln during the month of August 1255. On the eve of first day of that month,[2] a Saturday afternoon, a little boy Hugh, son of a widow named Beatrice,[3] aged eight years,[4] while running after a ball at play[5] fell by accident into a gong or cesspool[6] attached to the house of a Jew

---

[1] "Games and Songs of American Children," Boston, 1883. I drew attention to Mr. Newell's interesting version in the *Jewish Chronicle*.

[2] Gules of August (French ballad), a popular name for the 1st of August, also called Lammas. This used to be a popular holiday. "Gules" occurs transcribed in Hebrew characters in Mr. Davis's *Shetaroth*, No. 103, p. 232. The *Acta Sanctorum* gives the date of Hugh's martyrdom as July 27 (xxxiii. 494); and Matt. Paris favours that date. The king's itinerary, as given in Rymer and the Patent Rolls, rather favours the date of the ballad.

[3] Shirley, "Royal Letters," ii. 110.   [4] Matt. Paris.

[5] English ballads. Owing to their late date little confidence can be placed on this point, but it seems antecedently probable.

[6] The French ballad declares that the body was covered with ordure.

named Jopin,[1] or Joscefin,[2] two doors off the Jews House at Lincoln.[3] His body remained in this gong for some twenty-six days[4] subject to the disintegrating forces of its nauseous contents. Meanwhile there had assembled at Lincoln a number of the most important Jews of England[5] in order to attend the wedding[6] of Belleassez, daughter of the Rav, or Chief Rabbi of the town,[7] known to his Christian fellow-citizens as Magister Benedict fil. Mosse de Londres,[8] and to his Jewish flock as Rav Berachyah ben Moses,[9] known also in Jewish literature as Berachyah de Nicole, an important Tosaphist.[10] He was the greatest Jewish scholar of his time in England,[11] and to do honour to him most of the chief Jews of England attended the wedding. In the midst of their festivities their joy was turned to horror and dismay by the discovery on Thursday, the 26th of August,[12] probably the day after the wedding,[13] of the disfigured body of little Hugh, distended by the gases of corruption, which had risen to the surface of

[1] French ballad, Matthew Paris calls him Copin ; either name might be derived from Jacopin, diminutive of Jacob.

[2] There was a Josephin living at Lincoln at the time whose son, Chayim, married Bellaset. Davis, Nos. 154, 156.

[3] Local tradition reported by Mr. Haes.

[4] Annals of Burton. Matt. Paris says ten days, but this is quite discordant with his own date of the martyrdom.

[5] Matt. Paris, Annals of Burton, French ballad.

[6] Annals of Burton.

[7] Conjecture derived from date of Shetar. Davis, No. 156.

[8] Rymer, *Foedera*.   [9] Davis, *l.c.*

[10] Zunz, Neubauer, *ll.cc.*

[11] Meir of Norwich, poet, is the other chief name known from this period.

[12] Annals of Burton. French ballad allows for a considerable period to have elapsed between the disappearance of Hugh and the "summoning" of the Jews to Lincoln.

[13] Wednesday has always been a favourite day for weddings among Jews, and but little time can have elapsed or the assembly would have dispersed to their homes elsewhere.

the gong.[1] We can imagine the horror of the party when Joscefin, the father-in-law of the bride,[2] broke in upon the company assembled two doors off[3] with the news of the ghastly discovery. The corruption of the body burst the walls of the stomach as soon as an attempt was made to remove it,[4] and the entrails were dissevered from the body.[5] Instead of announcing the discovery to the proper officials, the Jews, on the advice of Peitevin,[6] the Dayan[7] and Hagin,[8] committed the fatal error[9] of attempting to conceal the body, or, at any rate, of removing it from the neighbourhood of the Jewry.[10] They cast it into Grantham's well,[11] where it was discovered after three days, on Sunday, 29th August,[12] by a woman passing by.[13] Among the crowd attracted by the discovery was one John of Lexington,[14] who was familiar, from tradition and his reading,[15] with the myth about the ritual murder of boys by Jews. As

[1] Conjecture to account for the appearance of the body just after the wedding.

[2] Conjecture (see note 2, p. 220).

[3] Local tradition.

[4] Conjecture to account for the disembowelling of the body, Matt. Paris.

[5] Or, as Mr. York Powell suggests, the entrails were removed by some Jewish physician when it was decided to remove the body.

[6] French ballad. His flight, as recorded by Tovey, seems to argue the consciousness of complicity.

[7] Deduced from reference in Tovey to his school.

[8] French ballad.

[9] Copin's confession cannot be explained without assuming some connection of the Jews with the matter.

[10] Tradition reports two places in which the body was found, in Jopin's house and in Grantham's well. The suggestion here made reconciles the two statements, and at the same time allows for a certain amount of complicity, or at least injudicious concealment, on the part of the Jews.

[11] Oulton, "Traveller's Guide," 1805, ii. p. 54.

[12] Annals of Burton.

[13] Annals of Burton. According to Matthew Paris it was the boy's mother who discovered the corpse ; this disagrees with the Burton Annals and with the French ballad.

[14] Matthew Paris.   [15] *Idem.*

one of the canons of the Minster[1] he saw the desir-
ability of claiming the body as a further attraction for
the cathedral,[2] and his plan was assisted by the seeming miracle by which a woman in the crowd removed
some obstruction to her eyesight[3] by wiping them
with some of the moisture exuding from Hugh's body.[4]
The parish priest attempted to compete with him for
the possession of the precious charge, but the superior
authority of Lexington overcame his protests.[5] In a
grand procession, grander than Lincoln ever yet had
seen,[6] the remains of little Hugh were transferred to
a stone coffin in the South Aisle Choir,[7] in which they
remain undisturbed for over 500 years.[8]

Meanwhile Lexington had, by combined threats and
promises,[9] induced Jopin to make such a confession[10]
of the complicity of the Jews as could be twisted into
evidence for making the boy a martyr of the faith.[11]
Here he was content to rest,[12] having obtained for his
cathedral an equal attraction to those of Norwich and
Gloucester and the abbey of Edmondsbury.[13] But
Beatrice, the mother of the poor little lad, was not

---

[1] Annals of Burton.

[2] Conjecture from his remark on discovering the body.

[3] Annals of Waverley, French ballad.

[4] Annals of Burton.

[5] Ibid.

[6] French ballad, Scotch ballad (Jamieson). Here is a point which
remained in the folk memory for over five hundred years.

[7] E. Venables, "A Walk through Lincoln Minster," p. 41.

[8] Pegge, l.c., Michel, p. 63.

[9] Matt. Paris, Annals of Burton.

[10] Paris, Annals of Burton, French ballad.

[11] Without a confession implicating all the Jews little Hugh could not
be raised to the position of a martyr. As a matter of fact, his name was
never formally received into the Roman martyrology. (See Michel, p. 51,
note 23.)

[12] Deduced from the fact that Jopin was not even tried till the king
arrived at Lincoln.

[13] See Jacobs, l.c., pp. 45, 75, 256.

content with this,[1] and hearing that the king was approaching Lincoln on his way from Scotland,[2] went out to meet him, and laid the case before him.

Henry III. hated the Jews, while making use of them as sponges to replete his treasury. He had but six months before[3] lost his power over them by selling them to his brother Richard. Here he saw his chance of both gratifying his hatred and replenishing his treasury. He hurried to Lincoln, seized all the Jews he could find there,[4] silenced the only witness who could declare the truth by hanging Jopin, after having caused him to be dragged round the city tied to the tail of a wild horse,[5] he brought the rest of the Jews up to London,[6] hanged those who refused to trust themselves to the tender mercies of a Christian jury,[7] holding its sitting in Lincoln, now all aflame with infuriated passions,[8] and only released the remainder after they had been imprisoned six months,[9] when the term of his agreement with Earl Richard was over and he had them again at his mercy.[10] The Franciscans, who constituted the noblest element in English life at the time, were on the side of the Jews—significant testimony to their innocence—but pleaded for them in vain.[11] The protracted nature of the inquiry, the

---

[1] French ballad.

[2] This would be in October 1255 (see itinerary of Henry III.; as given in *Foedera*, the king was at Alnwick 23rd September, at Westminster 18th October).

[3] 24th February 1255 (Patent Roll, 39 Henry III., m. 13).

[4] Matt. Paris.

[5] Matt. Paris, Annals of Waverley, Annals of Burton.

[6] Close Roll, 39 Henry III.

[7] *Liber de Antiquis Legibus* (Cam. Soc.), p. 23.

[8] Annals of Burton.

[9] Matt. Paris, v. 552, 12th March 1256.

[10] See note 3, above.

[11] Matt. Paris, v. 546; Annals of Burton attribute the intervention to the Dominicans.

severest punishment of the victim, the wide publicity given to the accusation, caused the martyrdom of Hugh and the cruelty of the Jews to become a fixed element of belief in the popular mind of England, which has retained the memory of the boy martyr down to the present day. It was a tale above all others likely to touch the tender human soul of Chaucer, and caused him to give utterance to the prayer with which I commenced this paper, in which I have endeavoured to put together, for the first time, into a consistent narrative, all the scattered evidence which history, archæ-ology, and tradition give as to the fate of little St. Hugh of Lincoln, boy and martyr.

"AARON SON OF THE DEVIL"

(From " The Jewish Chronicle")

IN making some investigations into the early history of the Jews in this country, my attention was called by a notice in Mr. Walter Rye's recent " Short History of Norfolk" to a caricature inscribed on the Forest Roll of the County of Essex in the fifth year of Edward I.'s reign (1277). On examination at the Record Office, both the caricature and the record which accompanies it proved to be of exceptional interest, and I am enabled to give a tracing of the former and a translation of the latter. For help in transcribing this unique document I have to thank the skill of Mr. C. Trice Martin, of the Record Office.

The entry is the record of an offence against the severe forest laws of the time committed by certain Jews and Christians of Colchester, whose names are mentioned, together with the amount of punishment inflicted. In the case of the Christians this consists of small fines, the amount of which is written in each case over the offender's name. I have placed these in square brackets after the name in the following trans-

lation, in which a little archaic colouring may not
perhaps be amiss :—

COLCHESTER to wit : By the same it was brought forward that a
certain doe was started in Wildenhaye Wood by the dogs of Sir John
de Burgh, Sen., which doe in her flight came by the top of the City of
Colchester, crossing towards another wood on the other side of that city.
And there issued forth Saunte son of Ursel, Jew of Colchester, Cok
son of Aaron, and Samuel son of the same, Isaac the Jewish chaplain,
Copin and Elias, Jews, and certain Christians of the said city, to wit :
William Scott [2s.], Henry the Gutter [2s.], Henry the Toller [2s.],
and others. And these with a mighty clamour chased the same doe
through the south gate into the aforesaid city, and they so worried
her by their shouting that they forced her to jump over a wall, and
she thus brake her neck, to wit, on Wednesday next after the feast of
St. Nicholas, in the fifty-second year of the reign of King Henry
[7th December 1267]. And there came upon them Walter the Gold-
smith, bailiff [half-a-mark], and Robert the Toller [2s.], beadle of the
same city, and others that are dead, and carried thence the game, and
had their will of it. And these came not, nor did their attorneys.
Thereupon it was ordered to the sheriff that he summon the aforesaid Jews from day to day, and a day was set to the bailiffs of Colchester for producing the others mentioned within three weeks from
Easter Day. And the aforesaid Saunte and Isaac put in an appearance, and being convicted were cast into prison. And the aforesaid
Cok stayeth at Lincoln, therefore was it ordered to the Sheriff of
Lincoln to produce him within one month from Easter. And the
aforesaid Saunte being led forth from prison was fined forty shillings
on the surety of Vives of Gipewis [Ipswich], Vives of Clare and
Mosse Panel of Haverhulle, Jews. And the aforesaid Elias came not,
nor was he to be found. Therefore let him be driven forth, &c.
And the aforesaid Isaac being led forth from prison was fined in four
marks on the surety of Joce of Cantuar [Canterbury], Jew, Abraham
son of Aaron, Isaac son of Chera, Jew, Saer son of Radulph of Colchester, and Richard Pruet of the same. And later came forward
the aforesaid Copin and Samuel, and are committed to prison, and
being led forth were fined, that is to say, Copin in two marks on the
surety of Vives son of Coperun and Aaron son of Leo, Jews ; and
the aforesaid Samuel in one mark on the surety of Jacob of London
and Saunte son of Ursel of Colchester, Jews. And the Sheriff of
Lincoln answereth nought concerning the aforesaid Cok the Jew, but

contemned the mandate of the Justiciars, &c.   Wherefore he is at
mercy one hundred shillings.

And the said Cok who came not ten marks
by taxation of the Justiciars.

The document tells its own story in tolerably plain
language, and sets before us a vivid picture of a hunting scene in the thirteenth century, when hunting had
the additional charm of being a criminal offence little
less than treason.   What more concerns us to observe,
however, is the fact that Jew and Christian are equally
seized with that mania for chasing anything that runs,
which has been the characteristic of Englishmen at all
times.   And the intimate association of the followers
of the two creeds gives us a truer, and at the same time
a more favourable, impression of the relation of Jew
and Christian than we usually obtain from the ordinary
histories.   As we shall see, two Christians stood bail
for one of the Jews who were engaged, and the way
in which the chief actors of the scene are mentioned
seems to imply that the Jews led the way in the chase,
though it is the Christians who eat the game, probably
because venison killed in the way mentioned was not
fitted for Jewish food.

But if in their social relation the Jews seem to have
been on equal terms with the Christians, their position
is quite different before the law.   It is the Sheriff of
the County who has to produce the Jews before the
Justiciars ; it is only the town-bailiff who is responsible for the others.   Again, it is the Sheriff of Lin-
colnshire who is responsible for the appearance of the
Jew who had escaped to Lincoln.   Still more marked
is the contrast in their respective punishments.   The
five Christians are only fined in an aggregate sum of
14s. 8d. (equal probably to about £20 at the present
time), while of the five Jews who receive their punish-

ment, four are imprisoned and fined £6, 13s. 4d., the
fifth, who evades the legal process, is ultimately fined ten
marks, *i.e.*, also £6, 13s. 4d., while the sixth disappears
and is outlawed, if that be the meaning of " exigatur."
These sums give a very inadequate idea of the intrinsic
value involved in them.   We must remember that the
average wages of unskilled labour was one penny a
day, that the price of a sheep was fourpence, and that
the annual rental of some Jews' houses at the time of
the Expulsion was as low as a shilling and half-a-crown.
Under these circumstances the £13, 6s. 8d., for which
the five Jews and their ten bails were responsible,
would probably purchase as much of the available
necessities and luxuries of the time as £400 would
nowadays.   This is an enormous sum to pay for ten
minutes' chase of a deer, and yet the forest laws had
been considerably lessened in severity by the Forest
Charter of 1217.

Turning from the incident itself to those who were
engaged in it, our attention is first arrested by the
names of the Jews concerned as principals or bails.
Saunte, the first on our list, was not an unfrequent
one among the Jews of the time, at least in its Latin
form of Sanctus ; we find a Sanctus of Edmondsbury
fined in 1183 for receiving sacred vessels in pledge.
It was probably introduced, like almost all the Jews'
names of the time, from France ; a Santo from Gurnai
is mentioned in 1204.   Saunte's father, *Ursel*, bore a
still more common one.   I find Ursels at York, at
Oxford, at Hereford, at Lincoln, at Bedford, and at
Wickford.   So popular was it that it was transliterated
directly into Hebrew signatures as אורשיל, under which
form it occurs in a Hebrew Starr at the British Museum
in the signature of an Ursell of Colchester, who was
probably father of the Saunte mentioned in our docu-

ment. *Cok*, the next name, is also sufficiently familiar, and, so far as I know, is distinctive as a Jewish name; Jews bearing that name occur at Bedford, Northampton, York, Canterbury, Winchester, and Devizes. It was probably a nickname, as Cok of Devizes is also known as Solomon, son of Simon. *Copin*, again, is a favourite name of the period. We have it at Edmondbury, at Worcester, and at York, while it was the name of the best-known of Oxford Jews and of the Jew accused of the murder of Hugh of Lincoln. *Vives* is one of the most interesting of the names borne by the early Jews in this country. It comes from France, as we find a Vives from Paris, and occurs in many variants, as Vivon, Vivard, Vivian, and (by a mistake in printed books) as Vines, *n* and *u* being indistinguishable in old court-hand. Persons bearing this name occur at London, Norwich, Pontefract, Canterbury, Shrewsbury, and Oxford, besides Clare and Ipswich, as here. In itself it is nothing more than a French translation of חיים, the source of the "Hyam" and "Hyams" of the present day. The Italian form, Vita, occurred in the name of the grandfather of Sir Moses Montefiore. But היים is also directly transliterated as Hiam, as in the second name of Sir Moses, or with the insertion of a guttural, as Hagin or Aggyn, so that from this *Shem-ha-kodesh* we have no less than eight *kinnuim*. Most of the remaining names are Biblical, Moses appearing under the form of *Mosse* (dissyllable; *ss* = *sh*), nearer to the Hebrew than our Greek form, and Joseph as Joce. *Coperun* or *Coperim* (it might be either) is unique; I cannot find another example in the 1500 names I have collected. The use of a family name by Moses *Panel* is not such a rarity, Bland, Crespin, Matrin, Parimer, Russel being among those I have observed. The last deserving notice is doubly interesting. *Chera* is the French *chere*, " dear," and is the name of a Jewess. Chera of Winton (Winchester) is mentioned in connection with some transactions with the Jews of Southampton (see *Jewish Chronicle*, No. 700), and two of her sons, Deulebenye and Elias, also occur, so that it is possible Isaac son of Chera may be a third brother. Why they were called the sons of their mother is a puzzle which is not peculiar to this case, but occurs in several others, as Abraham son of Avegay, David son of Comitissa, Leo son of Margaret, and the like. It is difficult to account for this curious form of nomenclature in any way not derogatory to the honour of the persons concerned.

So much for the names. As for the persons who bore them, in many cases this is the only time that history catches a glimpse of them, so far as I can learn. Saunte's father and Isaac's mother we have already referred to, but Saunte and Isaac themselves make no further appearance in the annals of the time. Cok and Samuel were probably the sons of the Aaron of Colchester who represented Bedford at the Jewish Parliament of 1240, and a Samuel fil. Aaron of Colchester is also mentioned in a document of 1220. Isaac is termed " Capellanus Judæus," a name which is paralleled by a Sampson le Chapeleyn, who was among the Jews of Canterbury expelled in 1290. The term probably implies the *Chasan* or Cantor of the congregation, but this Isaac seems to have been especially influential; he is fined the most of all the Jews who give themselves up, and no less than five persons hold themselves responsible for the payment. Still more interesting is it to observe that among the bails are two Christians, for Richard Pruet is evidently no Jew, and Saer (generally Saher) is a good old Saxon name, the modern representative of which was borne by the most renowned pugilist of the "sixties." As Isaac was so important a personage, he may have been the Isaac son of Benedict who represented Colchester at the Jewish Parliament of 1240. Or he may also be identical with the R. Isaac, who signed a deed of a conveyance of a house in Stockwell Street, Colchester, which was so ingeniously deciphered by Dr. Neubauer. Of the others mentioned, Vives of Ipswich was living in 1290 when his villa "in the suburbs" escheated to the king. Before leaving the *dramatis personæ*, attention may be called to the evidence they afford of the widespread and yet close connection of the Jews of the time. Here we have Jews assembled at Colchester from London, Canterbury, Lincoln, Ipswich, Clare, and Haverhill, the last three in Suffolk.

The caricature which accompanies the record presents almost as many points of interest as the document itself. In the first place, it is scarcely a caricature. Is it not rather a slightly exaggerated portrait? Certainly the scribe who jotted it down while the proceedings were going on has caught with great skill, though with equal animus, the characteristic features of the Jewish face as we find it on the Assyrian monuments and as it moves among us at the present day. The aquiline nose with the depressed tip, though here exaggerated, the thick underlip, the gleaming eye, the strong lines of the features, even the curly hair on the forehead, all are characteristic. That they were familiar enough in England at the time is proved by the fact that the monks of St. Albans were struck by the Jewish features ("Judaicam faciem") of a Saracen Emir who visited them during one of the pauses of the Crusades. If a portrait, of whom has it preserved the lineaments after 600 years? The name inscribed above, "Aaron fil.

Diaboli"—half in jest, half in grim earnest—for were
not all Jews "sons of the Devil" in the sight of good
Christians, tell us at best only the first name. The
only Aaron mentioned in our record is Aaron son of
Leo or Judah, for in translating their names the Jews
made much use of the animal metaphors in the blessings of Jacob and Moses, and in the former occurs
"Judah is a lion's whelp," and so יהודה became Leo.
Was it from some confusion of the "sacred" and
"secular" names of Aaron that caused the scribe to
write down in his impatience "son of the—Devil."
But another inquiry is suggested by the probable
occasion of the entry being written. The offence was
committed in 1267; the entry is made in 1277. Some
delay may have at first occurred owing to the unsettled
state of the Eastern counties, due to the "War of the
Disinherited," that followed the fall of Simon de Montfort. But ten years must have been exceptionally long
for the law's delay even in those days. Now, the last
entry on the roll would only be made when everything
had been settled, and it was probably entered after
negotiation for the return of the truant Cok fil. Aaron
had resulted in the payment by the Sheriff of Lincoln
of a fine of one hundred shillings for not producing
him. After this Cok seems himself to have come back,
and the whole proceedings were closed by his being
fined, the amount being put in in a couple of lines apart
from the original entry. This would give the clerk
time to draw his sketch, and he might well have been
curious about the man who had been absent ten years
from his native town and was willing to pay a sum
equivalent to £200 of our money for the privilege of
returning to live amongst his town and kinsfolk. I
am therefore inclined to believe that the sketch represents this Cok fil. Aaron. Whomever it represents, it

is the earliest dated portrait of a Jew in existence, those lately figured in the *Revue des Études Juives* being of the dates 1335 and 1347.

The portrait also gives us some details of the dress of Jews of the time.   He wears a cowl, and in this case the cowl does not make the monk, but simply implies one who does not work much out of doors.   In the Ellesmere MS. of Chaucer both the Clerk and the Doctor wear similar cowls.   Of unique interest, however, is the square patch on the cloak.   This is no less than the distinguishing mark of the Jews, which was ordained for all Catholic Christendom at the Lateran Council of 1215 and adopted in England by the patriot Stephen of Langton in 1222.   This is not only the earliest representation of it, but it differs in shape from the seven other examples collected by the industry of MM. Loeb and Ulysse Robert, which are all in the form of a quoit.   The one before us is in the shape of the two tables of the Law, as seen to this day in our synagogues, and as imposed by an enactment of 1274, which had been confirmed in 1277, the year in which our document was written.   It was to be of saffron taffety, six finger breadths long and three broad.   It was perhaps an unconscious tribute of Englishmen which made the distinctive mark of their Jewish fellow-countrymen to be that Law by which their lives were ruled, for adhering to which they were called and treated as " sons of the Devil," and for which so many of them died a martyr's death.

JEWISH HISTORY: ITS AIMS AND METHODS

(Discourse of Reception delivered to the Royal Academy of History, Madrid)

GENTLEMEN,—Permit me to thank you for the honour which you have conferred upon me in electing me Corresponding Member of your body. I cannot flatter myself I owe this honour to any personal merits of my own. It is, I take it, only an outward mark of the interest taken by you in the history of the people of Israel in Spain, an interest which has been vividly expressed in your *Boletin* by the admirable studies on Hispano-Jewish history by Senores Fidel Fita and Fernandez y Gonzalez. Indeed, if I mistake not, I welcome in my election one of the many signs that Spain has learnt with regard to the Jews, the highest and most difficult of all moral lessons, to forgive those we have injured. Spain now recognises that it was not the Jews, but her treatment of them, that was the *Tizon de España*. Permit me to add a few remarks on the present position of Jewish history, its aims and problems. In a body which counts among its members such authorities as Don Fidel Fita and Senior Fernandez y Gonzalez it would be an impertinence on my part to speak of the *rôle* of the Jews in Spanish history; but you may perhaps permit me to speak of the subject in its relations to Jewish history in general, of which I have been a loving student for many years.

The history of Jewish history has gone through three stages, as it seems to me, and is now entering upon a fourth. At first we have the picturesque treatment of the subject, in which a series of vivid pictures, often more vivid than veritable, summed up all that the historian had to tell of the Jews and their fortunes (Basnage, &c.). Thus, in this country, the history of the Jews was summed up in a series of pictures of the Jews of Toledo delivering up the keys of the town to the Moors; of Jewish financiers in their counting-houses, and Jewish savants in their studies and laboratories; of murder and violation of Jews for imaginary crimes, child murder or well poisoning; of rabbis and monks disputing for the relative merits of Talmud and Gospel; of St. Vincent Ferrer drawing crowds of terrified Jews into the folds of the Church with cross transformed into sword; of Torquemada flinging down the thirty shekels before the Reyes Catolicos, or, saddest scene of all, of the San Benito ascending the steps of the scaffold or the pyre to make a Spanish holiday. These scenes, often enough mythical in detail, were held to constitute Hispano-Jewish history, and to many minds they still form its staple.

While Christian writers described in this manner the history of the Jews, with a *parti pris* against the enemies of their faith, Jewish writers, equally excited by controversial feelings, painted pictures of the persecutions of Israel experienced at the hands of Christians (Jehuda ben Verga, Joseph Cohen, Usque, &c.). The indignation of the Jews answered the prejudice of the Christians, and history was equally absent from both.

Second Period.—In this period Jewish students were investigating in the writings of Jews themselves the inner spirit of their history. With commendable industry and no small amount of artistic feeling they devoted themselves to the task of describing the history of Judaism as developed by Jewish thinkers or poets (Jost, Zunz, Graetz). It is scarcely necessary to add that such a manner of treating the history of Judaism brings it in contact, in many points, with the history of Spain. For it was from Cordova, Toledo, Lucena, and Barcelona that many of Israel's deepest thinkers and most inspired and sweetest singers came during the Middle Ages. In point of fact, the names of Avicebron, Abraham ibn Ezra, Jehuda Halevi, and Maimonides, not to speak of less well-known names, are, or should be, equally the glory of Judaism and of Spain.

Of these contributions to the history of the Jews, especially the memorable work of Graetz, one may say, " *C'est magnifique, mais ce n'est pas l'histoire.*" They are not history in the true sense of the word, since they fail to explain the position of the Jews in the national history of the countries where they dwelt.

Third Period.—The third phase, or period, in the history of the Hebrews came when Europe, in occupying itself in the study of constitutional problems, could not fail to treat, if only incidentally, with the constitutional position of the Jews in the Middle Ages. This aspect of Israelite history was, naturally, for the most part, treated by Christian writers especially versed in constitutional history, as Madox and Blunt in England, Stobbe in Germany, and Bedarrides for France and Italy. Here, in Spain, your own historic activity has been concentrated so much on the publication of *fueros* and other constitutional documents, that it was not so difficult a task for Amador de los Rios to compile his political history of the Jews in Spain, for, excellent as it is in this respect, it has little claim to the other two epithets, "Social and Religious," that occur in its title.

Fourth Period.—It is precisely towards the elucidation of this social aspect of Jewish history that the
present, or fourth stage, of investigation is directing
itself. Hitherto, the attempt has been rather to accen-
tuate the differences between the Jews and their neighbours. Nowadays we are attempting to bring out the
resemblances, the common human nature underlying
both. The German proverb, *Wie Christelt es sich so
Jüdelt es sich* (As the Christian, so the Jew) best expresses the tendency of this new departure. Something has been done in this direction for Germany,
France, and Italy by Zunz, Berliner, and Güdemann,
especially the latter ; but very much more remains to
be done before an adequate *Culturgeschichte*, as the
Germans would call it, of the Jews can be written.
For this it is not sufficient to know the Laws, so much
depends on the way they are carried out. And before
the Laws come the Customs, which only rarely are
recorded in written documents. Painters talk of painting atmospheric effects ; we have to do very much the
same in dealing with *Culturgeschichte*. If it is difficult
to come to an understanding about social movements
of our own time, how much more also is it to know
those of times past. Hence there is a certain hesita-
tion in the attitude of Jewish historians, just at present, which may best be described by the French phrase
Elle se recueille pour mieux sauter.

Undoubtedly, for this aspect of social history every
scrap of information may be of importance. A single
phrase in the documents, the form of a proper name, a
difference of date, may throw a flood of light on social
matters. Hence, the fourth stage of Jewish historical
investigation, on which we are now entered, is engaged,
above all, with the collection of materials, which is
the bibliographic, diplomatic, and monographic stage.

In this connection it is to be remembered that before determining what MS. sources remain to be searched, it is first necessary to learn what has already been printed ; in other words, the first step must be bibliographical. Accordingly, in England we have compiled a volume of over 250 pages, containing merely the titles of works relating to Anglo-Jewish history (*Bibliotheka Anglo-Judaica*, by J. Jacobs and L. Wolf). More recently an even more extensive work, upon the same lines, dealing with Russian Jewish history, has appeared in St. Petersburg. In Germany they have been for some time engaged in publishing *Regesten* of the scattered details relating to the earlier history of the Jews in that country. And, with regard to the Iberian Peninsula, I have myself been engaged in compiling a bibliography of the history of the Jews in Spain, adding to the references of Amador de los Rios those occurring in works published subsequently to his, as well as those contained in German and Hebrew writings, which that distinguished historian omitted to consult.

But more even than to the summing up of old information in bibliographies, Jewish science is diligently occupied at the present moment in the search after new knowledge to be found in manuscript sources. In connection with this movement societies or institutions have been formed all over Europe for the collecting and printing of manuscript materials dealing with Jewish history. France initiated the movement by the foundation of the *Société des Études Juives*. In England an Anglo-Jewish Historical Exhibition was held in 1887, and the movement thus begun has been recently accelerated by the formation of a Jewish Historical Society in Germany. There has existed for some time a *Commission für die*

Geschichte der Juden in Deutschland, and similar societies have been founded in Russia, Roumania, and the United States. Much manuscript material has been brought to light by these societies, or by archivists in connection with them. In this connection reference may be made to many articles in the *Revue des Études Juives,* especially those by that model investigator Mr. Isidore Loeb ; to *Les Juifs de Languedoc,* published by M. Saige, with admirable *pièces justificatives ;* to the volume of Mr. Davis, entitled *Shetaroth* (Hebrew deeds of English Jews), published by the Anglo-Jewish Exhibition ; to the *Quellen* of the German *Commission ;* likewise, *Codice diplomatico degli Judei Siciliani,* of which the first volume has been published. It is scarcely necessary to add that my own researches in Spain were directed towards this end.

After the bibliographic and diplomatic stages of historic investigation comes the monographic. Every fresh document discovered, certainly every series of documents bearing on a single event, or single aspect of history, can afford opportunity for monographs. Already many of these have been written in Graetz's *Monatschrift,* in the *Revue des Études Juives,* and in your own *Boletin.* In connection with this subject I have another suggestion to make to those who have honoured me by associating me with them.

Among the works to which the Academy has given the stamp of its official approval I observe several relating to the Moors, but none relating to the Jews of Spain, who, after all, were not enemies, but only Spaniards of a different creed. Could not the Academy stimulate research on the Jewish history of Spain by proposing rewards for monographs on such subjects as the following :—

I. A *Corpus inscriptionum judaico-Hispanicarum,* towards which Don Fidel Fita has already made such admirable contributions.

II. The social relations of Jews and Christians, and of Jews and Moors, in Spain.

III. The *rôle* of the Jews in the economic and financial development of Spain.

IV. Marks employed to distinguish Jews in different parts of Spain at different epochs.

V. The historical data contained in Hebrew writings of Spanish Jews, especially the *Responsa* of important rabbis, like Solomon ben Adret, &c.

Various other subjects could be indicated, some of them more suitable perhaps for the Spanish Academy; as, a list of Spanish writers to supplement and complete the obsolete one of De Castro and others which have more relation with science, as, a comparison of the characteristics of Spaniards (especially the *Chuetas* of Mallorca) with those offered by the *Sephardim,* or Spanish Jews. Besides these themes many others of interest exist which have been treated by eminent savants, whose learned works have just appeared, or may be shortly expected to do so. The illustrious Dr. Steinschneider has recently published a list of Jewish translations made from the Arabic during the Middle Ages, a work consecrated in large measure to the Spanish Jews. The no less distinguished Dr. Neubauer has passed many years of his life in collecting Hebrew geographical names which occurred in the Rabbinic writings in mediæval times, and it is to be hoped that his work, when it appears, will include a list of Hebrew names of Spanish places which will replace, with advantage, the preliminary sketch made by Zunz. Finally, Dr. Kayserling has prepared a *Bibliotheca judaico española* containing a list of Jews who have written in Castilian. With all this there is much left to do, and I am convinced that a series of prizes offered by your Institution would be the best guarantee for the filling up of the missing information. I have, besides, the confidence that there will not be wanting Jewish Maecenates willing to add their forces to those of the Academy, so that prizes shall correspond to the difficulties of the subject.

This, then, is the fourth stage which Jewish history has now reached, the bibliographic, diplomatic, and monographic stage. With regard to the latter, there still remains the difficult work of comparison between one country and another; for it is a great mistake to think that the lot of the Jews was the same in all countries. There are general similarities, no doubt; thanks chiefly to the unifying influence of the Church on the one hand, and of Rabbinic law on the other. But local circumstances have influenced the lot of the Jews in various ways, and there still remains the difficult task of comparison between different countries.

It is only after the work of this fourth stage is finished, on which we Jews are at present engaged, that we can look to the fifth and last act of Jewish history. This will take the form of special histories of the Jews in each country, for with the vast accumulation of material which is now going on it will be impossible for another Graetz to give a history of Jews in general. Just as there has been only one Gibbon, there can only be one Graetz. If any general attempt is to be made, one may safely prophesy that it will take the form of a philosophy of Jewish history, which will form no inconsiderable part of the work for which all students of history are nowadays preparing the way. For it is the conviction that history will one day give the solution of life's problem that sus-

Q

tains us students of the past in our laborious and often dull undertakings. No philosophy of life will ever be considered adequate if it does not explain the life of the past as well as the present. History must thus be the Œdipus that will solve life's riddle. And the history of the Jews will form no unimportant contribution towards such a solution. It is the conviction of many others, besides us Jews, that a Divine purpose runs through the long travail of Israel. Jews alone form a bridge between ancient and modern times. If their history does not contain any inner meaning, then the life of man upon this earth has no rational aim.

It is on account of this general importance of Jewish history that it may claim special attention from all students of the past, whether Jews, or Christians, or free-thinkers. We Jews of Europe look to you historical investigators of Spain for that portion of Jewish history which is the richest and most interesting of all, and can only be studied in Spain itself. It is the earnest hope of many that, in the not distant future, there may be many who will be able to call themselves Spaniards as well as Jews. These will then be the natural guardians and investigators of Hispano-Jewish history. But till that time arrives, it is upon the historians of Spain, especially as represented by the Royal Academy, that the duty revolves of keeping pace with the rest of Europe in the scientific investigation of the history of Israel.